SHAKESPEARE THE AESTHETE

CONTEMPORARY INTERPRETATIONS OF SHAKESPEARE

Derek Cohen
SHAKESPEAREAN MOTIVES

Graham Holderness, Nick Potter and John Turner
SHAKESPEARE: THE PLAY OF HISTORY

Murray J. Levith
SHAKESPEARE'S ITALIAN SETTINGS AND PLAYS

Lachlan Mackinnon
SHAKESPEARE THE AESTHETE

Peter Mercer
HAMLET AND THE ACTING OF REVENGE

Further titles in preparation

Series Standing Order

If you would like to receive future titles in this series as they are published, you can make use of our standing order facility. To place a standing order please contact your bookseller or, in case of difficulty, write to us at the address below with your name and address and the name of the series. Please state with which title you wish to begin your standing order. (If you live outside the UK we may not have the rights for your area, in which case we will forward your order to the publisher concerned.)

Standing Order Service, Macmillan Distribution Ltd, Houndmills, Basingstoke, Hampshire, RG21 2XS, England.

Also by Lachlan Mackinnon
ELIOT, AUDEN, LOWELL: Aspects of the Baudelairean Inheritance

Shakespeare the Aesthete

An Exploration of Literary Theory

Lachlan Mackinnon

MACMILLAN
PRESS

First published 1988

Published by
THE MACMILLAN PRESS LTD
Houndmills, Basingstoke, Hampshire RG21 2XS
and London
Companies and representatives
throughout the world

Typeset by Wessex Typesetters
(Division of The Eastern Press Ltd)
Frome, Somerset

Printed in Hong Kong

British Library Cataloguing in Publication Data
Mackinnon, Lachlan
Shakespeare the aesthete: an exploration
of literary theory.
– (Contemporary interpretations of
Shakespeare)
1. Shakespeare, William – Criticism and
interpretation
I. Title   II. Series
822.3'3   PR2976
ISBN 0–333–43356–4

For Sarah

Contents

Preface

This book is centrally concerned with five plays, *All's Well That Ends Well*, *Troilus and Cressida*, *Macbeth*, *Measure for Measure* and *The Winter's Tale*. It began as a study of the problem plays, an investigation into how their abrasive failure to satisfy the generic requirements they set themselves and their resulting atmosphere of decadence came about and whether or not they could be regarded as successful. I was particularly concerned to make a positive case for *All's Well*, which is among the most undervalued plays in the canon. I soon realised that the problem of the problem plays was simply that they presented in exaggerated form tensions which run through Shakespeare's work, and this book results from the consequent broadening of my field of inquiry.

Each chapter is divided into three parts. Chapter 1 begins with a discussion of *All's Well*, looking particularly at the language of the play and what it reveals about the characters and their world, with especial attention to Helena as a competitive individualist in a decayed feudal society, before going on to consider how time in the play is used to speed up and slow down the action at various points. In the second section, I read *Troilus and Cressida* in a similar way, but compare it with Chaucer's *Troilus and Criseyde*, Henryson's *The Testament of Cresseid* and Walton's opera *Troilus and Cressida* to define more precisely what is unique to Shakespeare's treatment of the subject. I point in particular to the ironic effect by which the characters' behaviour is seen to be determined by their future reputations, a curious reversal of tragic destiny. To find a contrast with the contingent, fickle time of *All's Well* and the crowded time of *Troilus and Cressida* I turn in the third section to *Macbeth*, where I explore the divorce between the full, rewarding time of familial and sexual life, looking with care at the Macbeths' marriage as exemplary of this, and the empty time into which the tragic hero is projected. Noting that Macbeth is both sympathetic and villainous, and that similar conflicts of interpretation are created by the plays previously discussed, the first chapter ends by wondering how it is that Shakespeare's work should seem meaningful when there is so little possibility of agreement about what its meaning is.

The second chapter begins therefore with a general treatment of symbolism and allegory. It centres on Spenser's vision on Mount Acidale but contrasts his allegorical procedures with Milton's handling of allegory and symbolism both within his work (particularly *Paradise Lost*) and in his approach to questions of genre. The other poets I discuss in some detail include Marvell, Coleridge, Keats and Shelley. My aim here is to restore symbolism to its traditional station above allegory, in contrast to a number of influential modern critics, but to argue that we can see from the Mount Acidale vision that it held this position long before Romanticism.

In the second section of Chapter 2 my subject is *Measure for Measure*. Coming to focus on Isabella's silence at the end of the play, which I compare with Calantha's stoicism in Ford's *The Broken Heart* and with Epicoene in Jonson's play, I offer a reading hostile to allegorical or symbolic interpretations while admitting their attractions. Shakespeare achieves through realism the effect of the Romantic sublime, as described specifically by Kant.

The Winter's Tale is dealt with in the third section of Chapter 2. I suggest that although the play tantalises us with the possibility of symbolic meaning there is nothing in the text which bears such a reading out as more than a natural desire on the part of audiences and readers to unify the work they perceive. Again, I see the effect as sublimity, but I am also concerned to analyse and praise in detail what seems to me Shakespeare's most remarkable single scene, the sheep-shearing.

My conclusion returns to the broader questions of meaning as opposed to meaningfulness, and suggests that meaning narrowly understood is not a literary device. Shakespeare is therefore doing much the same as all writers, if rather more so. Again, I use Kant's concept of the disinterestedness of aesthetic experience to develop the view that it is perfectly possible for us to feel meaning in a work while being entirely unable to isolate or define it.

My focus throughout is on Shakespeare as a fully self-conscious artist, rather than the inspired, unreflective genius he is often taken to be. My subtitle is meant to point up the tentative, exploratory nature of the book, but my title presents an unlikely pairing of terms: we may find in Shakespeare, I believe, that the pure aesthete might because of his disinterestedness be also the man most deeply implicated in the common human world. The two do not seem to me to be contradictory.

Acknowledgements

I want to thank Dr Clare Robertson for her generous palaeographic assistance at a crucial moment and Dr Anna Bryson for her advice and hospitality. Conversations with Dr H. R. Woudhuysen of University College London, clarified aspects of Spenser, and the teaching of Mr Peter Conrad first stimulated me to think about some of the questions I explore here. Dr Michael Tweedy, Moberly Librarian of Winchester College, gave me both encouragement and information; I am also indebted to the staffs of the Bodleian Library, Oxford, and the University Library, Southampton.

A sentence and several ideas in this book first appeared in reviews written for *The Times Literary Supplement*, and I am most grateful to the Editor for permission to reuse this material.

For permission to quote from the Kinaston manuscript of *The Testament of Creseide* (shelfmark MS Add. C 287) I am grateful to the Bodleian Library, Oxford.

None of the above is responsible for any errors of thought or fact which may remain, for which I am to blame: neither is my greatest help and sharpest reader, to whom this book is dedicated.

The author and publishers wish to thank the following who have kindly given permission for the use of copyright material:

Methuen & Co., for the extracts from the works by William Shakespeare: *All's Well That Ends Well*, ed. G. K. Hunter (Methuen, 1967); *Measure for Measure*, ed. J. W. Lever (Methuen, 1967); *Macbeth*, ed. Kenneth Muir (corr. repr., Methuen, 1972); *The Winter's Tale*, ed. J. H. P. Pafford (Methuen, 1966); and *Troilus and Cressida*, ed. Kenneth Palmer (Methuen, 1982).

Oxford University Press and Houghton Mifflin Co., for the extracts from *Troilus and Criseyde* from *The Works of Geoffrey Chaucer*, ed. F. N. Robinson (2nd edn, 1966).

Oxford University Press for the extract from 'The Faerie Queene' from *The Poetical Works of Edmund Spenser*, ed. J. C. Smith and E. de Selincourt (1912; paperback, 1970).

Faber & Faber Ltd and Alfred A. Knopf, Inc., for the extracts from 'Of Mere Being' from *Opus Posthumous*, by Wallace Stevens, ed. Samuel Frech Morse, and for the extracts from 'Asides on the Oboe' from *The Collected Poems of Wallace Stevens*.

Faber & Faber Ltd and Random House, Inc., for the extracts from 'The Sea and the Mirror' from *W. H. Auden: Collected Poems*, ed. Edward Mendelson.

Faber & Faber Ltd and New Directions Publishing Corp., for the extracts from 'Notes from Cantos CXVII' from *The Cantos of Ezra Pound*, copyright © 1962 by Ezra Pound.

J. M. Dent & Sons Ltd, for the extracts from Samuel Taylor Coleridge, *Poems*, sel. and ed. John Beer (rev. edn, 1973).

Indiana University Press for the extracts from 'The Gypsy Ballads of Federĭco García Lorca' by Federĭco García Lorca.

Every effort has been made to trace all the copyright-holders but if any have been inadvertently overlooked the publishers will be pleased to make the necessary arrangement at the first opportunity.

A Note on Texts

For *All's Well That Ends Well*, *Troilus and Cressida*, *Macbeth*, *Measure for Measure* and *The Winter's Tale* I have used the most recent Arden editions, which are cited separately in the notes. Quotations from all other plays by Shakespeare come from *Complete Works*, ed. W. J. Craig (London, New York, Toronto: Oxford University Press, 1963 reprint of 1943 resetting) and will not be separately annotated.

In a handful of cases, as with 'decree' in 'Kubla Khan', I have changed the tenses of verbs quoted by themselves to fit them grammatically into my sentences. These instances will be obvious.

Chapter 1

I shall begin with the so-called problem plays, and in particular
All's Well That Ends Well and *Troilus and Cressida*. The plays earn
their soubriquet from Boas' identification of them as Shavian
dramas concerned with the woman question,[1] but the name has
stuck beyond that ephemeral occasion because the plays do present
a genuine enigma. They do not fall easily into generic categories
and they leave many auditors with a peculiar mixture of
uncertainty and disgust.

It is worth setting out from a detailed examination of the
language used by the characters in *All's Well*, to see how far this
itself contributes to such an unsatisfying effect. At the beginning
of Act v, where Helena enters with the Widow and her daughter
Diana, who have collaborated in the bed-trick at Bertram's
expense, she says,

> But this exceeding posting day and night
> Must wear your spirits low. We cannot help it;
> But since you have made the days and nights as one
> To wear your gentle limbs in my affairs,
> Be bold you do so grow in my requital
> As nothing can unroot you.
>
> (v.i.1–6)[2]

Presumably the Florentine women have just said that they are
happy to continue travelling. Helena's reply to them has a
nagging insistence on their suffering and fatigue. Their spirits are
worn low, ground down by the haste and lack of sleep their
journey has entailed: the repetition of 'wear' yokes spirits and
'gentle limbs' together, setting body and mind on the same
physical plane. That day and night are as one to them is an aspect
of the play's curious lack of time, to which I shall return, but the
phrase 'gentle limbs' is of particular interest because it echoes
Helena's concern for Bertram's 'tender limbs' (iii.ii.104) when she
learns that he has gone off to war. Those for whom Helena cares,

or in whom she has an interest, are conceived of as the vulnerable flesh to which the play's abrasive argument reduces them.

Helena reassures the women that she will repay them. In the context of this play, her words are more than a formal courtesy. Money has played a crucial role in the bed-trick, as we see when it is first mooted, in Act III Scene vii. Helena has told the Widow her story, and says that she cannot demonstrate it further unless she reveals herself to Bertram. The Widow replies,

> Though my estate be fall'n, I was well born,
> Nothing acquainted with these businesses,
> And would not put my reputation now
> In any staining act.
>
> (ll. 4–7)

Wondering what Helena takes her for, the Widow stands on the prerogative of age and birth to redeem herself from what she sees as 'these businesses', a contemptuous dismissal of the licentious behaviour of the young. 'Nor would I wish you' (l. 7), Helena replies, and urges belief. The Widow's next words move towards a grudging acceptance:

> I should believe you,
> For you have show'd me that which well approves
> Y'are great in fortune.
>
> (ll. 12–14)

'Fortune' rings dully here, stripped of its connotations of luck or providence. It only means money, and Helena latches onto that sense with her immediate

> Take this purse of gold,
> And let me buy your friendly help thus far,
> Which I will over-pay, and pay again
> When I have found it.
>
> (ll. 14–17)

The help which Helena wished first to 'borrow' (l. 11) she now proposes to 'buy', and that shift diminishes 'friendly' into mere 'favourable'. Helena cannot rely on the kindness of strangers.

When the Widow sees what Helena is after, Helena insists that she must perceive its rectitude (l. 30), instructs her as to what is to be done, and promises that to help Diana

> After,
> To marry her I'll add three thousand crowns
> To what is pass'd already.
>
> (ll. 34–6)

'I have yielded', the Widow answers. Helena has won her on two levels: while the overt argument has been moral, covertly money has already changed hands. The Widow's change of heart comes also partly from her annoyance at the trouble Bertram causes.

> Every night he comes
> With musics of all sorts, and songs compos'd
> To her unworthiness; it nothing steads us
> To chide him from our eaves, for he persists
> As if his life lay on't.
>
> (ll. 39–43)

Bertram's behaviour is not just irritating but embarrassing in the intimacy of a city. The comic vignette of mother and daughter urging the importunate aristocrat to go away gives the Widow her own reality, one she cannot share with the itinerant Helena. However, Helena finds in the Widow's irritation another excuse for haste:

> Why then tonight
> Let us assay our plot; which, if it speed,
> Is wicked meaning in a lawful deed,
> And lawful meaning in a lawful act,
> Where both not sin, and yet a sinful fact.
> But let's about it.
>
> (ll. 43–8)

Her gleeful, sententious, riddling couplets emphasise the finality of her aim, to regain her husband, but the half-line which follows on them disrupts their orderliness with the urgent business of conspiracy. Helena holds up the enigmatic nature of the bed-trick for observation as a neat resolution of moral problems, but cannot sustain that degree of detachment and is immersed in the necessities of the plot.

The relationship between Helena and her agents is mistrustful and ambiguous, then. She will only 'pay again/When I have found' the help she is buying. The Widow and Diana journey with her because of a sisterly solidarity in the face of Bertram's male gracelessness, but an atmosphere of now unjust doubt surrounds them to the very end of the play, when the King says to Diana,

> If thou beest yet a fresh uncropped flower
> Choose thou thy husband and I'll pay thy dower;
> For I can guess that by thy honest aid
> Thou kept'st a wife herself, thyself a maid.
> Of that and all the progress more and less
> Resolvedly more leisure shall express.
> All yet seems well, and if it end so meet,
> The bitter past, more welcome is the sweet.
>
> (v.iii.321–8)

The King's residual uncertainty about what has actually happened leads him into the blundering unpleasantness of that 'If', which he rapidly skips aside from by making her the same offer as he made to Helena. The image of a 'fresh uncropped flower' seems perilously fragile here, emphasising the dangers virginity runs throughout the play and the fear that Parolles has been right, that ''Tis a commodity will lose the gloss with lying; the longer kept, the less worth. Off with't while 'tis vendible; answer the time of request' (i.i.149–51). Now, if Diana still has what is 'vendible', she shall have its price. The King's 'guess' at what happened is right, but that it is a guess makes him appear momentarily prurient, speculating about who really slept with whom. His wish for 'more leisure' to clarify things is peculiarly ironic, and I shall return to it after examining the final couplet.

'All yet seems well', the King says, as though on further inspection it might turn out not to be so. Here, he echoes unknowingly a misgiving the audience feels about Helena's marriage, that Bertram has shown no sight of moral reform and that Helena is wasting her love. The 'meet' ending the King discovers is one which only 'seems well', while his final sentiment expresses the ostensible aim of tragicomedy, to save worth from danger.[3] The play scrapes home to its conclusion, but in such a way that the audience cannot be satisfied.

The King's wish for 'leisure' is a wish for precisely what the play cannot offer him. What the play lacks is any sense of time as potentially restorative, for to an unusual extent this is a play in which things simply happen. The plot consists of two distinct elements from folklore, 'the healing of the king' and 'the fulfilment of the tasks'.[4] Helena's reward for achieving the first is Bertram's hand in marriage, but she must undertake the second to secure it. Both elements have a distinctly fairy-tale element which is here denied by the way in which they are yoked together. The healing is achieved, but its consequences miscarry and require of Helena different gifts, in that what is now needed is not access to hidden knowledge but an ability simply to cope.

However, different as the two areas of narrative appear to be, Helena is a remarkably consistent character. When we first hear of the King's illness, Lafew tells the Countess that he has sent his doctors away, 'under whose practices he hath persecuted time with hope, and finds no other advantage in the process but only the losing of hope by time' (i.i.12–15). Here, time is merely the medium of contingent misfortune. 'Hope', which trusts to time, is found worthless, part of a simple 'process' which cannot stay the course of disease. Helena does not show any response to the news of the King's illness until her soliloquy some two hundred lines later, during which time we have learnt about her father, heard her express her love for Bertram in a despondent soliloquy, and watched her argue playfully with Parolles about virginity. Her question 'How might one do, sir, to lose it to her own liking?' (l. 147) can be seen as reflecting her own dilemma, and Parolles' advice to 'like him that ne'er it likes' (l. 148) will be strangely followed in Florence. These are only hints, though, for during a dialogue in which Helena defends virginity she is preserving the privacy of her thoughts. The space she defends is both physical and mental, an anticipation of her words to the Widow and Diana. As soon as she is alone, she bursts out,

> Our remedies oft in ourselves do lie,
> Which we ascribe to heaven; the fated sky
> Gives us free scope; only doth backward pull
> Our slow designs when we ourselves are dull.
> (ll. 212–15)

Viola, caught in an increasingly perplexing chain of events, says,

> O time! thou must untangle this, not I;
> It is too hard a knot for me to untie.
>
> (*Twelfth Night*, II.ii.41–2)

Helena knows no such faith, but rather relies on the will. Not to succeed would be a judgement on her slowness to act on the basis of desire.

> What power is it which mounts my love so high,
> That makes me see, and cannot feed mine eye?
>
> (*All's Well*, I.i.216–17)

Her love is high like a watchful hawk, but high also because it is above her station. Nature, to which she refers a line later, cannot, she is sure, allow her to see and not to eat, but the metaphor of the feeding eye stresses the carnality of her desire. What she remembers most when Bertram leaves is that she liked

> to sit and draw
> His arched brows, his hawking eye, his curls,
> In our heart's table – heart too capable
> Of every line and trick of his sweet favour.
>
> (ll. 91–4)

The language is suitably decorative and artistic in idiom. Helen's fantasies are woven round a physique rather than a spirit – understandably, when we consider what Bertram's character is like[5] – and have therefore a physical force impelling her love to rise and demanding that the eye, a creature of light, be fed like a stomach.

> Impossible be strange attempts to those
> That weigh their pains in sense, and do suppose
> What hath been cannot be.
>
> (ll. 220–2)

Unusual endeavour is possible only to those who do not reckon the cost of their efforts or try to work out the odds on success.[6]

> Who ever strove
> To show her merit that did miss her love?

The king's disease – my project may deceive me,
But my intents are fix'd, and will not leave me.

(ll. 222–5)

The past offers examples of girls who have won their loves by displaying their merits. The sense of display is important, for Helena wants Bertram to see her as she sees him. The full throwing-force of 'project' is present in Helena's scheme, which proceeds from erotic motives. Helena sets out to cure the King to win Bertram, grasping the opportunity chance has given her.

Opportunism is the keynote of her character.[7] She tells the King that she is prepared to die if her cure fails, 'But if I help, what do you promise me?' (II.i.189). 'Make thy demand', the King replies; 'But will you make it even?' (l. 190) she retorts, dogging him to a guarantee. 'Ay, by my sceptre and my hopes of heaven' (l. 191) the King affirms, angered into a double oath by the doubt she has cast on his good faith.

Then shalt thou give me with thy kingly hand
What husband in thy power I will command.

(ll. 192–3)

Her demand is already prepared and formed, and her insistence is mere legalism, as we gather from the King's assurance that it will take place, 'the premises observ'd' (l. 200). This is the language of contracts rather than vows, for the other side of opportunism is legalism.[8] Helena does not trust to time and has no reason to trust the King, for her assertion of individual will runs against the ties of traditional reciprocity between master and servant on which she might have relied. Unprotected by natural order, she must invoke a man-made law.

A similar effect is observed in the long final scene, where Bertram is brought to bay. At his entry he is invited to give his opinion of Lafew's daughter by the King, who is about to marry them off. Bertram speaks of her as having captivated his heart so

That she whom all men prais'd, and whom myself
Since I have lost, have lov'd, was in mine eye
The dust that did offend her.

(v.iii.53–5)

'Well excus'd' (l. 55), says the King, momentarily lost in admiration of what we know to be Bertram's gall. Bertram's retrospective sentiment is, we shall see, no kin to love. The King goes on to explain why Bertram's belated love is exemplary of the way in which we may 'Destroy our friends and after weep their dust' (l. 64). This sententious expansiveness is cut off by

> Be this sweet Helen's knell, and now forget her.
> Send forth your amorous token for fair Maudlin.
>
> (ll. 67–8)

The King's urgent desire to see the young married is partly a desperate grasping at the future he will not see, but he sounds dangerously cold and dismissive here. Helena is frozen into an object-lesson, her memorial a maxim. Assimilated to the past, she can have no place in the present.

Bertram betrays his over-confidence and his lack of true feeling for Helena by handing over her ring as his love-token for Maudlin. It turns out originally to have been given Helena by the King, but Bertram sticks to his fantastic denials.

> In Florence was it from a casement thrown me,
> Wrapp'd in a paper which contain'd the name
> Of her that threw it. Noble she was, and thought
> I stood ingag'd.
>
> (ll. 93–6)

This is Bertram as he would like to be, the cynosure of fair ladies. Remembering the picture of Bertram and his jongleurs haunting the Widow's house by night, we are entertained by the contrast, but our amusement changes to incredulity as Bertram elaborates, recounting how he told the lady that he could not honourably proceed with her. The little fiction redounds to his credit, but its manner betrays the unreality of the world he inhabits. He describes a scene of courtly love, the fine young knight singled out by the secluded lady, but what we have seen is something closer to citizen comedy, the fine young knight making a fool of himself in the managing hands of bourgeois women. The slip in social register marks the degree of illusion. Bertram has, importantly, learnt little from the unmasking of Parolles.

He is disbelieved and taken away under guard. The Gentleman

arrives with Diana's note; Bertram is brought back. The long, inconclusive confrontation between Diana and Bertram is made sense of only when Helena appears. The King asks,

> Is there no exorcist
> Beguiles the truer office of mine eyes?
> Is't real that I see?
>
> (ll. 298–300)

He immediately suspects that magic is being used, but Helena disabuses him. Bertram impores her pardon (l. 302).

> O my good lord, when I was like this maid
> I found you wondrous kind. There is your ring,
> And, look you, here's your letter. This it says:
> *When from my finger you can get this ring*
> *And is by me with child, &c.* This is done;
> Will you be mine now you are doubly won?
>
> (ll. 303–8)

The sarcasm of her first line is an embarrassment for Bertram, who has been reduced from his courtly, self-serving anecdote to the confession that he 'boarded' Diana 'i' th' wanton way of youth' (l. 210) to this direct reference to his behaviour in bed. Helena passes on to refer to the supposedly impossible conditions he laid down for a resumption of their married life and to explain that they have been fulfilled. Bertram's answer to her last question would seem to be a foregone conclusion.

Not a bit of it.

> If she, my liege, can make me know this clearly
> I'll love her dearly, ever, ever dearly.
>
> (ll. 309–10)

It is the King who forced him to marry her in the first place to whom he speaks, as though still half fighting to save his place at court, and his reply consists of another condition. Helena is still only 'she', unloved unless she can dissolve all mystery about what has happened. We know that she can, but may mistrust his promise to love her forever. That Bertram's last speech is conditional leaves a lingering suspicion that he doesn't really

mean what he says and shows him resting determinedly at the
level of law rather than honour.

The King's suspicion that magic may be taking place is swept
aside by Helena's brutal realism. Her triumph is half-hearted,
though, as her 'Will you be mine?' shows. It is still in the end a
matter of Bertram's 'will', and this is seen as suspended, put into
abeyance and let drift on a condition that he must know will be
met. What he shows is not submission but collapse, a loss of
personality which may only be temporary. The King takes charge
of the action again, uttering the wish for 'leisure' I touched on
earlier.

The one full emotional response we are shown is Lafew's 'Mine
eyes smell onions; I shall weep anon' (l. 314). He turns to Parolles
for a handkerchief. 'So, I thank thee. Wait on me home, I'll make
sport with thee. Let thy curtsies alone, they are scurvy ones' (ll.
316–18). Lafew's acceptance of Parolles as a companion is a
touching making-do. His tone is not the arrogant assumption of
Prospero's 'this thing of darkness I / Acknowledge mine' (*The
Tempest*, v.i.275–6), where the enjambement conveys the tone,[9] but
closer to Touchstone's 'a poor humour of mine, sir, to take that
that no man else will' (*As You Like It*, v.iv.61–2). It is at once kind
and cognisant of the unworthiness of that kindness' object;
Parolles' habitual 'curtsies' are only 'scurvy', the fool with whom
Lafew will 'make sport' not a very good one. That clear-
sightedness finds cause for tears in the main plot's ending, but
just as its kindness is mixed with knowledge so its joy is perhaps
mixed with grief.

There is a peculiar rightness in the perennial, surely erroneous,
intuition that this play is *Love's Labour's Won*.[10] At the end of *Love's
Labour's Lost*, the ladies dismiss their wooers for a year and a day to
perform various apt arduous tasks that will make them fit for
marriage. Berowne remarks that

> Our wooing doth not end like an old play;
> Jack hath not Jill; these ladies' courtesy
> Might well have made our sport a comedy.
>   (v.ii.882–4)

Might have done but does not, because the ladies have a sense of
the seriousness of life which the frivolous academicians lack. It
seems increasingly likely that the suited couples will be joined,

but the arrival of Mercade has given the play a sombre twist.[11] The King consoles Berowne,

> Come, sir, it wants a twelvemonth and a day,
> And then 'twill end.
>
> (ll. 885–6)

The King's optimism leaps over the intervening time as a simple lacuna, but Berowne knows that 'That's too long for a play' (l. 886). Berowne is granted more literary self-consciousness than the other characters, and can therefore see that his life is not falling into a tidy aesthetic pattern. Seriousness overrides the form of order he instinctively chooses, and he cannot reconcile his being with his vision.

The two songs the minor characters of *Love's Labour's Lost* end the play with at once express and resolve this dilemma. Ver sings about spring.

> When shepherds pipe on oaten straws,
>   And merry larks are ploughmen's clocks,
> When turtles tread, and rooks, and daws,
>   And maidens bleach their summer smocks,
> The cuckoo then, on every tree,
> Mocks married men; for thus sings he,
>   Cuckoo;
> Cuckoo, cuckoo: O, word of fear,
> Unpleasing to a married ear!
>
> (ll. 911–19)

This is the accustomed landscape of erotic pastoral, but seen in one aspect. The ambiguity it unfolds is that, although in nature like seeks like (the birds), this is the effect of an essentially promiscuous sexual impulse which mocks human arrangements and human continuities. Merely seasonal, its libertinism flouts man's timespan: the 'ploughmen's clocks' mark the time of repetitive labour but not the cycle of harvest and renewal, and we may suspect that those 'summer smocks' have been worn and dirtied before. The frivolous, brief time of cuckoldry is the time of the lyric impulse to which Berowne submits.

> The flowers do fade, and wanton fields
> To wayward winter reckoning yields[12]

was Ralegh's reply to Marlowe's promise that

> The shepherd swains shall dance and sing
> For thy delight each May morning[13]

– a less ambivalent and compassionate way of putting the same thing.

Hiems' song about winter presents an opposed picture.

> When all aloud the wind doth blow,
>   And coughing drowns the parson's saw,
> And birds sit brooding in the snow,
>   And Marian's nose looks red and raw,
> When roasted crabs hiss in the bowl,
> Then nightly sings the staring owl,
>   Tu-who;
> Tu-whit, tu-who – a merry note,
> While greasy Joan doth keel the pot.
>   (*Love's Labour's Lost*, v.ii.929–37)

The birds are now chastened incubators, and life looks inward to the communal hearth rather than out to the open field. 'Marian's nose looks red and raw' is a properly unsexy image for this praise of community. Winter is a time of familiar recurrences, 'the parson's saw' and crab-apples. This solidarity and collective will to endure are the purposes served by the sexual urge, even if that urge doesn't know it. The emotions here are villagey, gossipy amusement and gustatory rather than erotic.

The distance between the two songs is the distance Berowne and his companions are required to bridge. The songs seem to encapsulate two extremes of human being, the lovers must show that they reflect one being. In a sense, they must discover how the implications of the songs bring them together. 'Love's labour' turns out to have been frippery, not really labour at all. What might have been a comedy turns into a prologue – assuming, that is, that the right end of comedy is marriage.[14]

The two songs bring *Love's Labour's Lost* to a formal close; they give aesthetic order to the experience of the play: but the end is only formal. Similarly, *All's Well* might have been a tragedy. Where the atmosphere of the earlier play is brilliant and verbal, that of the later one is acrid and emotional. It comes to a putatively comic ending with what is in the end breakneck speed – thirty-and-a-half lines between Helena's entrance and the start of the epilogue – but an ending which is again only a beginning. Helena and Bertram are married, but they now have to make that marriage work. 'Love's labour', Helena's tasks, has indeed 'won', but the gain is hollow and places demands on the future. Both plays throw their emphasis forward into a time which is unbounded by the requirements of the stage.

The time both plays want is the proverbial time that heals. This time is often invoked in the course of Shakespearean comedy, but is perhaps at its most vivid in *Henry IV, Part II*. Justice Shallow's Gloucestershire is a place in which time has almost come to a stop.[15] When we first see Justice Shallow we cannot understand why he is there. We are by now well accustomed to Falstaff's intrusive irrelevance, but this is new:

> SHALLOW. By yea and nay, sir, I dare say my cousin William is become a good scholar. He is at Oxford still, is he not?
> SILENCE. Indeed, sir, to my cost.
> SHALLOW. A' must, then, to the inns o' court shortly. I was once of Clement's Inn; where I think they will talk of mad Shallow yet.
> SILENCE. You were called 'lusty Shallow' then, cousin.
> SHALLOW. By the mass, I was called any thing; and I would have done any thing indeed too, and roundly too. There was I, and Little John Doit of Staffordshire, and black George Barnes, and Francis Pickbone, and Will Squele a Cotswold man; you had not four such swinge-bucklers in all the inns of court again: and, I may say to you, we knew where the *bona-robas* were, and had the best of them all at commandment. Then was Jack Falstaff, now Sir John, a boy, and page to Thomas Mowbray, Duke of Norfolk. (III.ii.10–29)

Falstaff's time, as Auden points out on his essay 'The Prince's Dog',[16] is the timelessness of appetite. Falstaff cannot age or change – as, indeed, he will in the end die off-stage because when he died on-stage he got up again.[17] What we have here is the slow time of nostalgia, private rather than public history.

Kings and princes are remembered for what they do and say. What distorts Hal's character is his knowledge that the king can only be a partial man, and what makes us dislike him is his apparent eagerness to shed his private self. The actions and words he must commit himself to will be public and significant, expressing the impersonal nature of kingship and not his own personality. Historical time is tragic time because in it people assume roles already laid down and accept the dangers they entail. In comic time, characters are themselves, and the immortality they earn is that of anecdote rather than chronicle. Shallow is the folk memory in person, so what he remembers is names rather than deeds. We never hear whether 'Will Squele a Cotswold man' was anything more than a bit of a lad, but we know that he existed because he is given a local habitation and a name. Embalmed in sentiment, such characters cannot quite die, which is why Shallow's response to the news of old Double's death is an anecdote and a ruminative repetition, 'And is old Double dead?' (l. 58). The death comes in a series of 'soft aftershocks of calm' like those the old watchers feel in Geoffrey Hill's 'The Guardians' after the distant, ominously nuclear 'Thunderheads' of the world the dead have entered.[18] Their function, to 'Gather the dead as the first dead scrape home', is comic recollection perverted by contemporary menace.

There is an implication in *Henry IV, Part II* that the two times are to some extent socially divided. Not everyone can be a king, after all. We should remember, though, that Falstaff exists in both worlds, and that his arrival in Gloucestershire disrupts the idyll. The stoical courage of Feeble the woman's tailor is one way for a private man to meet his public fate, and has a submissive dignity which embodies the strength of the time he is naturally at home in. Another way is that of Ancient Pistol, who adopts the manners of another class. His Marlovian rhetoric reveals something deeply important about the Marlovian hero, but it is an idiolect which allows him to endure his ordinariness. At moments, his fantasy so possesses him that its is the only language in which he can be reached, as Falstaff knows when he adopts it to press him:

> O base Assyrian knight, what is thy news?
> Let King Cophetua know the truth thereof.
> (*Henry IV, Part II*, v.iii.102–3)

Falstaff's greatness is his insight into others' fantasies, but he understands Pistol so well because the latter is to be his heir.

Pistol is the last member we ever see of Falstaff's troupe, vowing

To England will I steal, and there I'll steal:
And patches will I get unto these cudgell'd scars,
And swear I got them in the Gallia wars.
(*Henry V*, v.i.92–4)

'Gallia' is a last hopeful sign from this diminished figure who complains of age and expresses mean criminal ambitions, because it belongs in Pistol's martial register. It sounds like a new access of confidence, and leads us to trust that he will be reinflated before long. Falstaff has not so much died as dissolved into a landscape of 'green fields' (*Henry V*, II.iii.18)[19] and a little of him survives in Pistol. Pistol is the lesser man partly because he inhabits a smaller linguistic world, but he has Falstaff's hold on life, which Feeble, we may suspect, does not. Feeble joins the anonymous dead of war, private persons swept up into losses too great for individual identification and recall, because that is how the humble take part in tragedy. Pistol survives by evasion, having the courage of his ignobility.

Falstaff, Shallow, Pistol, Feeble all inhabit proverbial time. Shallow's scrupulous 'Jack Falstaff, now Sir John' is a familiar, predictable sort of name-dropping. It is a tissue-thin fraud, of course, as Falstaff says (*Henry IV, Part II*, III.ii.330–62), but a fraudulence that Falstaff understands. Within one speech he laughs at Shallow for having claimed to know John of Gaunt and cites him as his own friend (ll. 346–53), and somehow Falstaff's revelation of Shallow's past as legendary makes his own look mythical rather than historical. Proverbs reassure us that things will be as we expect, and just so does Falstaff treat his past and the world.

History without unhistorical time turns into ritual. The gardeners in *Richard II* are caught up into the courtly atmosphere of the dreamy King, allegorists rather than proverbialists,[20] because the King's identification of his role with himself collapses the distinction between the two times. Hal's knowledge of the distance between himself and Henry V keeps the two times properly apart. The history plays offer Shakespeare an unusually good opportunity for dividing the two times on a social basis: by inserting Prince John of Lancaster into historical time and making Falstaff's cronies largely petty criminals, he avoids the dangers of idealisation my description courts, a danger run by both kinds of time. Historical time aspires to epic grandeur, private to sentimental resonance.

The absence of comic time from *All's Well* affects the meaning of what happens as perceived by the characters. Lafew, who proposes a retirement into privacy, shows the most openly emotional response because he is nearest to earning the space of feeling. For the King, with his need for 'leisure', the action has been what everyone else has found it, all elbows. The plot of *All's Well* has no motor but pure contingency, as we can see from its most interesting lacuna.

It is not at all clear how Helena comes to meet Bertram again. Helena's departure from France is prepared for by a soliloquy (III.ii.99–129) which brings together love and estrangement. Helena refers to Bertram as 'Rossillion' twice, 'poor lord' and 'my lord': the social distance which was sharply marked in the first scene is still present. 'My lord' might be an affectionate address, but here it is not, for it is a passing reference while Helena addresses the putative bullets he faces and urging them not to touch him. It is in this speech that she makes the reference to 'tender limbs' I cited earlier, and throughout her concern is for Bertram's physical integrity. He has shut himself away into a separateness she cannot pierce, and her soliloquy acknowledges this. Her letter to the Countess (III.iv.4–17) confirms this. Helena announces that

> I am Saint Jaques' pilgrim, thither gone.
> Ambitious love hath in me so offended
> That barefoot plod I the cold ground upon,
> With sainted vow my faults to have amended.

Helena blames her own assertive individualism for the trouble that has come to her, and chooses a doggedness in suffering emphasised by 'plod' and the wearily rhythmic pulse of that whole line.

> Write, write, that from the bloody course of war
> My dearest master, your dear son, may hie.
> Bless him at home in peace, whilst I from far
> His name with zealous fervour sanctify.

The distancing 'master' and the intimate 'son' reflect estrangement.

Helena becomes actively passive, paradoxically choosing to endure what she cannot change.

When Helena next appears, she has arrived in Florence and is identified by the Widow as a pilgrim. In forty-five lines (III.v.30–74) Helena learns of Bertram's presence and his infatuation with Diana. However, Helena already knew that Bertram was headed for Florence (III.ii.51 makes this clear), so the information that he is there can hardly count as news. By l. 96, Helena is inviting the Widow and Diana to dine with her, when 'I will bestow some precepts of this virgin,/Worthy the note' (III.v.99–100). It is significant that after her departure from France Helena is not permitted another soliloquy. Events press in on her and her resourcefulness is displayed by the lack of time for reflection. This leaves room for misgiving about her motivation. Effectively, the play comes to a standstill when she leaves France, and starts a second action when she reaches Florence. We never know whether she has tailed Bertram, but are entitled to believe that in some unconscious way she is drawn to where he is.[21] There is no question of providence playing a part, because it requires a trust that Helena, as I argued above, has rejected.

There is, then, a paradox in the form of *All's Well*. What looks like a tight tragicomedy in which the girl gets her man, loses him and recovers him, turns out to break into two halves which seem violently pushed together because of the lack of time between them. Only one scene intervenes between Helena's departure from France and her arrival in Florence. Shakespeare does not invite us to reflect on the time between – we are aware of it as a plodding stubbornness, a state rather than a sequence of events. Where time does appear is in the drag between bed-trick and final scene, the journey back to Rossillion.

In Act IV Scene iv the trick has been accomplished. Helena assures the widow and Diana that

> One of the greatest in the Christian world
> Shall be my surety; fore whose throne 'tis needful,
> Ere I can perfect mine intents, to kneel.
>
> (ll. 2–4)

Helena again shows trust in legal process rather than God's

justice ('Christian' is merely geographical here), and in law as an instrument rather than an end. By now Helena's business has become 'welcome' to the Widow (l. 16), but her assurance of this is oddly greeted.

> Nor you, mistress,
> Ever a friend whose thoughts more truly labour
> To recompense your love. Doubt not but heaven
> Hath brought me up to be your daughter's dower,
> As it hath fated her to be my motive
> And helper to a husband. But, O strange men!
> That can such sweet use make of what they hate,
> When saucy trusting of the cozen'd thoughts
> Defiles the pitchy night; so lust doth play
> With what it loathes for that which is away.
>
> (ll. 16–25)

Helena's 'thoughts' 'labour': again the physical and mental are conjoined. Here, she does refer to 'heaven' and 'fate', but the potential nobility of those images is tarnished by their context. 'Heaven' turns out to guarantee an economic future, 'fate' to make Diana Helena's 'motive', which she is because it is by meeting her that Helena is moved to undertake the plot. Helena appears heaven-sent to the Widow, but the 'intents' she still clings to are those of i.i.225, and the Widow and Diana are to her contingent conveniences. The Widow's 'love' is to be met with 'recompense'.

Helena's remarks about men have a curious distance. Bertram is generalised into a biological example, whose weaknesses render him subject to female manipulation. Helena is aware that Bertram's desire to an impersonal force, that, though 'sweet', it is 'use' that has been made of her. We are in a world of shared female expertise, not individual feeling.

Diana is now reminded that she must do more to fulfil the plan and willingly agrees. Helena ends the scene with

> We must away;
> Our wagon is prepar'd, and time revives us.
> All's well that ends well; still the fine's the crown.
> Whate'er the course, the end is the renown.
>
> (ll. 33–6)

The restoration time promises here is physical, and it may not be over-fanciful to suggest that we should hear a bumpy discomfort in 'wagon' undercutting it. Proverbial wisdom is evoked to dismiss current inconvenience, but there is also a sense that Helena uses the end to justify the means, which have included, after all, the lie that she is dead. There is little faith here, rather an insistence on seeing things through.

The opening of Act v Scene i, when we next meet these characters, has already been discussed, but there are now further points to be observed. Helena asks the Gentleman to take a message to the King, who turns out not to be there.

> He hence removed last night, and with more haste
> Than is his use.
>
> (ll. 23–4)

We are given the sense of a world outside Helena's concerns moving at its own pace. The unnecessary additional information invites us to imagine a bustle whose thoughts are elsewhere. 'Lord, how we lose our pains!' the Widow exclaims (l. 24). Her despondency is checked by Helena's

> All's well that ends well yet,
> Though time seem so adverse and means unfit.
>
> (ll. 25–6)

Helena insists that things will work out despite appearances, reiterating the proverb with the determination to make it come true that her resolve to go on to Rossillion displays. The proverb is here used to pacify the Widow while Helena gets on with plotting. It is noteworthy that Helena speaks to the Widow as though possessed of wisdom, yet shows no trust in that wisdom herself.

The play's time suddenly and inopportunely slows, which is as exhausting for the audience as it is for the characters. As we have already observed, the last scene ends with surprising abruptness after Helena's reappearance, another disconcerting alteration in tempo. This jerkiness serves to disrupt further the unifying and consolatory pattern of tragicomedy, enacting the contingency which has played so large a part in the plot. That feeling of casual occurrence extends throughout the play, and affects even what might be thought of as the home of moral order, the old world represented by the King and the Countess.

When we first see the King he is engaged in *Realpolitik*. Austria has warned him that Florence will seek his aid, 'and would seem/To have us make denial' (i.ii.8–9). The King consents,

> And Florence is denied before he comes;
> Yet, for our gentlemen that mean to see
> The Tuscan service, freely have they leave
> To stand on either part.
>
> (ll. 12–15)

While not getting his own hands dirty, the King is willing to allow volunteers to join either side. He strikes a careful balance between external and domestic demands, as the Second Lord recognises:

> It well may serve
> A nursery to our gentry, who are sick
> For breathing and exploit.
>
> (ll. 15–17)

The 'nursery' is, of course, a place for infants. The gentry are thwarted youths grown 'sick'. The pause at the line-ending suggests a purposeless *ennui* before 'sick' is given direction, but in such a way as to confirm France's aimless claustrophobia. Foreign war acts as domestic safety-valve.

The appearance of the King's new ward Bertram offers his own spirit a 'nursery': 'It much repairs me / To talk of your good father' (ll. 30–1). Retreating into nostalgia, the King finds a space wider than that afforded by 'our young lords' (l. 33). The memory is not truly restorative, as it tends to exacerbate the King's exhaustion.

> 'Let me not live', quoth he,
> 'After my flame lacks oil, to be the snuff
> Of younger spirits, whose apprehensive senses
> All but new things disdain; whose judgments are
> Mere fathers of their garments; whose constancies
> Expire before their fashions'. This he wish'd.
> I, after him, do after him wish too,
> Since I nor wax nor honey can bring home,

I quickly were dissolved from my hive
To give some labourers room.
(ll. 55–67)

The clothing-imagery has an obvious reference to Bertram in his
association with Parolles, but the reported words are unforgiving
of the new. One cannot imagine such a father ever having talked
understandingly to his son, and part of the problem in France is
the inflexibility of older standards. The imagery of the bee-hive
explains why this should be so. The state has become a process
from which infirmity excludes the King, its activity busy and
purposeful but alien. The possibility of individual achievement in
historical time has gone, and there is no consolation. To be
'loved', as the Second Lord reminds him that he is (l. 67), is not
enough. 'I fill a place, I know't' (l. 69). He now inquires about
Helena's father, but forlornly, as he knows him to be dead.

The King's purposeless continuing to be may be seen partly as
the melancholia of terminal illness, but it suggests a deep
wrongness in the country. Youth is blocked and age unsatisfied:
somehow, what matters has been let slip.

When Helena first meets the King, she adopts a language that
we do not hear from her elsewhere.[22] The King refuses to believe
that she can cure him, and she rejoins that

> Inspired merit so by breath is barr'd.
> It is not so with Him that all things knows
> As 'tis with us that square our guess by shows;
> But most it is presumption in us when
> The help of heaven we count the act of men.
> Dear sir, to my endeavours give consent;
> Of heaven, not me, make an experiment.
> (II.i.147–53)

'Inspired merit' seems a faintly odd way for Helena to describe
herself, even if in an analogy, given what we already know of her
intentions, and her remarks about heaven are ones which she will
not see as applying to herself. Advising the King to 'make an
experiment' of heaven is a suitably modern idiom for her to fall
into, though it obviously runs against biblical precept (e.g.
Matthew 4:7). That it does so will, in a multiplication of ironies,
not cause the experiment to misfire. Helena slides in and out of

the hieratic register proper to kings, but her sliding signals its desuetude. The King asks whether Helena is 'so confident' (l. 158) and is assured that, 'The greatest Grace lending grace' (l. 159), he will be cured within two days.

> Upon thy certainty and confidence
> What dar'st thou venture?
>
> (ll. 168–9)

the King asks.

> Tax of impudence,
> A strumpet's boldness, a divulged shame,
> Traduc'd by odious ballads; my maiden's name
> Sear'd otherwise; ne worst of worst, extended
> With vildest torture, let my life be ended.
>
> (ll. 169–73)

Helena first puts in jeopardy her reputation, that for which in the heroic world a person will surrender all, but, realising that such an offer is not enough, offers her body as well. Physical rather than moral agony is the only efficient guarantee.

> Methinks in thee some blessed spirit doth speak
> His powerful sound within an organ weak;
> And what impossibility would slay
> In common sense, sense saves another way.
> Thy life is dear, for all that life can rate
> Worth name of life in thee hath estimate:
> Youth, beauty, wisdom, courage – all
> That happiness and prime can happy call.
> Thou this to hazard needs must intimate
> Skill infinite, or monstrous desperate.
>
> (ll. 174–83)

'Skill' might mean moral percipience, but practical (medical) capability seems more likely.[23] The 'blessed spirit' is judged by its willingness to throw away 'Youth, beauty, wisdom, courage', the talents it has been given. Helena is rated at the size of her stake. There is a worrying undertone of the King's having been haggling which stresses the empirically minded mistrust that is his natural attitude.

Lafew's speech when the King's cure is first heard of is of particular interest: 'They say miracles are past; and we have our philosophical persons to make modern and familiar, things supernatural and causeless' (II.iii.1–3). This should remind us of Donne's worries about astronomy.[24] What Lafew describes in precisely the passage from folkloric trust to contemporary reason that the King's contract with Helena has exemplified. When the King appears, he gives Helena 'a second time' 'The confirmation of my promis'd gift' (ll. 49–50).

The King now offers Helena the pick of his wards.

> Fair maid, send forth thine eye. This youthful parcel
> Of noble bachelors stand at my bestowing,
> O'er whom both sovereign power and father's voice
> I have to use. Thy frank election make;
> Thou hast power to choose, and they none to forsake.
>
> (ll. 52–6)

The King is now operating at the level of fairy-tale, to which the success of Helena's cure has raised him, a level on which she herself will insist – 'Gentlemen,/Heaven hath through me restor'd the king to health' (ll. 63–4). Realistically, though, the King's power appears capricious and arbitrary, the more so when we reflect that he is being manipulated by Helena. The King claims to be liberating her from her social station and granting her a peculiar liberty, but this is what she has planned. There is no question of a real choice, for we know that Bertram is her object.

When she has picked Bertram out, and the King instructs him to marry her, he replies,

> My wife, my liege! I shall beseech your highness,
> In such a business give me leave to use
> The help of mine own eyes.
>
> (ll. 106–8)

Regrettably, he commands our sympathy here. He is obtuse and wrong – Helena is plainly a desirable bride – but he is being treated unfairly. The King's liberality to Helena means ignoring his personality, and Bertram wants to be set on the same level as her. We shall see later that the help of his own eyes isn't much good to him, but that is not the point. For a moment, Bertram seems as much picked on as picked out.

He maintains our sympathy with his fuller explanation. The King asks if he knows what Helena has done, implicitly whether he is aware of her merits. 'Yes, my good lord, / But never hope to know why I should marry her' (ll. 109–10). Where the King has claimed an authority at once constitutional and familial, Bertram insists on his autonomy, as he has every right to do given that we have seen the King spurning his place in the kingdom and know that under his reign youth has been bottled up and refused engagement in the affairs of the state. The King attempts to repossess the kingdom as his household, but the ties on which such government depends have already broken down and cannot arbitrarily be reinstated.

Bertram forfeits our sympathy when he next speaks. The King repeats what Helena has done, and he asks,

> But follows it, my lord, to bring me down
> Must answer for your raising? I know her well:
> She had her breeding at my father's charge –
> A poor physician's daughter my wife! Disdain
> Rather corrupt me ever!
>
> (ll. 112–16)

It emerges that his grounds are snobbish ones, but still based on individualism. He conceives of himself as set over against the world, his station independent of the monarch's wishes, and uses crudely financial terms to disparage Helena's background. Snobbery is the residue of fealty in a desacralised world, and the King misses the point with his ''Tis only title thou disdain'st in her, the which / I can build up' (ll. 117–18). Bertram has already in effect rejected the King's power to 'build up' social rank, and sees it as given only by birth. A system capable of flexibility and generosity has become a rigid determinism, and legitimises his own selfishness rather than taking legitimacy from the King's power.

The beautiful irony of all this is that we have actually seen magic work through Helena almost without her knowing. The language she uses and her manipulative exploitation of the magic should trouble us, but her capacity to embody what heals goes beyond her personality. Just as desire in this play is an impersonal, physically grounded force, so the appearance of goodness transcends the individual will. I shall return to this instance of Shakespearean doubleness,[25] wanting for the moment simply to register its presence.

The King uses against Bertram the argument that virtue is given irrespective of rank. This argument carries all its traditional force as the human face of feudalism, but is devalued again when he says,

> If thou canst like this creature as a maid,
> I can create the rest. Virtue and she
> Is her own dower; honour and wealth from me.
>
> (ll. 142–4)

He invites Bertram to find Helena sexually enticing, to accept her not as a person but as a potential being, a virgin rather than a woman. To this invitation he adds a bribe. Bertram's answer insists on her individual being, even if this is still conceived in terms of social rank. 'I cannot love her nor will strive to do't' (l. 145). To the King, Helena is merely a 'creature', a created thing over whom he has quasi-divine powers. Where to the King she is therefore plastic, to Bertram she is abhorrently rigid. The paradox by which royal prerogative appears more generous than the assertion of individual liberty is rapidly submerged as the argument turns into a battle of wills, the King replying, 'Thou wrong'st thyself if thou shouldn't strive to choose' (l. 146). He is now precisely denying the freedom Bertram claims.

Bertram refuses to recognise the claims of either royalty or magic: the King interprets both as only concerning himself. The King's command of his proper language is uneven, and about to break down. Helena attempts to withdraw, and the King tells her, 'My honour's at the stake, which to defeat, / I must produce my power' (ll. 149–50). Bertram's stubbornness reduces the argument to its lowest level, that on which he has always seen it, partly because the King has already thrown away his authority. It is not authority but 'honour' which is now imperilled, 'power' which is to arbitrate.

Bertram has no option but to submit. When he has done so, the King's 'Good fortune and the favour of the King / Smile upon this contract' (ll. 177–8) attempts to restore the moment to the level of ritual and tradition, but by now we can only feel the inappropriateness of this manoeuvre. When he says, 'As thou lov'st her / Thy love's to me religious; else, does err' (ll. 182–3), his language is that of Inquisition; authoritarian rather than individualistic, but with an authoritarianism which is challenged by individualism and does not flow from unassailable origins.

In both halves of the play, Bertram is victim not agent. When he decides to spurn Helena and go to the war, he says that 'Wars is no strife / To the dark house and the detested wife' (ii.iii.287–8). His reaction to Helena is patently unjust and short-sighted, but here injustice finds its own desolate poetry. The image opens a world of extended domestic suffering we find nowhere else in the play, and makes us feel the inward force of his resentment just as there is *joie de vivre* in his last shot at Helena gone out of earshot,

> Go thou toward home, where I will never come
> Whilst I can shake my sword or hear the drum.
>   (ii.v.90–1)

Bertram shaking his sword is a diminutive, childish figure who has no sense of war's reality. The make-believe he inhabits is not a generous reconstruction of the world like Falstaff's but a petulant unawareness of regenerative possibilities. War is only fun, domestic life unchanging and monotonous.

To call Bertram childish is to imply that he needs to grow up. His failure to do so in the course of the play flouts expectations which tragicomic form encourages. The exposure of Parolles ought to be educative, but we have no evidence that it is. After the scene of the exposure (iv.iii) we see the two together only once, in the final scene, where they do not speak to each other, and Bertram's comment on Parolles in Act iv Scene iii is to reiterate the 'cat' of 'I could endure anything before but a cat, and now he's a cat to me' (ll. 229–30: cf. ll. 255, 266). A cat's independence of being resists Bertram's fantasies about the world. A cat is also 'a spiteful and backbiting woman' (*OED*, quoting this instance), and as such recalls his image of Helena. Bertram does not have the imaginative resources to deny the facts he keeps bumping into: Parolles' revealed unworthiness is not a moral lesson but a reminder of the otherness of other people, with which Bertram does not know what to do.

Bertram's ineducable mean-spiritedness (we saw earlier how his attempted self-exculpations are derivative, clichés of romance) persists into the last scene. Events bludgeon him into submission, and there is no sign of a change of heart. The play offers Bertram no space to enjoy his own being, because the momentum of events never lets up on him, and no space ever to discover his own nature. He cannot change because he is denied the time to change. Similarly, the king remains, as we have seen, a determined matchmaker, trying to wed Bertram and Maudlin, then offering Diana her pick of a husband. The king learns nothing from the action, and expresses the lack of necessary 'leisure'.

The character who comes closest to self-recognition is Parolles. As his name indicates, this fantastic scarfed figure belongs to a different dramatic world, that of Jonsonian comedy.[26] Parolles is ostensibly a type, a vainglorious, dishonest soldier with courtly airs and graces to which his merits give him no title, but when he is alone on stage after his exposure he finds room to disclose himself and to sound the bottom reach of the play.

> Yet am I thankful. If my heart were great
> 'Twould burst at this. Captain I'll be no more,
> But I will eat and drink and sleep as soft
> As captain shall. Simply the thing I am
> Shall make me live. Who knows himself a braggart,
> Let him fear this; for it will come to pass
> That every braggart shall be found an ass.
> Rust, sword; cool, blushes; and Parolles live
> Safest in shame; being fool'd, by fool'ry thrive.
> There's place and means for every man alive.
> I'll after them.
>
> (IV.iii.319–29)

At the end of Act III Scene vii, Helena's broken line signalled her resolute adherence to plotting, her unwillingness to rest in the couplets of contemplation. Parolles' broken line signals his witty opportunism, for he and Helena are mirrors to each other.[27] Both survive by persistence, each securing desired ends by opportunistic adaptation. Here, Parolles is glad not to have a 'great' heart, to be trivial, because he cannot die of shame. 'Captain' was only a role, one he can set aside without imperilling his own existence. 'Simply the thing I am / Shall make me live': this is an emphatically physical presentation of enduring selfhood which cuts below any idea of personality to something as impersonal as desire. It is like feeling the solidity of one's own breastbone. This bedrock recognition cheers Parolles up.[28] He rises to an almost prophetic pitch for the next two lines, paradoxically reaffirming moral order. This proximity to the proverbial we shall see restated later with Lafew. Parolles has been 'fool'd', made a fool of, but he has also been made into a fool and can now profess folly. The equivocation by which the passive turns into an active force is what enables him to 'thrive' in the certainty that there is room for everyone in the world. Parolles' unworthiness lets him see the generosity of the natural order whose parasite his wit empowers him to become.

Humiliation extends Parolles' imaginative horizons: the 'thing' he is closes them. Parolles is too wary to rely on the wisdom he has acquired. At his next appearance he presents himself as the butt of circumstance, 'muddied in Fortune's mood' (v.ii.4), but he meets the Clown's relentlessly physical expansion of his metaphor with truculent irritation. 'I spake but by a metaphor', he objects (ll. 10–11), rejecting the freedom wordplay enacts. Of course, Lavatch is not a sentimentally imagined rustic but a scabrous, lavatorial curmudgeon: the implications of the scene are tantalisingly just out of the characters' grasp. 'Pray you, sir, deliver me this paper' (l. 15) Parolles insists, and in that insistence we recognise the old 'thing'.

Parolles' tone changes when he introduces himself to Lafew as 'a man whom Fortune hath cruelly scratch'd' (ll. 26–7), angling for the pity Lafew's 'we must do good against evil' (ii.v.48) leads him to expect. Lafew at first offers money alone, but draws nearer when Parolles identifies himself (v.ii.38), replying with a pun on his name (the kind of free-floating wit Parolles resists), an exclamation and 'Give me your hand. How does your drum?' (l. 40). Lafew knows what has happened but takes no advantage of his knowledge, telling Parolles to 'inquire further after me. I had talk of you last night; though you are a fool and a knave you shall eat. Go to; follow' (ll. 49–51). Lafew's emotional reactions are, as I argued above, apt to a more broadly comic world but inadequate to the demands of this one. 'I praise God for you' (l. 52), Parolles says, as well he might if he had not so clearly picked out his target. Parolles shakes down his own windfalls, but has the impudent brilliance to hit the register in which Lafew is at home. We may feel that Parolles is the parasite Lafew deserves.

Parolles' name binds him to an identity, as does Volpone's, but where Jonsonian nomenclature is reductively typical 'Parolles' has open-endedness. Parolles is Protean in a world where words have become bargaining-counters or tools, and the ultimate reality, as we see from the King's dealings with Bertram, is force. Parolles and Helena both exploit language to secure what they want, neither evincing respect for the traditional orders whose dictions they may from time to time adopt.

It is easy to see why the play might be regarded as dealing with a modern 'problem' in a modern way. Through Helena and Parolles we experience an atomised society whose decayed social and moral orders breed an aggressive individualism. If the play seems to be being treated partly as a socio-economic fable, this is because its emphasis on money and the replacement of vows by contracts does suggest historical parallels. However, I do not want to suggest that the play expresses Shakespeare's nostalgia for the golden age, and I hope also to avoid the suggestion that the characters' language is alone sufficient to represent the play's world. Obviously the plot is at least as important, and I want now to consider Shakespeare's use of tragicomic form.

Helena's personality emerges with startling clarity at the end of Act I Scene i:

> Our remedies oft in ourselves do lie,
> Which we ascribe to heaven; the fated sky
> Gives us free scope; only doth backward pull
> Our slow designs when we ourselves are dull.
>   (ll. 212–15)

The natural order of the stars may be mechanistically determined, but man's freedom moves beyond such trammels except 'when we ourselves are dull'. Although Helena can speak to the Countess of loving heaven (I.iii.187–8), her true love, 'Religious in . . . error' (l. 200), is for Bertram, her 'idolatrous fancy' (I.i.95) substituting desire for acquiescence in providence. It is noticeable that Helena assents to the Countess' idiom as she will employ the King's and, as I said above, important that though she believes in the magical efficacy of her father's potion (I.iii.237–45) she puts it to personal ends. We see her doubly because we are conscious that she has to wriggle and manipulate to escape the restrictions of class and background that threaten her autonomy.

We must also be impressed by the power of her love and her sheer tenacity. It is clear that her desire is strongly physical, and I have indicated the ways in which she confuses the carnal with the spiritual. That her desire is physical does not demean it – indeed, her love appears as a hunger for fixity in a shifty universe. That Helena is self-seeking does not necessarily demean her, for she has no one to look out for her and no adequate moral currency in which to demand payment. What is perhaps most affecting is Bertram's worthlessness, the implication that love need not be deserved to be earned.

Indeed, Helena's desire for Bertram is fruitful and productive: it makes a baby (v.iii.307). This is what raises her above Parolles, whose desire is solipsistic, its end his own perpetuation. The bitterness of the ending, therefore, is shaded by an intimation of the traditional marital conclusion of comedy, particularly Shakespearean comedy. The play has offered the possibility of tragedy, the opposition of obtuseness to self-sacrifice, and now it offers a chance to comedy. That it does so is not entirely an effect of Helena's will.

In the lag between bed-trick and conclusion, time does indeed 'backward pull', almost as though it were rebuking Helena's self-assertive insolence. But it isn't: dull contingency and not a teaching Fortune delays the action; the brake on Helena's intentions is not a matter of her being either 'dull' or demanding. In the first part of the play Helena tries to engineer a miraculous comedy, and in the second she works for the potentially redemptive effect of tragicomedy, and in neither case does she succeed. Things run athwart her wishes.

The gap at the centre of the play denies the necessity of tragicomedy. The second plot is started by chance – Helena, as we saw, uses the language of fate to the Widow, not to herself – and the bridge to it is provided by the invisible working of Helena's desire. We cannot know whether or not she consciously trailed Bertram because she cannot know, acting under the compulsion of need. Helena's want of Bertram is as painful as Parolles' hunger. The outcome of the play is the result of powers working within the characters of which they may be conscious but are not in charge. This is in one way a powerfully modern psychological effect, but in another it is purely aesthetic and timeless.

In *All's Well*, desire itself takes a tragicomic form. Tragicomedy generically requires the satisfactions at which this play's desirers aim, for while procreation and self-perpetuation may be morally distinct they are both desirable ends for comic characters. Falstaff has no wish to breed: Beatrice and Benedick are clearly designed to. One participates in the generative cycle as repetitive sameness; the others as movement. Parolles' and Helena's desires both aim at comic ends, then, and having been endangered naturally takes a tragicomic form.[29] What disturbs us is not their fulfilments but their relationships with the people through whom their ends are achieved.

Lafew tempts us to sentimentality, partly because he is so moved by the aesthetic harmony of the *dénouement*. This is why he is tested by juxtaposition with Parolles, who shows that his virtues are dangerous liabilities and that his vision is limited. Feeling sorry for him as a parasite's victim yet despairing of him as a caught cony, we cannot finally share in his emotions. His tears are blinding because they are blind to the reality of Helena and Bertram.

Bertram remains the thing he is. Where desire for Helena and Parolles is dynamic, forcing them to act, for him it is static. All his rushing around leaves him in the same place, fantasising narcissistically about the desire he is helpless not to attract. He gets the child unintentionally and by the wrong woman, for his sexual conduct is only appetite, fickle, satiable and ashamed. It is not at the end of the play clear whether he has been moved inwardly or not: we feel that only a miracle could make it so, and the play does not encourage us to expect miracles.[30]

Tragicomedy is achieved, then, despite the characters, who are opaque to us. We can never really understand Helena's passion because we can see every reason for it to die, none for it to live but its own strength. Similarly, Parolles' determination to live acknowledges its own baseness and cannot therefore command our entire sympathy. Unable to penetrate or entirely to like anybody in the play, we are unhappy about the conclusion we yet want. We share the distance between the formal and the emotional with the characters, happy at the satisfaction of desire but obstructed by the characters' objective, resistant thickness. For them as for us, tragicomedy is still latent, a potential explanation and justification of the action which is always in view but never in touch.

All's Well That Ends Well puts moral and social assumptions into question and shows the replacement of fixed ideals by the circulation of desire mitigated only by contract. It also puts into question the possibility of its own stability, being placed at such a distance from its putative genre that we are made conscious how much we would like formal and moral expectations to cohere. Resisting assimilation to genre, it takes on the abrasive existence of its characters, who resist assimilation to plot, and presents us with the thinglike density of life while reminding us that that alone cannot be enough to satisfy the imagination.

II

Helena's reputation grew during the eighteenth century to the point at which Schlegel could invoke Griselda.[31] Hazlitt found 'great sweetness and delicacy'[32] in a character Coleridge untypically for his age thought 'not very delicate':[33] Coleridge thought Bertram had much to be said for him,[34] and that Shakespeare needs to shape our sympathy by having the other characters extol Helena's virtues. 'We get to like Helena from their praising and commending her so much.'[35]

The sense that we have to 'get to like' Helena is a tribute to Shakespeare's lifelikeness, but it also suggests the rubbing along the play imposes on cast and audience alike and further implies that this is imposed on the relationships between them. Moralising on Helena's reported death, the First Lord says that 'The web of our life is of a mingled yarn, good and ill together; our virtues would be proud if our faults whipp'd them not, and our crimes would despair if they were not cherish'd by our virtues' (IV.iii.68–71). The tension between honour and shame in Bertram's character is exemplary of a tension in the world. The First Lord's moral teleology does not, however, help us with the whole of the play, because it carries an intimation of the circular binding we feel in the Epilogue, when the King tells us that 'All is well ended if this suit be won, / That you express content' (ll. 2–3). The play world cannot give value to what has happened, and it is for us to judge. What might be openness is in the King's mouth a desperate plea for our cooperation.

A similar effect is achieved in *Troilus and Cressida*, where the audience's co-operation is never sought by the characters[36] though solicited by the play's smutty cynicism. In *All's Well* we see a comedy without comic, regenerative time; in *Troilus and Cressida* we see tragedy accelerated into meaninglessness.

One of the most important things about the story of Troilus and Cressida, for Shakespeare as for Chaucer, is that it is retold. We are concerned here not with its genealogy, the way it made space in the matter of Troy for unclassical ideals of sentiment and conduct,[37] but with the phenomenon that once the story exists it keeps getting told. Why that might be so can be seen by examining two derivations from the Chaucerian account.

Henryson's *The Testament of Cresseid*[38] begins with a confident generalisation:

> Ane dooly sesoun to ane cairfull dyte
> Suld correspond, and be equivalent.[39]

Henryson joins inner and outer, mind and circumstance, in a way that defines precisely the scope of his poem, as we shall see. The weather was properly atrocious when he sat down to write it, as he assures us. It was night, and the moon shone so brightly

> That I micht see, on every syde me by,
> The northin wind had purifyit the air,
> And shed the misty cloudis fra the sky.[40]

The clarity of this is so compellingly naturalistic that we might overlook how the fact that the worst of the weather has passed symbolically anticipates the focusing of Henryson's imagination in the wake of greatness. The naturalism is pursued: it was so cold that Henryson had to 'remuf aganis my will'[41] from his oratory to the inner 'chalmer'.[42] This secularisation is obviously important. In the inner room,

> I mend the fyr, and beikit me about,
> Than tuik ane drink my spreitis to comfort,
> And armit me weill fra the cauld thairout.
> To cut the winter-nicht, and mak it short,
> I tuik ane quair, and left all uther sport,
> Writtin be worthy Chaucer glorious,
> Of fair Cresseid and worthy Troilus.[43]

The emphasis on physical comfort as Henryson, apparently a bachelor though 'expert' in love young and old,[44] settles down to read, reflects on both Chaucer's and his own creations.

When Henryson had read through *Troilus and Criseyde*, 'To brek my sleip ane uther quair I tuik'.[45] This deliberate wakefulness may use the traditional associations of night to embody the poet's access of creativity, but it also helps blur his own originality. The new book is one

> I quilk I fand the fatall desteny
> Of fair Cresseid, that endit wretchitly.[46]

Henryson moves deliberately to deny his own responsibility for the story he is to tell, a move which Chaucer had found invaluable.

> Quha wait gif all that Chauceir wrait was trew?
> Nor I wait nocht gif this narratioun
> Be authoreist, or fenyeit of the new
> Be sum poeit, throw his inventioun.[47]

As he has already spoken of the time 'quhen I began to wryte / This tragedy',[48] we know that 'this narratioun' is his own. The tension between 'authoreist' and 'fenyeit of the new' is crucial. The Chaucerian device of 'myn auctour' is deliberately confused with legitimacy so as to pour scorn on the modish poet who forges his own stories. The question whether Chaucer himself genuinely assented to poetry as a relay-race has already challenged this tone, however. By casting doubt on Chaucer's truthfulness and expressing complete uncertainty as to where his own story comes from Henryson gives the latter an objective reality, so allowing himself simply to appear as the executant. We are ostensibly invited to enjoy Henryson's performance.

The realism of *Troilus and Criseyde* penetrates Henryson's beginning. That realism is concentrated in Chaucer's medieval Troy, where courtly love flourishes among cushions and gutters and the presiding genius is Pandarus. The scenes in Troy are Chaucer's most novelistic because they combine mental exploration with a thickness of contingent detail. We are made to feel that Troilus and Criseyde are people like ourselves, and have the elementary fictional pleasure of identification.[49] *Troilus and Criseyde* is not a novel, though: the very word insists on the newness of what is related, and one of the poem's most telling features is that it is not the first recounting of the story.

The Testament of Cresseid is presented, then, as a reader's directed daydream. As such, it pays tribute to Chaucer by drawing new vitality from his original power. Henryson makes us feel that we want to know what happened next by ignoring Chaucer's ending and proposing that we resist his withdrawal of the characters from our attention. Reading *Troilus and Criseyde* is for Henryson not only an imaginative stimulus but a creaturely pleasure. The night may be the symbolic domain of imagination, but it has a bitterly Scottish chill. We are made to join in Henryson's ultimately punitive fantasy because he makes himself into a realistic fictional character. The balance between self-portrayal and impersonal narration shows us literature acting on life with moving depth. The easy give-and-take between Chaucer and Henryson has a warmth and human intensity denied to Emma Bovary reading her novelettes. Where Flaubert is agitated by the thinness to which literature reduces life, Henryson apparently celebrates their intercourse, seeming to show what Matisse would mean by an art the businessman could sink into as into an armchair.[50]

Walton's *Troilus and Cressida*[51] explores the spiritual, emotive side of the story by inviting the characters to escape into music from the constraints of their destiny. The artistic catastrophe which ensues reveals much about that destiny. At the beginning of the first act, we see the Trojan priests and people in conflict, the people being dominated by Antenor, who will in due course betray the city. The irony is tired and snobbish, the situation beside the point, the tension structurally irrelevant to the opera. Troy is shown as riven and fractious, which may be right for a moribund state but makes a nonsense of the story. If everyone in Troy is pursuing self-interest, nothing more than greater emotional intensity can privilege Troilus and Cressida in our eyes.

As Chaucer has it,[52] Troilus and Criseyde are imperilled by public unity. When Troilus proposes to Criseyde that they should steal away together, she says,

> 'But that ye speke, awey thus for to go
> And leten alle youre frendes, God forbede,
> For any womman, that ye sholden so!
> And namely syn Troie hath now swich nede
> Of help. And ek of o thyng taketh hede:

> If this were wist, my lif lay in balaunce,
> And youre honour; God shilde us fro meschaunce!
>
> 'And if so be that pees heere-after take,
> As alday happeth after anger game,
> Whi, Lord, the sorwe and wo ye wolden make,
> That ye ne dorste come ayeyn for shame!
> And er that ye juparten so youre name,
> Beth naught to hastif in this hoote fare;
> For hastif man we wanteth nevere care.
>
> 'What trowe ye the peple ek al aboute
> Wolde of it seye? It is ful light t'arede.
> They wolden seye, and swere it, out of doute,
> That love ne drof you naught to don this dede,
> But lust voluptuous and coward drede.
> Thus were al lost, ywys, myn herte deere,
> Youre honour, which that now shyneth so clere.'
>
>   (IV.1555–75)

Criseyde goes on to worry that 'My name sholde I nevere ayeynward winne', but the essential point is clear.

It is also beautifully muffled. Criseyde appeals to Troilus' public image, and insists that he would lose if it his plan went through. He should not desert 'For any womman' – an almost parenthetical self-denigration which contributes to our picture of Criseyde – particularly when Troy so needs him. Additionally, Criseyde's life would be in danger if the plan came out, like Troilus' honour. The instinct for self-preservation betrays itself helplessly. It is important, she goes on, to think what will happen after the war, how cross Troilus will be if he is unable to go home 'for shame'. Before jeopardising his name, Troilus should stop and think, because 'hastif man ne wanteth nevere care'. This finger-wagging proverbial advice is transparently rhetorical in context. Most importantly of all, 'the peple ek al aboute' would say Troilus had deserted not for love but for fear. So you would lose all your bright honour, 'myn herte deere': Criseyde is genuinely concerned for Troilus as well as herself, but the arguments she has used betray her shallowness.[53]

In *Bérénice*,[54] Titus is tempted to throw everything up for Bérénice.

Ah! lâche! fais l'amour, et renonce à l'Empire.
Au bout de l'univers, va, cours te confiner,
Et fais place à des coeurs plus dignes de régner.
Sont-ce là ces projets de grandeur et de gloire
Qui devaient dans les coeurs consacrer ma mémoire?
Depuis huit jours je règne; et, jusques à ce jour,
Qu'ai-je fait pour l'honneur? J'ai tout fait pour l'amour.
(IV.iv.1024–30)

Paradoxically, Titus owes this heroic conception of himself to
Bérénice. Brought up in Nero's court, Titus would have become a
debauchee had it not been that

Bérénice me plut. Que ne fait point un coeur
Pour plaire à ce qu'il aime et gagner son vainqueur?
(II.ii.509–10)

Bérénice claims that she 'n'aime en lui que lui-même' (I.iv.160) but
the nature of that self is not so simple as she would make it
appear. Its being depends precisely on its capacity to renounce
her, as she comes to understand and to make clear in her final
speech to Antiochus.

Prince, après cet adieu, vous jugez bien vous-même
Que je ne consens pas de quitter ce que j'aime
Pour aller loin de Rome écouter d'autres voeux.
Vivez, et faites-vous un effort généreux.
Sur Titus et sur moi réglez votre conduite:
Je l'aime, je le fuis; Titus m'aime, il me quitte.
Portez loin de mes yeux vos soupirs et vos fers.
(v.vii.1495–1501)

It is necessary to become a moral exemplar. Antiochus knows well
that she will have no use for him in the circumstances. As he
himself has earlier put it to Arsace,

Penses-tu seulement que, parmi ses malheurs,
Quand l'univers entier négligerait ses charmes,
L'ingrate me permît du lui donner des larmes,
Ou qu'elle s'abaissât jusques à recevoir
Des soins qu'à mon amour elle croirait devoir?
(III.ii.802–6)

Antiochus is too passively, desperately in love to win her: Titus' glory overpowers his. Titus cannot marry Bérénice and remain emperor, but he could not abdicate and remain the man she loves. She can in the end only recommend a tragic attitude to Antiochus, styled on that into which she and Titus are thrown.

Troilus threatens to be Antiochus, and Criseyde implores him to be Titus. Troilus is, as his name suggests, irrevocably tied to Troy. To give up everything and trail after Criseyde would be to become ridiculous even to himself. 'Sorwe and wo' would indeed be mingled in self-loathing exile: Criseyde's tone attempts to jolly Troilus along, but there is a serious truth under it. Love has made Troilus a better soldier, as it should. In renouncing the stereotype, Troilus would enter a new world of feeling Criseyde fears.[55] However, there are important differences between Racine's and Chaucer's understandings. Racine's characters are ennobled by the inhumanity with which they must treat themselves; Chaucer's are humanised by their weary relation with literary and moral dignity.

Troilus persists, reiterating his proposition.

> 'For evere in oon, as for to lyve in reste,
> Myn herte seyth that it wol be the beste.'

He is ready to sacrifice everything, but she will not let him. "What lif is this?" she asks sensibly, before accusing him of lacking faith in her. Antiochus observes that

> Titus m'accable ici du poids de sa grandeur:
> Tout disparaît dans Rome auprès de sa splendeur;
> Mais, quoique l'Orient soit plein de sa mémoire,
> Bérénice y verra des traces de ma gloire.
>
> (III.ii.793–6)

The Orient seems a dull, mean place against his will: 'What lif is this?' indeed. Criseyde has an unsettling realism which complicates judgement. Troilus submits stoically:

> 'At shorte wordes, wel ye may me leve:
> I kan na more, it shal be founde at preve.'

Somehow this couple muff their way into doing the right thing.

Criseyde invokes the judgement of society rather than moral values, which reflects her own social nature and anticipates her disintegration when deprived of social support. Troilus becomes heroic because of a comic resignation in face of his mistress' loquacity. Their mutal incomprehension proceeds from their characters, and seems to have the inevitability of fate.

It is vital to this effect that Troy should be a community. Chaucer makes it such partly by cluttering the place with things. Walton and his librettist, Christopher Hassall, do not show us a united public world against which the lovers' privacy might be tested. The mistrust of the common people shown at the start is part of an attitude which undermines the whole work.

Troilus himself appears in the first scene and, in this context all too characteristically, invokes Aphrodite, 'In my heart abiding'.[56] The music prolongs and embellishes 'heart' to establish it as a value, but this unfortunately is to take Troilus at his own estimation. The comedy Chaucer finds in Troilus' sudden conversion to love is omitted, and we see a one-dimensional heroic lover where Chaucer offered a further perspective. This affirmation of Troilus' idea of himself will be repeated when he tells Pandarus that 'love is loath to wait'[57] (an amazing reversal of characterisation) by placing a similarly indulgent emphasis on 'love'. The music takes Troilus' side as it will take everybody's, with a cold-hearted promiscuity quite unlike creative generosity.

It will, for instance, take Diomede's part late in the second act, when he first sees Cressida. His wondering, unaccompanied lines of admiration form a moment of pure feeling and, although the intention may be to remind us of Cressida's overwhelming attractions, the effect is to make Diomede rather sympathetic. Indeed, unlike Troilus, he makes his own music. Diomede's wonder is on a level with the duet between Troilus and Cressida, 'We were alone',[58] which lyrically enshrines their erotic experience and abstracts it from the plot. All the characters aim at such moments, of which the debased form is Pandarus' loving appreciation of 'my smooth address',[59] a phrase lingered on and repeated so as to show that he, if meanly, shares the values of others and has none of his own. Pandarus is presented as a witty young man about town, but one too sentimental to be dangerous, too self-indulgent to be much of a pander.

The most impressive yet revealing passage in the opera comes at the end of the second act, when behind closed curtains Troilus and Cressida enjoy each other while the music enjoys itself. This orchestral interlude moves into the brooding, drowsy dawn music and words, which are themselves undercut by the martial drum. Here, Walton achieves a feeling comparable with the Chaucerian, but too late. The orchestral interlude is an erotic fantasy made pornographic by the conditions of staging: we cannot help wondering what the curtains are hiding from us.[60] The equivalent passage in Chaucer[61] avoids these dangers by being physical and mental, enumerating (in general terms) the features of Criseyde's body as well as Troilus' response. The continuity of verse ties the night into the plot, forcing it to share the world with other kinds of experience.[62] Walton's reverie is bodiless and tawdry because sex and spirituality are clumsily juxtaposed rather than interpenetrating.

The third act rapidly degenerates into a shambles. Troilus and Cressida have tried to keep in touch, but their correspondence has been intercepted by Evadne, who has the moral sensibility of Juliet's nurse. Responsibility for the plot being handed over to this evil genius, Cressida is at least partly absolved of moral blame and largely deprived of dramatic conflict. She is permitted a musically beautiful moment of loneliness and longing which has no point or focus because she is the victim of external agency rather than of her own nature. The Cressida riddle has been abandoned rather than solved, so that when she sings 'Leave me to my fate'[63] the orchestra will pound home her heroism while we are increasingly uncertain what her fate is to be. She so dithers between Troilus and Diomede that when the chorus reproach her for her infidelity it is literally impossible to tell whose side they are on. 'You must not die for me',[64] Cressida tells Troilus, but 'die' is gratuitously singled out and stressed as though she had some other sacrifice in mind. Cressida's death earns a moment of musical ebullition before harsh, percussive tones drown it, but one wonders why.

The opera botches the plot so that everyone becomes pardonable, a tasteless evasion of the story's severity. The characters are sentimentally encouraged to express selves less rich than the composer assumes. Where Chaucer explores the thinness of his characters and their role-playing, the opera throws away the significance on which it parasitically depends. Had Edith Sitwell written the libretto,[65] the strident, bitty hollowness of her poetry would have interacted effectively with the heartlessness of the music, because Troilus and Cressida are inherently unmusical beings, with inner lives too disorganised for the Walton-Hassall world of jostling narcissistic egos. Pandarus, though ostensibly cheapened by the score, turns out to be the same as everyone else in understanding that the only meaning of the plot is to provide occasions for feeling.

The opera's attempt at a radical transformation of the story necessarily fails, where Henryson's careful accommodation of its prior existence gives him a greater freedom. Henryson acknowledges that he is a reader, just as Chaucer himself is a reader of Boccaccio. The part played by 'myn auctour' is familiar, and generally acknowledged as crucial if we are to discuss Chaucer's attitude: the clearest instance of this is the moment at which Chaucer must deal with Criseyde's change of heart. The change is fully apparent in the *Litera Criseydis* (v.1590), with its confused final stanzas:

> 'Come I wole; but yet in swich disjoynte
> I stonde as now, that what yer or what day
> That this shal be, that kan I naught apoynte.
> But in effect I pray now, as I may,
> Of youre good word and of youre frendship ay.
> For trewely, while that my lif may dure,
> As for a frend ye may in me assure.

> 'Yet preye ich yow, on yvel ye ne take
> That it is short which that I to yow write;
> I dar not, ther I am, wel lettres make,
> Ne nevere yet ne koude I wel endite.
> Ek gret effect men write in place lite;
> Th' entente is al, and nat the lettres space.
> And fareth now wel, God have yow in his grace!
> La vostre C.

(ll. 1618–31)

This is the last direct appearance Criseyde makes in the poem, having already yielded to 'this sodeyn Diomede' (l. 1024). The penultimate stanza is disjointed ('disjoynte' means separation and dilemma), crowded, and contrives to end by addressing Troilus in the only terms he cannot understand from Criseyde, those of

friendship. The sad slackening and lingering retentiveness of
feeling here is quickly hidden by further incoherent apologies.
Criseyde is sorry that her letter is so short (six stanzas to the
fifteen of the *Litera Troili*); she dare not write at length from where
she is; she was never much good at writing anyway; important
things can be said in few words; it's the thought that counts.
These excuses fail to hang together as her personality fails to
cohere (the leprosy to which Henryson consigns her is the
physical emblem of this), but in their brokeness they show why
she is lovable. The confession that she never wrote well is a
feigned artlessness, in that she has, and knows she has, already
broken her word, but it is also true. Criseyde is incapable of
brazening things out, so that the longer she goes on the more she
discloses. Ironically, she writes far too much, and her remarks on
the power of compression and implication rebound on her. We
feel that she is helpless in front of desires she does not understand.
'Entente' has a peculiar force here, as its main meaning is
'meaning' but it carries also its originally French sense of
'understanding', a sense toward which it gestures, particularly in
proximity to the French signature. Criseyde's meaning reaches
out for Troilus' understanding but cannot reach it directly: or,
rather, the meaning that is understood is not the one she
intended.

Chaucer prepares us for the sense of Criseyde's helplessness
when she is wooed by Diomede.

> And after this the storie telleth us
> That she hym yaf the faire baye stede,
> The which he ones wan of Troilus;
> And ek a broche – and that was litel nede –
> That Troilus was, she yaf this Diomede.
> And ek, the bet from sorwe to releve,
> She made hym were a pencel of hire sleve.
>
> I fynde ek in the stories elleswhere,
> Whan thorugh the body hurt was Diomede
> Of Troilus, tho wepte she many a teere,
> Whan that she saugh his wyde wowndes blede;
> And that she took, to kepen hym, good hede;
> And for to helen hym of his sorwes smerte,
> Men seyn – I not – that she yaf hym hire herte.
>
> (v.1037–50)

The movement in these two stanzas is enormously complex. Chaucer starts by laying the responsibility for what he is to relate on 'the storie', which means that the feelings he will express are not so much about his own heroine as about one of her possible appearances. Criseyde the exile overloads her protector Diomede with gifts. The 'faire baye stede', once Troilus', is followed by a brooch that was also his. 'And that was litel nede': Chaucer is anguished by the superfluity of this evidence of betrayal, but what we understand is that the weight of gifts is meant to buy off Criseyde's guilty conscience. The 'sorwe' of which Criseyde relieves Diomede is only a form of words – we never hear it developed – with which he enmeshes her, but she takes his courtliness with a desperate, endearing literalness as she makes him wear her favour. Diomede is turned into the knight he never was (we can almost picture him staggering under the unexpected booty) so that Criseyde can reassure herself that she is behaving properly. She hopes that the more strongly she asserts the uniqueness of this relationship the less guilt she will feel. We realise that she was never really in love with Troilus, not as he loved her, and that her guilt is felt as a nagging ache rather than laceration.

In the second stanza, Chaucer almost wearily refers to 'the stories elleswhere', as though shaking his head over the massive documentary evidence offered by the prosecution. He also begins to distance Criseyde, who now appears in a number of broadly consistent versions but is herself absent. That Troilus grievously wounds Diomede in battle is almost thrown away, because only Criseyde's behaviour is at issue here. The effect of the summariness is to remind us strongly, though, that Criseyde does not exist alone, that there is a world going about its business around her. Seeing Diomede hurt, Criseyde is said to have wept, and it is said that 'she took, to kepen hym, good hede'. Here the stanza begins to expand in meaning, for, although the words can be read as 'she took great care to preserve him' and to deal with her nursing him, 'kepen' can also mean 'keep', and we are offered a large vista of the anxious Criseyde busying herself to hold on to the shallow, impetuous man who wanted her body. 'His sorwes smerte' might just be the pain of his war-wounds, but it is also the term he uses to hint at his desire for her. The last sacrifice Criseyde would make for him would, in the latter case, be her heart, which we already sense to be worthless to anyone but her.

The self-regard such a reading implies is distressing and sympathetic rather than contemptible. However, the reading is again undercut by Chaucer's 'Men seyn – I not', his confession of ignorance. People may say what they will, but Chaucer cannot speak against her.

Chaucer can remove himself from Criseyde by presenting his poem in three terrestrial worlds – Troy, the battlefield and the Greek camp – which are observed with successively diminishing intimacy. To this aspect of the poem the celestial sphere is irrelevant. The elevation of Troilus at the end does, though, reorganise our whole perception, suddenly removing us from the whole earth and trivialising the lovers' tragedy in a larger perspective. The vanishing of Criseyde is emotionally satisfying but enigmatic. In his effort to solve the enigma, Henryson transfers to the characters Chaucer's ignorance. When his Troilus sees Cresseid,

> sho was in sic ply he knew hir nocht.
> Yit than hir luik in-to his mind it brocht
> The sweit visage and amorous blenking
> Of fair Cresseid, sumtyme his awin darling.
>
> Na wonder was, suppois in mynd that he
> Tuik hir figure sa sone, and lo! now, quhy;
> The idole of ane thing in cace may be
> Sa deip imprentit in the fantasy,
> That it deludis the wittis outwardly,
> And sa appeiris in forme and lyke estait
> Within the mynd as it was figurait.[66]

What happens is below consciousness. Troilus is reminded of Cresseid, whom he once (the 'sumtyme' is bleakly over) loved, but does not recognise her. Henryson's explanation is a subtle account of the way in which perception can be distorted by memory. The odd effect of this is that Troilus sees Cresseid better in what comes from the imprinting of memory than in the leprous woman before him. Deluded, he sees right without knowing it. Henryson's explanation, like his whole poem, may seem obtusely helpful: there is an unwillingness at such moments to leave questions unresolved which makes his world narrower than Chaucer's. On the other hand, we may properly wonder whether

Troilus ever saw in Criseyde more than a projection of his own desires. The romantic lover we are shown learns how to feel from a convention figured in books and art.[67] Chaucer makes subtle comedy out of the dissonance between the unapproachable lady of convention and the young widow who could easily fit into the fabliau world to which Pandarus often seems to point. Henryson's generalisation is less sententious than it seems, then, for it points up an important feature of his original.

Ignorance and delusion are not what Henryson intends to leave us with. *The Testament of Cresseid* is forthrightly moral in its conclusion. When Troilus leaves,

> 'Quhat lord is yon?' quod sho, 'have ye na feill,
> Hes don to us so greit humanitie?'
> 'Yes,' quod a lipper-man, 'I knaw him weill;
> Shir Troilus it is, gentill and free'
> Quhen Cresseid understude that it was he,
> Stiffer than steill thair stert ane bitter stound
> Throwout hir hart, and fell doun to the ground.[68]

Where Troilus has been inadequately reminded of her, she has entirely failed to recognise him. Again there is an aptness: as we saw earlier, she never really shared Troilus' feelings. Troilus has been so charitable because he was reminded of Cresseid, and that she sees it as 'humanitie' reminds us of their common frailty. To the leper who identifies him, though, he is simply 'Shir Troilus', a knight who is appropriately 'gentill and free'. Troilus is 'worthy' when he first appears in this poem,[69] in what seems a heavy-handedly Chaucerian way, but now we see that here, as in *The Canterbury Tales*, the word is examined from several different angles as the narrative progresses. Cresseid's swoon allows her to compose herself for confession and testament. 'Stiffer than steill', she is cold and rigid with horror at her own forgetfulness (though the phrase may also, of course, qualify the dignified Troilus or the ache that pierces her).[70] She has betrayed Troilus again. She dies, and when Troilus learns of her death he too swoons, saying, 'I can no moir;/Sho was untrew, and wo is me thairfoir!'[71] This restatement of the facts says all that need be said. It is only 'Sum' who attribute to Troilus the moralising verse on her gravestone.[72]

Henryson's final stroke is to turn to his audience.

> Now, worthy wemen, in this ballet short,
> Made for your worship and instructioun,
> Of cheritè I monish and exhort,
> Ming not your luf with fals deceptioun.
> Beir in your mynd this short conclusioun
> Of fair Cresseid, as I have said befoir;
> Sen sho is deid, I speik of hir no moir.[73]

If it were a only terrible warning against infidelity, neither Henryson's poem nor the story itself would amount to very much. 'Worthy' is again ambiguous, but the only poetically interesting moment in this stanza until the last line. Cresseid is dead and the account closed, but the death here is the one she has undergone in Henryson's narrative, not the actual death of an historical character. Once dead she is only exemplary, and therefore of no further interest. Henryson acknowledges against his overt purpose that what is really interesting is the woman as she was alive. His poem divides interestingly between the scenes in which he shows a deep understanding of Chaucer's implications and the less psychologically involving passages such as the allegorical, externalised judgement of the gods. The gap between the lived texture of the story and the rectilinear moral implications Henryson inherits from Chaucer, but by ending with a death rather that immortality he prevents his whole story from leaving us with tantalising reverberations.

Criseyde/Cresseid/Cressida (who may have been Briseis):[74] the variety of spellings reminds us of the extraordinarily complex history this story has. The recensions at which we have looked show how the consciousness that this is an oft-told tale infiltrates successive accounts of it and how to rebel against the inherited plot, as Walton's opera does, is to throw away freedom of interpretation for the sake of spurious novelty. Gilbert Highet tells us that Shakespeare's *Troilus and Cressida* is 'a dramatization of part of a translation into English of the French translation of a Latin imitation of an old French expansion of a Latin epitome of a Greek romance'.[75] Robert Kimbrough goes on to show that we must take into account the other line of descent through Boccaccio, and to show how widely disseminated the subject was in sixteenth-century English drama.[76]

There is a moment in Shapespeare's play[77] when the characters assume their destinies. One by one, Troilus, Cressida and

Pandarus mockingly try out the literary roles they will ironically take on, through which we are compelled to see them. 'Let all constant men be Troiluses,' says Pandarus, 'all false women Cressids, and all brokers-between Pandars. Say "Amen".'

TROILUS. Amen.
CRESSIDA. Amen.
PANDARUS. Amen. Whereupon I will show you a chamber with bed, which bed, because it shall not speak of your pretty encounters, press it to death. Away.

Exeunt [TROILUS and CRESSIDA].

And Cupid grant all tongue-tied maidens here
Bed, chamber, pander to provide this gear!

(III.ii.200–10)

The triple agreement is a shared joke only, and therefore brings out the heart of Shakespeare's treatment. *Troilus and Cressida* is a tragedy of private life in which the central characters have no privacy: indeed, Pandarus urges them to 'press' the bed not because it will be discreet but as a punishment for its refusal to testify to their raptures.[78] We expect Pandarus to make salacious jokes and know before the characters go to bed that their joys will be deluded. Pandarus turns to the audience in and out of character: he already is what he has just hoped not to become. Cressida's vow to be true has already been menaced by her admission that

I have a kind of self resides with you,
But an unkind self, that itself will leave
To be another's fool.

(ll. 146–8)

This 'kind of self' is hardly a self at all but a mere consciousness of instability, which makes Cressida rather less than a dramatic character. Earlier still in the same scene, Cressida has wondered why she has so easily admitted to her love. 'Who shall be true to us / When we are so unsecret to ourselves?' (ll. 123–4). Cressida's problem here is one not of concealed or misunderstood motives but of absolute transparency. She is depthless to herself, unlike

Ajax, who does not even know what pride is (II.iii.154) and is told
by Agamemnon that for that reason 'Your mind is the clearer' (l.
155). Achilles, who has clung to 'privacy' (III.iii.190–1), is able to
say when brought out of it that

> My mind is troubled, like a fountain stirr'd,
> And I myself see not the bottom of it.
>
> (ll. 306–7)

One way, then, of assessing the characters of *Troilus and Cressida*
is to look at their self-consciousness. The most difficult to
manoeuvre and the most private are those who claim truthfully
not to see what is going on in their own minds.

The capacity of consciousness to withdraw into itself, and the
lack of it, are crucial to the behaviour of both Cressida and Troilus
in Act v Scene ii, the scene of betrayal. When Cressida was
handed over to the Greeks in Act IV Scene iv, Diomedes told her
that 'to Diomed / You shall be mistress, and command him wholly'
(ll. 117–18), and told Troilus, who rebuked him, 'When I am
hence / I'll answer to my lust' (ll. 129–30). Although this primarily
means 'at my good pleasure',[79] we cannot but hear a sexual
undertone. On arrival in the Greek camp, Cressida kisses the
assembled company. Ulysses is moved to exclaim,

> O, these encounterers, so glib of tongue,
> That give accosting welcome ere it comes,
> And wide unclasp the tables of their thoughts
> To every ticklish reader: set them down
> For sluttish spoils of opportunity
> And daughters of the game.
>
> (IV.v.58–63)

He sees immediately that she has no reserve and that she is 'glib',
too easy, too incautious in speech. By Act v Scene i the rumour
has reached Thersites that Diomedes 'keeps a Trojan drab, and
uses the traitor Calchas' tent' (ll. 95–6). That Thersites does not
realise who the whore is, as we wonder that it has come to this
already, is in character, for his generalised loathing needs no
particular object.

When Cressida appears from Calchas' tent, then, the betrayal
has already happened, or is still happening. Just as Chaucer

leaves open the question of whether Criseyde's emotions were engaged, Shakespeare makes it hard for us to pin down the moment of turning. What has happened is what was always going to happen: if it comes from Cressida's character, it has almost happened before the play starts. 'Now, my sweet guardian. Hark, a word with you' (v.ii.7). Cressida initiates a whispered conversation as we, Troilus, Ulysses and Thersites look on. The first words we hear of it are Diomedes' 'Will you remember?'

> CRESSIDA. Remember? Yes.
> DIOMEDES. Nay, but do, then,
> And let your mind be coupled with your words. (ll. 12–15)

Memory, continuity: the qualities Cressida does not possess. She is puzzled by the instruction, which Diomedes repeats and expounds, tying her mind to her speech. She has been betrayed by glib words to which she is now committed. She begs Diomedes not to tempt her (l. 18).

> DIOMEDES. Nay then –
> CRESSIDA. I'll tell you what –
> DIOMEDES. Fo, fo, come, tell a pin; you are forsworn. (ll. 20–2)

Cressida tries to change her words for new ones, a ploy Diomedes brutally dismisses.

> DIOMEDES. What did you swear you would bestow on me?
> CRESSIDA. I prithee, do not hold on me to mine oath;
> Bid me do anything but that, sweet Greek. (ll. 25–7)

Cressida clearly means that she has promised to sleep with Diomedes, but her language resists any kind of commitment. Speech is definite and defining; Cressida is neither.[80]

Diomedes is about to storm off. 'Hark, a word in your ear' (l. 34), says Cressida, beginning the conversation again to her own certain loss. She wants to yield and therefore submits to domination by language. This is hardly a novelty in Shakespeare's theatre. The prologue to *Tamburlaine the Great, Part I*[81] promises that

> From jigging veins of rhyming mother-wits,
> And such conceits as clownage keeps in pay,

> We'll lead you to the stately tent of war,
> Where you shall hear the Scythian Tamburlaine
> Threatening the world with high astounding terms,
> And scourging kingdoms with his conquering sword.

Tamburlaine's words may be 'high astounding', as is the mighty line, but they are also potent. The first character in the play to speak is Mycetes, who is 'insufficient to express' because 'it requires a great and thundering speech' (i.i.2–3). Even a lesser such as Theridamas can earn from this inarticulate nonentity the praise 'Thy words are swords' (l. 74). Theridamas rapidly finds Tamburlaine's 'persuasions . . . pathetical' (i.ii.211): Tamburlaine promises to show his 'vaunts substantial' (l. 213). Tamburlaine's magniloquence extends to dismissing 'all the curses which the Furies breathe' (ii.vii.53). Tamburlaine's rhetorical empery is, of course, as thin as the rhetoric that constitutes it, and Shakespeare cheerfully guys him as Pistol. However, its magnificence also masks an essential seediness. If language is only an instrument of power, truth and the possibility of lapidary wisdom vanish. Diomedes is a minor erotic Tamburlaine who happily abuses the notion of truth to serve his ends, and as such he is characteristic of his world.

Aware that Cressida's relation to language is tenuous, Diomedes insists on a token (*Troilus and Cressida*, v.ii.60). Cressida fetches the sleeve Troilus gave her.

> CRESSIDA. O all you gods! O, pretty, pretty pledge!
>   Thy master now lies thinking on his bed
>   Of thee and me, and sighs, and takes my glove,
>   And gives memorial dainty kisses to it,
>   As I kiss thee – Nay, do not snatch it from me:
>
>   [DIOMEDES *snatches the sleeve.*]
>
> He that takes that doth take my heart withal.
>   DIOMEDES. I had your heart before: this follows it.   (ll. 77–83)

Diomedes' brutality picks up the note of his entrance to the scene. 'Calchas, I think? Where's your daughter?' (l. 3), he asks peremptorily. Here, he ignores entirely Cressida's past, her little fantasy of a passive Troilus, which we can see is inaccurate, for he is watching as this half-serious wavering goes on. Cressida binds her heart to an object, a token, where Diomedes insists that tokens are outward signs of intentions already formed. His rough-and-ready approach to character is the 'sodeyn' quality Chaucer gave him. Cressida's plea that her heart goes with the sleeve declares her lightness and disintegration in a way Diomedes cannot understand. She is not quite a Trojan drab, because her inconstancy of purpose, her flickering sensibility, make her more interesting if less palpable.

Cressida's final speech here summarises her predicament:

> Troilus, farewell! One eye yet looks on thee,
> But with my heart the other eye doth see.
> Ah, poor our sex! this fault in us I find:
> The error of our eye directs our mind.
> What error leads must err; O, then conclude,
> Minds sway'd by eyes are full of turpitude.
> (ll. 106–11)

She is divided by conflicting desires and generalises them into female superficiality. Her conclusion, that such a mind must be full of wickedness, falls uncomfortably pat. It is as though she accepted herself as an unsatisfactory creature and resolved on infidelity because it expressed her being. This extraordinary sense of the self as so riven that it can act only by departing from truth and certainty is not the wisdom it might be. 'What's aught but as 'tis valued?' Troilus asks earlier, and is told by Hector that 'value dwells not in particular will' (ii.ii.53–4). Troilus sees a world of dead things given value by desire, Hector one where value inheres in objects.

Troilus presses the point:

> I take today a wife, and my election
> Is led on in the conduct of my will:
> My will enkindled by mine eyes and ears,
> Two traded pilots 'twixt the dangerous shores
> Of will and judgment – how may I avoid,
> Although my will distaste what it elected,
> The wife I choose? There can be no evasion
> To blench from this and to stand firm by honour.
> (ll. 62–9)

'Today' as it might be any day I marry, a matter of 'election' in which it is perhaps significant that the other partner's will is not involved. Value is conferred by desire. 'Will and judgment' could imperil the choice made by the senses, which must therefore guide the will to the end they have chosen. The will, though a danger, can be directed: judgement has simply to be avoided. Once committed, though, will and judgement are honour-bound to stand by what has been chosen.

The self is conceived here as prey to involuntary forces which influence the will against judgement. What emerges from this internal conflict appears as choice and must be defended as 'honour'. For Troilus, the die is only cast once and everything is staked on the one throw. 'Honour' proceeds from self-assertion and self-definition, rather than relating to the inherently honourable. His judgement of Cressida's faithlessness rests on this shaky foundation, then: she has not stuck by the choice of her desires, and has therefore renounced 'honour'.

Both Troilus and Cressida are changed by their liaison. When we first see her, Cressida has firm views on personal identity. Pandarus tries to persuade her that Troilus is a better man than Hector:

PANDARUS. Do you know a man if you see him?
CRESSIDA. Ay, if I ever saw him before and knew him.
PANDARUS. Well, I say Troilus is Troilus.
CRESSIDA. Then you say as I say, for I am sure he is not Hector.
PANDARUS. No, nor Hector is not Troilus in some degrees.
CRESSIDA. 'Tis just to each of them; he is himself.   (I.ii.64–71)

Cressida reduces Pandarus to tautology and holds him there. This confidence about the identities of others is reflected in her view of herself. Pandarus says that she is 'such a woman, a man knows not at what ward you lie' (ll. 263–4). Her teasing prevents his being sure who she is, and her bawdy response ('Upon my back, to defend my belly' – l. 265) deflects the question. Her first soliloquy ends with her self-commitment to a role:

That she was never yet that ever knew
Love got so sweet as when desire did sue . . .
Then though my heart's content firm love doth bear,
Nothing of that shall from mine eyes appear.
                                        (ll. 295–6, 299–300)

Cressida resolves on the pose of detachment which will force Troilus to beseech her. Up to this point, she appears as teasing but confident. She believes that people are who they are, and that she can prevent her own feelings from appearing to Troilus. This confidence is, as we have seen, erroneous, and it is at the moment when her feelings break out that she begins to recognise the problem of her selfhood. The part she establishes for herself early in the play turns out to have been provisional, contingent on Troilus' love for her, and essentially unstable.

In this sense, Troilus is right to insist that first choice is final. He wishes to foreclose the otherwise seemingly endless shifting of identity which he phrases most tellingly in the puzzled 'This is, and is not, Cressid' (v.ii.145). Cressida's infidelity sets up a 'madness of discourse/That cause sets up with and against herself!' (ll. 141–2). Her duplicity threatens his own identity, setting his soul at war with itself (ll. 146–7). Importantly, he began the play with some doubt about who was who.

> Tell me, Apollo, for thy Daphne's love,
> What Cressid is, what Pandar, and what we.
> (i.i.98–9)

It is ironic that he should invoke the god of poetry in a play which will answer his questions, and that he should do so with reference to a girl who escaped the god by turning into a natural object. Cressida behaves similarly. She renounces what holds civilisation together, consciousness and commitment, contracts deliberately entered into, for the free range of desire. This regression makes Troilus look stiff and awkward in the pose he assumes when Ulysses wonders ingenuously whether he is 'half attach'd' (v.ii.160) to what he says about Cressida.

> Ay, Greek; and that shall be divulged well
> In characters as red as Mars his heart
> Inflam'd with Venus. Never did young man fancy
> With so eternal and so fix'd a soul.
> Hark, Greek: as much as I do Cressid love,
> So much by weight hate I her Diomed.
> (ll. 162–7)

Troilus has become a single self, able to produce 'characters' but ones written rather than spoken. He can set his love on one side, existent but inoperative, because his will is inflamed by what his eyes have seen. He can stylise himself as a uniquely resolute lover and killer at the same time because he has at last an active part to play.

Cressida flattered herself by imagining a passive, lachrymose Troilus kissing her glove. His inertia explained her wavering, it may be felt, as it may be supposed that had she known of Troilus' presence she would have acted differently with Diomedes. Whether her motive would have been fear or fidelity does not matter, because in either instance she is dependent on others for support. Shakespeare thus bears out Chaucer's analysis of her as a social being.[82] Troilus can now appear to himself, be his own audience and reduce Ulysses to the generic 'Greek'. When Pandarus brings Cressida's letter, Troilus looks it over and says that all it contains is

> Words, words, mere words, no matter from the heart;
> Th'effect doth operate another way.
>
> (v.iii.108–9)

He can now see language as instrumental and detect a self antecedent to it, as he has discovered such an identity for himself. In Chaucer, ten lines pass between the *Litera Criseydis* and the moment

> That Troilus wel understod that she
> Nas nought so kynde as that hire oughte be.
>
> (v.1641–2)

Chaucer's leisurely narrative has room to follow the unfolding of Troilus' thoughts as the drama cannot.

Drama compresses and congests what poetry could dilate. The play crowds together the affair of Troilus and Cressida and the wrath of Achilles, the medieval expansion of the Homeric original, so that they comment on one another. The Prologue tells us that we are

> Beginning in the middle, starting thence away
> To what may be digested in a play.
>
> (ll. 28–9)

We cannot see the beginning or the end, though we know what they are, and that we cannot affects the play radically.

Editors take the final exchange with Pandarus to be a late insertion:[83] R. A. Foakes points out that the play could almost end with Troilus' 'Hector is dead: there is no more to say' (v.x.22).[84] This brings the play to hysterical arrest. The full ending changes the emphasis with Troilus' 'Stay yet' (l. 23) and vow to massacre Greeks, followed by Pandarus' last appearance. The propriety of this is twofold. Troilus' insistence on continuing to speak can be directly compared with Othello's 'Soft you; a word or two before you go' (*Othello*, v.ii.337) at the moment when Lodovico seems to have closed the play. Othello insists on directing the attention of all those round him back on himself and his own feelings, presenting himself as a sympathetic tragic figure who is now going to do the decent thing.[85] Troilus must be the same because the play cannot leave the last word to him. He is not a fit authority to end with, as he has for private reasons enclosed himself in a single stylised role which claims to speak for the community. As his own feelings pour out, we are reminded that time goes on, that the play contains a future. 'There is no more to say' seals the play-world from us, which may be appropriate to its subject's antiquity but is wrong for the play we have seen.

It is much more fitting that Pandarus should reappear and be spurned. Troilus can thus make clear that he has really entered the martial, heroic world, while the seam of sheer unpleasantness that runs counter to it throughout the play finds its logical outcome in an appeal for sympathy to any procurers in the audience. The unpleasantness is that of unredeemed nature, the force let loose by the Trojan War. We know that that war begins with adultery, that 'All the argument is a whore and a cuckold: a good quarrel to draw emulous factions, and bleed to death upon' (ii.iii.74–6). The 'argument' of the Trojan War and that of the relationship between Troilus and Cressida can both be so summarised. Public and private worlds are both disordered: Shakespeare finds his subject a knitting of the two. Ulysses speaks of 'The providence that's in a watchful state' (iii.iii.195), the cognisance taken by an inquiring government of all that is under it. Against this totalitarianism Achilles cannot maintain his privacy. Nature is let loose as violence and turmoil at all levels.

Against this background, many readers have found Ulysses' speech on order in Act i Scene iii, particularly ll. 81–134, a salutary corrective. 'Take but degree away, untune that string, / And hark what discord follows' (ll. 109–10). The traditional association of music with cosmic order is powerfully expressed and persuasive. We may take leave to doubt how far Ulysses means what he says, though, as the context is a debate and Ulysses is celebrated for his argumentative slipperiness. What he says may be true, and the atmosphere of the Greek camp at this point bears it out, but Ulysses does not have the certain ground on which to base his argument because he has submitted to the conditions of free discussion with his respectful obeisance to Agamemnon and Nestor in ll. 60–1. The effect is peculiarly moving. By describing what happens when order is gone, and because of the coincidence of that with what we see, Ulysses makes us long for it. His purpose is to encourage a stratagem, but in doing so he invokes values of whose absence we are necessarily conscious.

Ulysses' speech is equivocal. Submitting to debate, Ulysses enters the exchange of ideas in which words are tokens used by power. He is only a politician. The world he inhabits is such that even the most customarily admirable language appears only by contingency. This uprooting has profound consequences for the idea of truth as either veracity or constancy, as we have seen with Cressida at the private level. The play comes after a moral fall, the theft of Helen, which is mirrored in a linguistic fall. Some modern theorists would have us believe that language is necessarily fallen, that the 'madness of discourse' is all we ever find,[86] and what we have so far seen of this play might seem to bear them out.

There is, however, another perspective. Troilus and Cressida occupy a surprisingly small part of the play which bears their names. We are insistently reminded that we are *in medias res* at every point by shouts and flourishes which disrupt the moments on stage and return us to the war. It is in war, particularly heroic, Homeric war, that some human values find their highest expression, as Shakespeare knows. His handling of the problem is seen most clearly in the treatment of Ajax and his combat with Hector.

Robert Kimbrough points out that

In both the *Iliad* and the medieval legend, Hector and Ajax had fought in single combat; however, that Aeneas should visit the Greek camp with a challenge from Hector, that the challenge should be presented in a chivalric manner, and that Ulysses should arrange for Ajax to be selected to answer the challenge are all new in Shakespeare.[87]

Aeneas' visit to the Greek Camp in Act I Scene iii sets up the parallel plot. It shows us both how divided the Greeks are and how courtly are the Trojans. Shakespeare thus reminds us of what in roomier literary forms can be everywhere apparent. One further advantage of the second plot is that it gives Ulysses something to do. Shakespeare is clearly interested in that devious intelligence, both for its own sake and because of its relevance to other concerns in the play, but it cannot be shown without being exercised. The cynical adeptness of debaters in this play may have been intended to appeal to the Inns of Court audience for whom the play might well have been performed,[88] and Ulysses offers a peculiarly striking instance of that facility. The challenge delivered by Aeneas makes the Greeks set about finding a champion, which makes possible an examination of the heroic ethos.

Ajax first appears in the play as a subject for discussion in Act I Scene ii, where Alexander describes him to Cressida. He is a man of 'crowded humours' (l. 22) to whom Cressida's response is that he 'makes me smile' (l. 32). It is also important that he is described as having overcome Hector in battle (ll. 34–7), because this will lead us to have high hopes of him later. We learn next, in Act I Scene iii, that Ajax has 'grown self-will'd' (l. 188), a condition he will not maintain for long, and become a mockery Achilles. The challenge is delivered, and Ulysses recognises that the 'blockish' (l. 375) and 'dull brainless' (l. 381) man can be used as a stalking-horse to 'pluck down Achilles' plumes' (l. 386). The plan will work 'hit or miss' (l. 384), and Ulysses shows no concern at all for Ajax' fate. What we know so far is that Ajax is a topic for jokes and extremely stupid – something Ulysses is qualified to judge. What we are not quite ready for is the Ajax we see.

We find Ajax with Thersites, who runs rings round him. Thersites holds back the details of the proclamation that Ajax is seeking, and is repeatedly struck (at II.i.11, 42 and 55 at least). Were it anybody but Thersites, we should find Ajax unsympathetically oafish. As it is, none of our loathing for Thersites rubs off on him, and we feel in a general way that Ajax' heart is in the right place. The feeling is generalised because there is no point for it to focus on: Shakespeare gives us simply an impression that Ajax may have more to be said for him than has so

far been indicated. Achilles and Patroclus manage to send
Thersites packing, which is important because Achilles' superiority
to Ajax is made clear. Our incipient liking for Ajax must be
balanced by a recognition that he need not have resorted to
violence had he been a brighter man, that he is potentially
dangerous. Achilles, who has been withdrawn longer than Ajax,
yet knows what was proclaimed: again, Ajax is shown to be
inferior.

In Act II Scene iii Ajax is buttered up by the other Greeks. He is
a man 'of sweet composure' (l. 240), Ulysses tells him.

> And here's a lord – come knights from east to west
> And cull their flower – Ajax shall cope the best.
>
> (ll. 263–4)

Ulysses casts his final compliment into a jaunty, simple minded
rhyme of the kind likely to register with the slow-witted hero. It is
not clear how often we should remember that Ajax is by name a
privy,[89] but the joke is probably inescapable throughout. It should
be said in defence of this likely execrable pun that Shakespeare's
'fatal *Cleopatra*'[90] is at the centre of his omnivorous use of words:
Shakespeare is concerned not to exclude the irrelevant but to
show that everything naturally coheres.

Ulysses arranges in Act III Scene iii that the Greek leaders
should pass by Achilles' tent and speak disdainfully to him. Ajax'
'Ha?' (l. 67) is marvellously expressive. He has begun the exchange
by addressing Patroclus but is unable to follow it up. This is not
simply because he is too slow to think how but because he could
never do so. He is now in such a state of vanity and exaltation
that he is beyond words.

> THERSITES. Ajax goes up and down the field, asking for himself.
> ACHILLES. How so?
> THERSITES. He must fight singly tomorrow with Hector, and is so
>   prophetically proud of an heroical cudgelling that he raves in
>   saying nothing. (III.iii.243–8)

'Languageless, a monster' (l. 263), Ajax can no longer recognise
whom he is talking to (ll. 259–61) and merely 'wears his tongue
in's arms' (l. 269). Ajax can be seen completely, as his feelings can
only express themselves in actions and he has no mental resources.

Apart from a brief railing at 'opinion' (ll. 263–5), Thersites devotes his speeches at this point to detailed description.

The mirth Ajax provokes is almost loving. Taking him off, Thersites desists from generalisation. His performance as Ajax (ll. 250–61) shows in him a capacity for actorly involvement in another's being that nothing else about him would lead us to expect. His loathsomeness is a little diminished by it.

Ajax is not a problem for himself. Where for Cressida lucidity shows nothing, and that void is troubling as it hints at discontinuity and instability at the core of selfhood, for Ajax it acts as a blessing. When his duel with Hector takes place, it is remarkably brief or notably spectacular: only three lines are spoken between the start and end of their combat (IV.v.113–15). It may be that the fight takes some time, and that the audience's attention is focused on this ritualistic externalisation of feeling. If so, there is comedy in Ajax' 'I am not warm yet; let us fight again' (l. 117). Hector refuses to fight any more because of his kinship with Ajax. Ajax' reply has a remarkable dignity:[91]

> I thank thee, Hector.
> Thou art too gentle and too free a man.
> I came to kill thee, cousin, and bear hence
> A great addition earned in thy death.
> (ll. 137–40)

He recognises Hector's nobility at once, and finds the most succinct possible phrasing for his own motives and ambition. This nobility persists when Hector takes his leave:

> If I might in entreaties find success –
> As seld I have the chance – I would desire
> My famous cousin to our Grecian tents.
> (ll. 148–50)

Ajax may simply mean that he is not often able to beseech Hector, but there is a more general sense that he knows how seldom his words will achieve anything for him. This momentary pathos touches the rest of this scene and Ajax' last words, when in Act V Scene ix the death of Hector at Achilles' hands is announced:

> If it be so, yet bragless let it be:
> Great Hector was a good a man as he.
>
> (ll. 5–6)

In part, this is simply irritation that Achilles has achieved what he has not, but by this point Ajax has earned enough of our respect for his words to carry some authority. This is secured by showing Ajax to us in varied contexts that allow his dignity to outstrip his comic thickheadedness.

Ajax acquires dignity just as Achilles sheds it in the brutal slaying of Hector. Achilles is brought out of his sulk by the death of Patroclus, rather than by Ulysses' scheming. Where deliberate contrivance has been abortive and frustrating (and the plot 'has no central momentum'[92]) accident dominates. In the stalking of Hector we see Achilles turn accident to his advantage.

When they first fight, Hector desists and courteously lets Achilles go. 'I do disdain thy courtesy, proud Trojan' (v.vi.15), says Achilles, an intimation of what is to come. In Act v Scene vii we see Achilles telling his Myrmidons what to do when Hector is found. They are to encircle him and fence him in with their weapons because 'It is decreed Hector the great must die' (l. 8). 'Decreed' impersonates fate, but speaks only for Achilles' will. While the encounter between Ajax and Hector was chivalric, what is now being prepared is cold-blooded liquidation.

And that is what happens. Hector has just disarmed, weary of battle, when Achilles and his troop enter. Achilles tells him that

> Even with the vail and dark'ning of the sun
> To close the day up, Hector's life is done.
>
> (v.viii.7–8)

The hero's death is part of an inexorable natural process. Hector is already a dead man. His reply, 'I am unarm'd: forego this vantage, Greek' (l. 9) looks for a courtesy it does not find. 'Strike, fellows, strike: this is the man I seek' (l. 10). Hector has no dying speech, but is brutally snuffed out.

Achilles addresses his Myrmidons:

> On, Myrmidons, and cry you all amain
> 'Achilles hath the mighty Hector slain.'
>
> (ll. 13–14)

This is only formally true in that, as we have just seen, Hector dies at the hands of a group. The Myrmidons' share in the deed is subsumed by their leader's reputation, however, and significantly none of them complains. Achilles represents a more efficient, modern way of waging war than the single-combat tradition of Ajax and Hector. Hector manifests the glory of that tradition, Ajax its stupidity and potential inconsequentiality.

It is, indeed, as a study in stupidity that we remember Ajax. At first, Ajax is really an arrogant loutish fool. Contact with Hector seems to ennoble him and brings out a side we can admire. We must acknowledge, though, that if Troy is to be taken Ajax is not the man to do it. And Troy is to be taken: part of the effect of this play depends on our knowing that that is so. It is commonplace to set Shakespeare among those Elizabethans who elevated the noble, doomed Trojans over the cunning, amoral Greeks, and this play gives much evidence for that view. Indeed, the true tragedy it contains is the inevitable destruction of Troy, a disaster too large for any of the characters to comprehend. It also presents a complex view of the relation between selfhood and social context.

All the characters find themselves without support. I suggested above that the world disrupted by both adultery and war is one in which nothing remains settled. In Cressida we see a self that speculates on its own motives but cannot see them, for they are desires which lie below consciousness, which believes in its own transparency. Desires only exist for her when they have taken on a verbal form,[93] and by then it is too late to act to change them. In Ajax we see a self too stupid to know that it has motives at all, one that is therefore easily manoeuvred by the knowing Ulysses (Ajax' search for a 'great addition' from Hector's death is simply heroic commonplace). Achilles is aware that he cannot see to the bottom of his own mind, but this greater degree of self-knowledge does not help him morally. Paradoxically, where we feel some sympathy for Cressida and some humorous but affectionate regard for Ajax, no matter what he really is, Achilles is baldly repellent. His cold, calculating, butcher's approach to war gets things done in a way only Ulysses can rival, and we know that these things must be done, but we cannot like the means.

Troilus recognises the dilemma of his world and picks one fixed attitude. Love for Troilus is a way of salvaging selfhood from the world's disrepair. This is why he can see Helen as 'a theme of honour and renown, / A spur to valiant and magnanimous deeds'

(II.ii.200–1): courtly love creates by its absolute demands a world of fixed values in which action has meaning. It is, of course, a sign of both Troilus' and the convention's limitations that what he praises here is what has radically destroyed the world's order. Warning Cressida against temptation, he says he trusts her,

> But something may be done that we will not;
> And sometimes we are devils to ourselves,
> When we will tempt the frailty of our powers,
> Presuming on their changeful potency.
>
> (IV.iv.92–5)

Troilus knows that human nature is potentially unstable and involuntary. Man is weaker than he supposes, and should not trust his own strength. This is why Troilus is as he is.

> CRESSIDA. My lord, will you be true?
> TROILUS. Who, I? – alas, it is my vice, my fault.
>   Whiles others fish with craft for great opinion,
>   I with great truth catch mere simplicity;
>   Whilst some with cunning gild their copper crowns,
>   With truth and plainness I do wear mine bare.
>
> (ll. 99–104)

Troilus cannot help being faithful. Others are cunning in the pursuit of fame, where he is thought simple, but the head he shows the world is genuine and not made to look worth more than it is.

One man who might be said to use 'craft' to gain reputation is Ulysses. Ulysses may know how fleeting reputation is, his advice to Achilles hints.

> Perseverance, dear my lord,
> Keeps honour bright: to have done is to hang
> Quite out of fashion, like a rusty mail
> In monumental mockery.
>
> (III.iii.150–3)

'For Time', he continues, 'is like a fashionable host' (l. 165). This cynical view is obviously presented to bring Achilles back to war, but it expresses the atmosphere of the play. One thing succeeds another: there is no final, definitive action or stance to shape the whole, and the plot moves forward by chance. Even Ulysses' attempts to motivate it miss their aim. His advice here denies the traditional conception of heroic immortality, in which what a man has done lives forever. It strikes at fears proper to Achilles, a hero rusty with disuse, and is therefore psychologically apt as well. Its effect, though, is to undermine its own force. If no reputation lives without repetition, at death all reputation ends. Heroism is futility. It is ambiguous whether Ulysses knows this or is only saying it, for his words are always tactical. Ulysses has an inscrutable detachment which riddles his being with doubt: dramatically, he can only appear as an instigator, an amoral servant of a political cause.

Troilus would be more than that, which is why he attaches importance to honour as an enduring quality: 'This is the monstruosity in love, lady: that the will is infinite, and the execution confined: that the desire is boundless, and the act a slave to limit' (III.ii.79–82). It is not just a question of sexual limitation. Love wants a total possession the human condition denies it. Equally, to love is to be circumscribed (as Othello discovers)[94] and so endangered. Placing his trust in Cressida, Troilus places it at risk, and knows that he does so. In her defection he finds, as we saw, a new role, a new fixity as the lover seeking revenge. He is caught up again into the whirlwind of destruction. His last speeches slide from speaking for a community to speaking for himself to railing at Pandarus because this fixity is itself only provisional. Pandarus ends the play promising to bequeath his diseases to the audience because he speaks for the fickle, appetitive world disclosed by the collapse of order.

But all this is po-faced stuff when we remember the rancorous farce the play makes of Homer and Chaucer. *Troilus and Cressida* decries heroic dignity by allowing only the boneheaded Ajax and the doomed Hector to show it, and questions the nature of personal identity, but, more, it pokes fun at the stuffy classics. Troilus and Cressida are destined to become stereotypes, but they have nothing to do with that. Their ridiculous, petty and furtive *amour* will become the *locus classicus* of infidelity, but in so doing it is denatured. These tragic figures are made so by what is made of them: the destiny which runs through the play and directs its course is not an archaic Fate which has already, immutably decreed, but the demands of the future. Troilus and Cressida must behave as they do because we know they will have done so, and the same holds for Achilles and Hector to the same degree.[95] Against that certainty, their flickering equivocal consciousness of self and other seem almost irrelevant.

The cynical, derisive attitude the play shows to its own subject – the lack of coherent plot and the paradoxes of characterisation – extends to the portrayal of the Trojan War as brutish, myopic and botched. One of the curiosities of a tale told often is that each successive telling claims to be nearer the truth, the origin, than its predecessors. Chaucer achieves this effect by admitting honest doubt over Criseyde's motives and her feelings, in contradiction to received opinion. Henryson questions the veracity of Chaucer's version. Where poems can ironically reflect on one another's shortcomings, drama must embody what it says. The doubt Chaucer feels about Criseyde Cressida feels about herself. Her unconscious becomes conscious for her only when it achieves a verbal trace, just as Criseyde's can be left unresolved by disavowing the usual verbal form ('Men seyn'). The dissolution of consciousness into linguistic accident this hints at mirrors the larger fact that Troy's story only matters because of how it is told. If Homer's narrative had not carried memorable conviction the war would have been forgotten. For us, it exists only as a verbal form.

But because it exists as such for us the story-teller is constrained. If, as Walton and Hassall try, he shucks this constraint his work will fall to pieces. Just so, if Cressida evades commitment she cannot know who she is. *Troilus and Cressida* presents an existential dilemma as a series of recognitions for us to make, a world without values which we must judge as we will.

III

The characters of *Troilus and Cressida* refuse to know what kind of world they live in and therefore what is true of themselves. Achilles escapes this generalisation but, as we have seen, earns no credit thereby. The characters of *All's Well*, particularly the King and Helena, are surprisingly articulate about their circumstances, and again articulacy is not of itself morally improving. Some of the most touching moments in Shakespeare are almost inarticulate, like the action of the servant who fetches flax and egg-whites to treat Gloucester's injuries.[96] It is with that sense of inarticulate appeal that I shall be concerned as I try to analyse what makes the play-world knowable to us in a way it is not to its inhabitants, and quite what our moral relation to Shakespeare's characters is.

The polarities which structure *All's Well* and *Troilus and Cressida* are notably simple. In one play we see traditional authority fallen into decadence, and the rise of self-seeking opportunism to fill the vacuum. This pattern hardly surprises us, and nothing in the play suggests that it is to be understood directly as true of its audience's world. The change is seen in both public and private spheres. The King decides to hold off from involvement in Italy but offers his young gentlemen their own choice. Helena can rely on no familial support and must therefore act in her own interests. The consequence of this is a rebarbatively competitive and untranquil world whose artistic expression is profoundly troubling. Tragicomedy, which depends on a rhythm of renewal, is seen as the deliberate construction of will.

Equally, *Troilus and Cressida* shows a traditionally noble world fallen into seamy disrepair. Our relation to this world is different, as the nobility belongs to our expectations. If we think of the Homeric world as inherently admirable we shall be shocked by the disgusting creatures who turn out to be its constituents. If, on the other hand, we look forward to the denigration of the heroic, if we share the fashionable cynicism often attributed to the putative Inns of Court audience, we shall be dismayed by the dignity which can attach to somebody like Ajax, someone utterly unlike us: where we are knowing, suspicious and intelligent, he is ignorant, gullible and thick. Whatever expectations we bring will be disappointed.

The literary expression of that disappointment is incoherent tragedy. Troilus, as and where he is, cannot but be injured by Cressida's perfidy. At the same time, his response seems curiously inhumane and mechanical, again because of what he is. What happens could not be otherwise because we already know the outcome, but in this world of accidental happenings it turns out to depend more on Diomedes' rough way with words than on Cressida's own duplicity. The characters are pulled forward into tragedy without earning our respect.

It is perfectly easy to see how the plays might be read as protofeminist inquiries. Helena and Cressida are both victims in

lack of individuality

male-dominated societies, and their actions are forced on them by the way in which men behave. However, Bertram compels our sympathy, and Diomedes is rightly annoyed by Cressida's 'fooling' (v.ii.101). The plays divide our sympathies because their worlds are bad for everybody. In both plays, the characters are denied the room to be fully themselves, and their cramped diminution is carried over into our response.

An enlightening contrast to the two plays can be found in *Macbeth*.[97] In this, the most nearly orthodox of Shakespeare's tragedies, there is again the sense of human potentiality denied, but our reaction to it is entirely different. The place to begin an examination is with the Macbeths' marriage, and in particular Lady Macbeth's appeal to the murderous spirits to 'unsex me here' (i.v.41). She wishes to feel no 'compunctious visitings of Nature' (l. 45) and to lose her womanhood. Dissociated from herself, she will use a weapon that may 'see not the wound it makes' (l. 52). Immediately, this speech is dramatic and shocking. It looks forward to the image of a baby's brains dashed out while feeding at her breast (i.vii.54–8), which will confirm our picture of her as unnatural. Disavowing her body, she disowns her feelings, and acquires a murderous detachment.

This shedding of sexuality is part of a web of imagery surrounding Duncan's murder. Macbeth means to do the deed like a rapist, 'With Tarquin's ravishing strides' (ii.i.55), another displacement of the kind he recognises in his wife when telling her to have male children only, 'For thy undaunted mettle should compose/Nothing but males' (i.vii.74–5). She has disowned all femininity, and becomes brutal masculine energy. The Porter tells us that drink 'provokes the desire, but it takes away the performance' (ii.iii.28–9); Lady Macbeth announces that 'That which hath made them drunk hath made me bold' (ii.ii.1), but is unable actually to commit the murder. Drink and drugs stimulate a libidinous drive which cannot be fulfilled, and that Lady Macbeth's explanation depends on Duncan's resemblance to her father (ii.ii.12–13) shows how joined are criminal and sexual prohibitions in her mind. Her fear is that murder is a kind of incest, for murder is in this play a sublimation of eroticism.

Lady Macbeth has a sexual vitality to which, we take it, Macbeth responds. In committing murder, though, what he loses immediately is sleep,

Sleep, that knits up the ravell'd sleave of care,
The death of each day's life, sore labour's bath,
Balm of hurt minds, great Nature's second course,
Chief nourisher in life's feast.

(II.ii.36–9)

Sleep is a tutelary domestic presence, a housewife sewing, bathing, healing and cooking. Or, rather, sleep is dispersed among the evidence of housewifery. What is lost is not now primarily sexual but homely.

Homeliness colours Macbeth's sense of his life's futility late in the play, when he knows that the proper accompaniments of old age, 'As honour, love, obedience, troops of friends, / I must not look to have' (v.iii.25–6).[98] The rights of marriage are parallel to the mutuality of friendship, and we are reminded of the touching vanity he showed early on when havering over the murder:

He hath honour'd me of late; and I have bought
Golden opinions from all sorts of people,
Which would be worn now in their newest gloss,
Not cast aside so soon.

(I.vii.32–5)

This Macbeth, still pleasantly ruffled by the attentions he has received, must be prodded on by his wife's taunts. Macbeth was 'a man', she says, when he dared to kill (l. 49), but not now that he hesitates. The imputation against his virility is enhanced by her use six lines later of the dashed-dead baby, her own unfeminine resolve. She is more of a man than he is. Lady Macbeth shifts the grounds of argument from homeliness to sexuality.

When Macbeth comes home from the wars, his wife insists on managing the business of murder herself (I.v.66–73). She does so because she knows her husband's character, which she analyses in soliloquy after reading his letter. The letter is affectingly domestic: 'This have I thought good to deliver thee (my dearest partner of greatness) that thou might'st not lose the dues of rejoicing, by being ignorant of what greatness is promis'd thee' (ll. 10–14). As soon as he has good news, he bursts to share it with his wife and cannot let it wait on his own arrival. (Later, he will tell her of his hallucinatory dagger, as III.iv.61–2 show.) The prophecy he has heard becomes a little present for her, an earnest of their shared future. The strong equality of the Macbeths' marriage is plain. It gives Lady Macbeth an expert insight into her husband's make-up:

>   Thou wouldst be great;
> Art not without ambition, but without
> The illness should attend it: what thou wouldst highly,
> That wouldst thou holily; wouldst not play false,
> And yet wouldst wrongly win.
>
>   (I.v.18–22)

'Th'milk of human kindness' (l. 17), a natural, maternal compassion, holds him back from violence. The Macbeth we are shown here is disarmingly ordinary:[99] not innately wicked, but muddled and inconstant. He is ambitious but lacks drive, and wishes to be well thought of ('holily' here suggests the opinion others will have of him). While not cheating, he is not averse to an error in his favour. Macbeth's vices here are minor venalities, but we shall see how dire their consequences may be. In this sense, the morality of *Macbeth* is very harsh-minded indeed.

We know from Macbeth himself already what his wife now tells us: in the immediately preceding scene he has muttered aside,

>   Stars, hide your fires!
> Let not light see my black and deep desires;
> The eye wink at the hand; yet let that be,
> Which the eye fears, when it is done, to see.
>
>   (I.iv.50–3)

Let that come to pass, to show itself in the world, the bringing about of which the eye which desires it fears to see, is the sense of this syntactically compressed passage. The compression and difficulty are entirely appropriate because they enact the difficulty with which Macbeth can articulate this thought even to himself.

The murder takes place in a bedroom by night. It is the pursuit of erotic ends by other means. We see a dinner-party disrupted by Macbeth's stagily rhetorical addresses to the Ghost, and have the deeper sense of a violated household. It is no surprise that Macbeth complains of the Witches, how

Upon my head they plac'd a fruitless crown,
And put a barren sceptre in my gripe,
Thence to be wrench'd with an unlineal hand,
No son of mine succeeding.

(III.i.60–3)

It is peculiarly galling to him that he will not be able to pass on what he has gained. The implication of the speech is that he would have happily 'mine eternal jewel/Given to the common Enemy of man' (ll. 67–8) had it been for his own children's sake. Macbeth speaks with the pain of thwarted parenthood. The most immediate way of striking at Macduff he will be able to think of is to have his wife, children 'and all unfortunate souls/That trace him in his line' (IV.i.152–3) murdered.

There is, then, an important set of images of sexuality and domesticity which surrounds the Macbeths and of which much more might be said. It is more germane now, though, to look at the shape of the play which contains this unfortunate couple. In the study, the Macbeths dominate it to a degree the stage makes impossible by presenting us with a variety of other sights. The procession of apparitions produced by the Witches is peculiarly interesting. Macbeth is not sure what the Witches' power is but, 'Howe'er you come to know it' (IV.i.51), he charges them at peril of enormous natural convulsions to answer his questions. What he sees brings him no peace. Rather, it determines him that 'From this moment,/The very firstlings of my heart shall be/The firstlings of my hand' (ll. 146–8). To draw back and contemplate the future is impossible for him, and he suffers immersion in the dramatic requirements of the role he has taken on. The interpolations in the play, the Hecate scenes, are sensitive to this dilemma: there is nothing of any relevance to add to the plot, so they turn the witches into melodramatic spectacle with singing and dancing. By their excrescent irrelevance they point to the unified dynamic of the play. They are less successful than Shakespeare's own arresting presentation because they speak not to Macbeth's fears but to the audience's, and by mythologising the Witches they paradoxically naturalise them to reason. The Witches become what we should expect, and are therefore lessened.

Shakespeare's Witches are haunting because their nature is simply not clear. Their habitual occupations, stealing chestnuts and tormenting sailors, are alarmingly trivial, surprisingly close to

Puck's activities (*A Midsummer Night's Dream*, II.i.34–57). Their malice is folkloric rather than cosmic. It is Macbeth who interprets them as egging him on to fulfil a prophecy there is no reason to suppose they are any more capable of understanding than was the oracle at Delphi. Banquo knows that they may be 'The instruments of Darkness' (I.iii.124) but does not grant them active malignity. That the fulfilment depends on the listener is reflected in the almost accidental manner in which the final prophecies come true. The woods that come to Dunsinane are as little woods as they could be, and Macduff's miraculous delivery is the result of mere obstetric technique.

The flatness of what prophecy intimates – Macbeth's boredom and the trivial signs – is echoed by the dullest scene in the play, Act IV Scene iii. We watch the exiled Scots resolving to deal with Macbeth, as they must if the play is to be in any sense a tragedy, with no sense of dramatic surprise except for the passage (ll. 50–114) in which Malcolm tests Macduff by pretending to be more villainous than Macbeth. Nothing has prepared us for his performance, and we share Macduff's horror, but when it is over the scene resumes a turgid sanity. Partly, this is a teasing reminder that for the other characters evil is dramatically manifest, but that for us it is interesting, even likeable. The external view of evil leads Malcolm to act it out as a serial confession of elementary viciousness: his sense of what evil might be like has none of the complexity we gain from watching Macbeth. This moral innocence is reflected in the descriptions of Macbeth we are offered. He is a 'Hell-kite' (IV.iii.217), a 'tyrant' (V.ii.11 and V.iv.8, for example), a 'Hell-hound' (V.viii.3) and a 'butcher' (V.ix.35). He is a moral emblem, a political outrage, a criminal: all in a sense true, but inadequate to his reality.

Macbeth's final appearance is as a severed head (V.ix.20–1). For those on stage, this severance means that Macbeth's body can no longer run around doing evil, and he becomes a pathological specimen, one of 'our rarer monsters' (V.viii.25). For the audience, however, it means that the mental existence we have shared is at an end.

Our deepest experience of Macbeth is participation in his consciousness, and the intensest form that takes is in his last reflective speech. Macbeth is told of his wife's death, and replies chilly that 'She should have died hereafter' (V.v.17). She was always going to die: in a better world she would have lived longer. Either is possible and satisfying, neither conveys emotion.

> To-morrow, and to-morrow, and to-morrow,
> Creeps in this petty pace from day to day,
> To the last syllable of recorded time;
> And all our yesterdays have lighted fools
> The way to dusty death.
>
> (ll. 19–23)

Time has become monotonous repetition. Duncan dead, nothing new can happen, and Macbeth is immobilised. The external expression of this is that 'They have tied me to a stake: I cannot fly, / But, bear-like, I must fight the course' (v.vii.1–2). The other characters are the retributive agents of a mechanical plot which treats Macbeth as an animal and will end with his dismemberment. To the end of history, time persists as sameness. The past too is a flattened landscape. The past of all men has only opened a space in which the unknowing have gone to their deaths. But this past is also his own (if 'our' is royal) and that of his marriage: in either instance, all that has been achieved is the killing of victims for whom no compassion is felt but the need for whose deaths is no longer apparent. The act which should have given significance took it away.

> Life's but a walking shadow; a poor player,
> That struts and frets his hour upon the stage,
> And then is heard no more: it is a tale
> Told by an idiot, full of sound and fury,
> Signifying nothing.
>
> (v.v.24–8)

Life has dwindled into acting. The actor here is an automaton who parrots the script and exits. Just as Cressida could be fixed by Diomedes' insistence that she be committed to what she said, so Macbeth is trapped by his deeds and his words. What externalises or expresses the self turns out also to limit and define it. From Macbeth's point of view, the script is just words. The 'idiot' may be either the actor or the writer, but the latter seems more likely. Macbeth feels a meaningless destiny working itself out through him, 'Signifying nothing'. Not only has it no meaning, but the only possible statement it can make is one of ultimate nullity. Macbeth's life is not only informed by meaninglessness; it shows it off as an actor displays the role he is given.

At this moment, we can see what an elegant meditation on tragedy *Macbeth* is. Viewed externally, its hero is a good man who is tempted, falls and is destroyed by an inexorable destiny. The play is so short because there is nothing to happen. Once Duncan has been killed, Macbeth has committed himself to the tragic parabola that ends with his own death, and the length of time that takes is immaterial. Macbeth knows immediately the King is dead what the meaning of the crime is for himself, his loss of domestic bliss, and can only wait for events to take their course. The drama becomes curiously desultory, a series of events that loosely conspire to destroy him. The play has a clear retributive framework and, as I argued above, a tough-minded morality, but neither seems quite to be the point.

The tragic structure is organised round prophecy and fulfilment but, as we have seen, neither prophets nor their agents are very plausible as servants of higher powers. Their acts are too contingent, almost laughably accidental, for us to be certain that a struggle of universal importance is going on.[100] Macbeth does not incarnate a primal dilemma as does, say, Oedipus, because he is in many ways too ordinary a man. We feel sympathy rather than awe as we watch his decline.

As Macbeth surrenders to tragedy, he becomes detached from himself. His life becomes a meaningless spectacle and he engages in a series of improvisations. The resolve to act immediately on impulse is one of these, just as his response to Banquo's ghost is histrionic as well as felt. Macbeth is condemned to see the thing through without gaining either pleasure or wisdom. Where the dithering, uncertain Macbeth of early scenes is in the middle of things, the Macbeth of the later part of the play exists largely as a reviled name, a corporeal identity from which his mind retreats into solipsistic wistfulness. Lady Macbeth, who is more full-bloodedly villainous to begin with, undergoes a more severe dissolution of personality: the crime is much more shocking to her than to Macbeth because, for all her bravado, she knows less what it means. She brushes aside Duncan's likeness to her father without pausing to consider its implications, where Macbeth knows that he is acting like a rapist. Lady Macbeth takes on her husband's weakness and collapses, where he is seen to have the strength she has only assumed, because his knowledge took more account of human nature. She believed that the body could be disowned; he knew that he could never escape from a relation to it.

And to the body's concerns. I have argued that Macbeth exists only as an exterior for the other characters. Feigning wickedness, Malcolm speaks of himself as one

> in whom I know
> All the particulars of vice so grafted,
> That, when they shall be open'd, black Macbeth
> Will seem as pure as snow; and the poor State
> Esteem him as a lamb
>
> (IV,iii.50–4)

Malcolm's evils will show like flowers.[101] This revelation of a hidden interior will bleach Macbeth's reputation. The opening may also suggest dissection, though, presenting both Malcolm and Macbeth as moral cadavers. For Malcolm, wickedness exists in the world and must be incarnate to be perceived. The irony is that Macbeth is not so easily read: not, at least, by him.

Lady Macbeth decides what is to be done after reading Macbeth's letter. At this moment he arrives, and there is a brief discussion in which she tells him to leave everything to her (discussed above). One of the reasons she does this is that she fears her husband's transparency: 'Your face, my Thane, is a book, where men/May read strange matters' (I.v.62–3). Because he is guileless, Macbeth can betray what moves him – presently, the desire for Duncan's death, we take it. But being read he can be understood, and because he can be understood he can be manipulated. Nobody else in the play claims such inwardness with Macbeth, which is a tribute to the strength and intimacy of their marriage. Before the possibility of promotion arises, the Macbeths live in loving mutuality.

We find in *Macbeth* the disorder at both public and private levels that we found in both *All's Well* and *Troilus and Cressida*, but there are significant differences in presentation. In the problem plays, disorder exists before the drama begins, while in *Macbeth* it has been put down and returns through the characters' choices. Tragedy for Macbeth is not an experience but a process. As soon as he has become a murderer the process takes over. The tragic moment is private – it happens off-stage in a bedroom. It destroys meaning for the Macbeths, but the other characters act together to restore it. In so doing, they must reduce Macbeth to an image of ultimate evil in order to exorcise him. The kind of collaborative action Malcolm leads cannot happen in worlds where Bertram remains impenetrably self-centred or Troy and Greece at war. For a higher cause, that of Scotland, characters sort out their differences and re-establish common values. The paradox is that we are half willing to cry out against this. Macbeth is more engaging than any of his enemies, and the way in which they speak of him not only diminishes him but suggests that they lack moral perception. The commonplaceness which attracts us to Macbeth is repulsive in Malcolm because in him it does not grow. Macbeth rises to a kind of vision, even though one logically entailed by the premises from which he set out.

Those premises are both a set of concepts and a house. In *Macbeth* Shakespeare makes concrete ideas of homeliness and love which are almost too humble for drama. The Macbeths' marriage is a realistic one, their shared ambition overpoweringly normal. They appeal to us indirectly, through the connotations of their words and the horror entailed by their loss, but the intimacy can neither be stated nor shown. To subject it to display would be to wrong it: we should have the embarrassing revelation of marital secrecy Lady Macbeth contrives when she excuses Macbeth's behaviour in front of the Ghost.

Such intimacy is preconscious and rare. 'There's no art/To find the mind's construction in the face' (I.iv.11–12), Duncan laments of Cawdor's treachery, but he has 'built/An absolute trust' (ll. 13–14) where it would perhaps better be intuited. In marriage, Lady Macbeth and Macbeth are in touch with themselves, each other and the world. They transgress their limitations and pay for it in division and death. The problem-play worlds might be described as post-tragic, for in them division is the given state of things. Language is instrumental, just as Macbeth's register after Duncan's death moves between recognisably dramatic and lyric idioms to adjust his relation to the world. Macbeth is not very interested in self-expression because what selfhood he has is double, the external identity in which his wishes return to him as terrible facts and the empty consciousness which can only wait for its own extinction. Macbeth is animated when he knowingly joins the two, listless when he does not. Lady Macbeth has not acted, only wished, so her motives return as the torments of madness. Lady Macbeth never gets far enough outside herself to have two identities but rests in one uncertainty.

What is common to the three plays, then, is an emphasis on the tenuity of the connection between character and action. The character who acts easily, Ajax, is stupid (yet, perversely, noble); the character who does not (Cressida, Macbeth) is in the end characterised, made into a 'character', by action. Those who seek ends outside themselves may, like Ulysses, be merely manipulative, or only seem so, like Helena, but the distinction between seeming and being is difficult because of the conditions drama imposes. For there to be a play at all, the characters must do things, act in every sense of the word,[102] but for them to be more than creatures of the plot they must resist action, preserve a consciousness in excess of the play's demands. The distressing effect of the problem plays arises from their inability to find consciousness a home; the agony of *Macbeth* comes from consciousness' ability to leave home.

The equivocal, indeterminate consciousnesses who inhabit these plays do not, of course, typify all Shakespearean characterisation. They exist for the sake of dramatic effects, and those effects depend on the expectations we bring to the plays. From *All's Well That Ends Well* we are led by the title to expect a tragicomedy, in *Troilus and Cressida* we know that we are going to hear again a familiar tragic narrative, and from *The Tragedie of Macbeth* the title,[103] foreknowledge or the play's first few minutes would individually be sufficient to alert us to the genre confronting us. In *All's Well* we find tragicomic form produced by human will in an acridly unpleasant world. *Troilus and Cressida* wearily goes through the motions, but speeds them up so that they look farcical. *Macbeth* offers us a tragic hero less noble, more like us, than we are prepared for, and a criminal more intriguing than any of his executioners: it divides us by separating moral judgement from emotional complicity. The characters turn against the dramas to which they are limited.[104]

But it is on those dramas that they depend for their very existence. None of these characters could satisfactorily convey himself in dramatic monologue, because each is affected by the impact of others, and seen in a different light. Ajax cannot be stupid and noble simultaneously: the two qualities may inhere in him but they must find successive expression. In solitude, this would be seen as shapeless meandering rather than as a coherent poem. Each speech might be regarded as a poem of self-disclosure, but is questioned and revised by what surrounds it. None of the characters we have looked at is easily summarised in a phrase. Indeed, the difficulty is acute: to ask what Troilus or Helena or Lady Macbeth is 'like' is to ask for an impossibility.[105] Some, such as Cressida and Macbeth, are aware of this problem within themselves, and are dissatisfied with any answer their worlds offer them. The further difficulty posed for us is that the plays are not unintelligible. We know that Macbeth is wrong to kill Duncan. We know that Bertram is culpably egocentric. We know that Cressida is guilty, that her traditional image does contain a truth about her. How is such knowledge possible? Is it even knowledge? A thoroughly sceptical reader might argue that we know nothing of the kind, that our freedom to judge is so great that any judgement is possible. Shakespeare offers us worlds without values, and we must place them there. I have argued that this is largely the case with *Troilus and Cressida*, and that it is a deliberate part of Shakespeare's intention, but in *All's Well* and *Macbeth* it seems to me that our possible responses are not unbounded. They are directly contradictory. The 'problem' of the problem plays is an extreme instance of the general problem of Shakespeare's universality.

Shakespeare is a universal writer in two ways. First, his work seems to contain more variety of language, situation and character more intensely realised than that of any but a handful of other writers, none of them English. Secondly, his work appeals to audiences who may know nothing of its context, who may indeed find the generic expectations I have assumed alien to their own cultural assumptions.[106] For the first there is no accounting. Whether we explain Shakespeare – or try to explain him – as an individual genius or as a site traversed by languages, a peculiar reticulation in the mesh of discourse, the scope of the undertaking is too great. It is not infinite, for there are only so many Shakespearean works, and we can parcel them out as we will, but no limitation on his creativity (or productivity) is clearly apparent. The question is not how Shakespeare was able to do what he did but how he was able to make his multifariousness comprehensible and attractive. The universality of response that Shakespeare commands may be explained by the plays' ability to satisfy our expectations, by their each somewhere containing, even in scattered form, the lines along which they were intended to be understood. This is an attractive hypothesis but still problematic. That Shakespeare's meanings are not single and clear is one of the few almost universally acknowledged truths about him but, as I have said, so is the simplicity with which we seem to know what the work means in a few primary ways.

All's Well and *Troilus and Cressida* depend for their greatest efforts on a peculiarly subtle, almost decadent relation to dramatic form. It is fitting that they deal with decadent worlds. *Macbeth* gains its power from the things that terrify Macbeth, witches, hallucinations, insomnia and so forth, but adds to this a more complex play with ideas about at-homeness, with oneself, with others and with the world. In all three cases, the subtle effects are close to the obvious ones. The problem plays are troubling and decadent because that is how they ought to be, *Macbeth* simple and complicated at once because that is the nature both of its content and of its conveyance to us through form and language. To clarify these questions, I shall approach them from another angle, moving away from Shakespeare to examine some other major writers' uses of symbolism and allegory before looking at how he avoids either.

Chapter 2

Describing the 'pleasure-house' to which he proposes to take Emilia, Shelley tells her and us in *Epipsychidion*[1] that

> Some wise and tender Ocean-King, ere crime
> Had been invented, in the world's young prime,
> Reared it.
>
> (ll. 488–90)

The obvious meaning of 'Reared' is 'raised', but its placing at the start of a line and the metrical emphasis of the reversed foot suggest some exceptional constructive energy. The word can also suggest 'nurture', and in that subordinate sense it is implied that the building is the joint work of man and nature. 'Ocean-King' brings the two together, as does the contrast between the loving overtones of rearing and the technical ingenuity of 'invented'.

This ambiguity points us to the relation this 'pleasure-house' has with the 'pleasure-dome' of 'Kubla Khan'.[2] Coleridge tells us that Kubla 'decreed' his building and abstracts the gardeners and masons involved in the work by giving 'were girdled round' a passive construction.[3] Something happens to the 'twice five miles of fertile ground', but it is as a consequence of Kubla's decree ('So') and not of collaborative human enterprise.

> So twice five miles of fertile ground
> With walls and towers were girdled round.

Coleridge goes on to tell us that

> It was a miracle of rare device,
> A sunny pleasure-dome with caves of ice!

The tension between 'miracle' and 'device' is that between dome and caves. The 'miracle' is Kubla's creation, the 'device' the contrivance of situation. The extravagant artifice seems divinely inspired, a commingling of human and natural orders. It is therefore a work of the Romantic Imagination, drawing on the

78

strength of nature and man's own mental powers to do its work.[4] However, the imagination is here used naïvely, for Kubla shows no sign of knowing what he has done and the dome is not gathered into eternity but imperilled by time.

> And 'mid this tumult Kubla heard from far
> Ancestral voices prophesying war!

Ancestors who prophesy join past to future in an arch which embraces the present and negates it by promising destruction, showing the wisdom of history as bloodshed. The only way of saving the dome is through conscious, sentimental re-creation, a transmutation embodied in the Abyssinian maid, whose song is the creative principle.[5]

Kubla has an heroic, primitive energy. He is Jehovah decreeing light, an irresponsible, self-moving beginner of things. The maid is distinctly feminine: we are not told that she is beautiful, and there is no trace of the erotic in Coleridge's description, but the grace with which she is described implies her attractiveness. She does nothing but sing, and it is the power of her song that matters. Coleridge wants to 'revive within me/Her symphony and song', to make live again what is now dead. 'In a vision once I saw' the maid, but the vision has faded. That it came from outside rather than within is guaranteed by the maid's being 'Abyssinian', a figure of foreignness from an unplumbable abyss. Because she is external, Coleridge can only ingest her song, which might be revived 'within me'. 'Could I' intimates by conditionality that this is impossible. However, were this to happen, 'To such a deep delight 'twould win me' that the poet would rebuild dome and caves 'in air'. The depth ties this rapture to the sacred river Alph, which rises from unknowable profundities 'measureless to man' to appear 'momently', a word which unites brevity and momentum into a hurtle of divine energy. That dome and caves are rebuilt 'in air' stresses the element of conscious contrivance together with the publicity of the poet's achievement. 'Air' is also the medium of song and poetry. The form the re-created landscape takes is identical with the medium in which it occurs.

The process of imagination here is complex and comes in stages. Coleridge has had a vision which revealed the music of creation, and is reminded of this as he thinks about Kubla's creation. (That the vision happened 'once' distances it, making its occasion irrelevant.) If he can successfully re-create within himself the conditions, originally external, from which that music sprang, it will again be as though outside him, something by which he can be wooed and won to a 'delight' which literally takes him outside himself. In that knowingly separate and deliberate re-creation of visionary trance Coleridge can become the indubitably great poet who can 'build . . . in air', make permanent the insubstantial. 'And all who heard should see them there', for the synaesthetic power of language possesses the listener as the revived vision would have possessed the poet, now a transfigured, demonic figure who has been in Paradise.[6] The hint that such a creature has returned like Lazarus tells us that the deliberate revival of the creative principle is also a resurrection without which the poet's experience is deathly.[7]

Obviously, the poem reflects more simply the young Coleridge's excitement about poetry and his sense of his own powers. In writing he discovers a strength in himself he had not known he possessed, a vision he is ambitious to have again. There is, though, a worrying ambivalence about the creative will here, a sense in 'Could I' that to try would be to fail, that inspiration is not voluntary. Imagination is at once autonomous and dependent on an external model, as Coleridge navigates between the solipsism on one hand and the determinism on the other that menace his whole career.[8] The poem is a statement and anticipation of failure, even though it proclaims the poet's ultimate capacity to re-create the world in which man and nature coexist (as dome and caves) in the most immaterial form (air) and thus to save it from the menace of history.

Not only does the poet create transcendent forms; he becomes one. Poetic fury turns the poet into a paradisal figure, a symbol[9] for man's fulfilment. The transfigured world he creates is a manifold unity perceptible in a hearing, at a glance, where Kubla's creation takes time to traverse ('twice five miles'): one effect of the poem is to suggest a connection between the symbolic and the typological. Kubla Khan is the type whose fulfilment is the poet.[10]

In adapting the pleasure-dome to his own purposes, Shelley gave two accounts of its origin. One is the acceptance that it was man-made, an acceptance that, as we saw, carries within it an organic ambiguity. Another is that

> It scarce seems now a wreck of human art,
> But, as it were Titanic; in the heart
> Of Earth having assumed its form, then grown
> Out of the mountains, from the living stone.
>
> (*Epipsychidion*, ll. 493–6)

The Titans precede the Olympian gods, and by associating the building with them Shelley confers on it an immemorial antiquity. The building was created so long ago that it might almost have existed forever. Originally it had a Platonic 'form' which was in 'the heart / Of Earth'. The house is the earth's poem and properly organic, having 'grown'. It comes from 'the living stone': Shelley takes a cliché and restores it to pristine vigour. The mystery of the house's making is the mystery of life and death coming together. Its material is inert, dead, yet living, expressive of a creative shaping intention.

Shelley is led to suppose this because the house has all the signs of antiquity.

> For all the antique and learnèd imagery
> Has been erased, and in the place of it
> The ivy and the wild-vine interknit
> The volumes of their many-twining stems.
>
> (ll. 498–501)

The imagery is clearly allegorical, but it can no longer be read. This might inspire a faint melancholy, as in Arnold's 'Stanzas from the Grande Chartreuse'. Arnold comes to the Chartreuse not to vilify,

> But as, on some far northern strand,
> Thinking of his own Gods, a Greek
> In pity and mournful awe might stand
> Before some fallen Runic stone –
> For both were faiths, and both are gone.[11]

Arnold is chilled and immobilised by the moment at which meaning takes flight, leaving runes the weather will gradually efface. Shelley is less bothered, for rather than the impersonality of climate the destructive force for him is the bacchanal of ivy and vines. When the flowers fade, the sky

> Peeps through their winter-woof of tracery
> With moonlight patches, or star atoms keen,
> Or fragments of the day's serene.
>   (*Epipsychidion*, ll. 504–6)

From the house one can see glimpses of the undying light of
which Shelley wrote in *Adonais* that

> The One remains, the many change and pass;
> Heaven's light forever shines, Earth's shadows fly.[12]

Whether by day or night, to look out from the house is to see that

> the Earth and Ocean seem
> To sleep in one another's arms, and dream
> Of waves, flowers, clouds, woods, rocks, and all that we
> Read in their smiles, and call reality.
>   (*Epipsychidion*, ll. 509–12)

The vision Shelley has here is one of primordial unity. Sea and
land are joined together eternally (more so than by the mortal
'Ocean-King') and the world is their shared dream. This collective
consciousness 'smiles', and we err by attempting to 'Read' it. Our
'reality' is divided and scattered like the light which accepts the
world's conditions,[13] and is divided partly by our attempt to see it
as legible, open to interpretation, rather than as a given unity
within which we ourselves are contained.

It is easy to imagine a reading which would find in this passage
a symbol repressing the knowledge of its origin in allegory. That
'the living stone' now brings forth plants would be seen as an
assertion of the organic over the constructed, the lamp over the
mirror. That the allegorical signs have become unreadable is here
in the poet as much as in the world. Indeed, that Emilia is a real
woman who replaces the sun, moon and comet which have
constituted Shelley's emotional life[14] could be seen as another such
arbitrary arrest of allegorical process. *Epipsychidion* claims to
transcend writing and attain presence, but we see beneath the
illusory claim to totality the ceaseless temporal undoing of
allegory, which constantly refers us to other signs and makes no
claims to embody the signified at any one moment.[15]

The attractions of such a reading are plain and widely felt at

present. It answers one of the central problems posed by poems
that claim symbolic truth, which is how we as readers are to
understand them. Presumably such truth should be compelling
and unitary, so that the symbolic poem by which we were not
utterly persuaded would be simply false in its own terms, and so
also that we could not accept two symbolic poems which contained
different views of the world. Shelley's view that truth is
necessarily scattered in this world might seem to help but, as
Chesterton observed, 'If we talk of a certain thing being an aspect
of truth, it is evident that we claim to know what is truth; just as,
if we talk of the hind leg of a dog, we claim to know what is a
dog.'[16] The pyrrhonist drive of Jacques Derrida and those who
think like him arises from a dissatisfaction with claims to unitary
truth (essentially, the phenomenological assertion of a present
self)[17] which finds no possibility of getting itself said in a language
which does not continually reiterate such a claim (the logocentrism
of which Western tradition is accused). To such a view the symbol
is only a mystification, a mask for allegory.[18]

Such a reading could plausibly be sustained by showing that
the now-defaced allegorical signs stand at the beginning of the
building's history. Furthermore, that Emilia's reality replaces the
allegorical, astronomical women of the past is not entirely
convincing. 'After the first death, there is no other',[19] and the
same goes for infidelity. Shelley wills her to be different, and uses
the rhetorical opposition of allegory and symbol to achieve this.
The defaced signs now share in the genial light of a timeless
wisdom, loosed from the specific literalness of interpretation. If it
is the case that allegory constantly refers us back to a lost origin,
its extension in time mirrors the ceaseless rhythm of interpretation
which, once existing, cannot find the lost original meaning where
its own undecidability would rest. Meaning strikes like inspiration,
but he on whom it falls is doomed. After all, Shelley tells us of the
Poet in *Alastor* that as he wandered he gazed

> And gazed, till meaning on his vacant mind
> Flashed like strong inspiration, and he saw
> The thrilling secrets of the birth of time.
>
> (ll. 126–8)

With this insight poetry can do nothing, and must return to
narrative: 'Meanwhile an Arab maiden brought his food' (l. 129).[20]

The trouble with such a reading is twofold. First, it beggars belief that all poets at all times should have been radically mystified, that the true subject of their poems was poetry and not whatever they claimed. Secondly, it misunderstands what Shelley writes. In the bower he describes, the allegory was once intelligible, at the moment it came into being, and that moment was one when the contraries of nature were one, the rock lived and the earth dreamed. We can still see such unity when we look out at the surrounding landscape, for the bower is a numinous spot, and know that the dispersed world 'we call reality' is the dream of a higher consciousness. This may only 'seem' (l. 509) to be the case, but seeming is in the circumstances all that is possible. Shelley implies that the opposition between symbolism and allegory is mistaken because they have a common source in the unity of truth, which is itself incommunicable.

Interpretation threatens the quiddity of its objects, always turning them into something else. A famous instance of this comes in the sixth book of *The Faerie Queene*,[21] when Sir Calidore disturbs Colin Clout and the dancing Graces on Mount Acidale. Calidore, 'rapt with plesaunce, wist not what to weene';

> Therefore resoluing, what it was, to know,
> Out of the wood he rose, and toward them did go.
>
> (VI.x.17)

The dancers vanish immediately, but Calidore presses on to Colin and 'Drew neare, that he the truth of all by him mote learne' (st. 18). Though the vision has fled, the poet is trusted to expound it.

Spenser can seem the most elusive of the great English poets, particularly when contrasted with his pupil Milton. Where Milton's lines seem to be hammered out of their author's personality, Spenser is conventionally granted sweetness and little more. This view does not explain why Milton, Wordsworth, Keats, Tennyson and Eliot, to name a few examples at random, should have turned to him for lessons in versification, or why he should have seemed an exemplary figure.

Spenser's versification, with his love for circling, repetitive rhyme-schemes such as those of the Spenserian sonnet or the *Faerie Queene* stanza, marries a reluctance to move forward with an intensity of intellectual exploration which is obviously educative for any poet who wishes to achieve durable form, but his slightly archaic focus on alliteration reminds us that his art is half popular, drawing on medieval romance. These deep characteristics of his verse, as much as particular local attractions, arouse profound responses.

More importantly, though, Spenser takes himself seriously: that is, poetry is not for him a youthful diversion, and with the publication of *The Shepheardes Calender* he announces that he will be the English Virgil.[22] The significance of this is partly historical, as a decisive blow in the struggle between ancient and vernacular tongues, and partly exemplary, in that it insists that the past can be emulated. Its only superiority is to have come first, and Spenser licenses high ambition by his example.

The function of 'E. K.' in *The Shepheardes Calender*, as Spenser's first expositor, deserves a little examination. One way of dealing with him is to see him as a member of the Cambridge circle to which Spenser belonged, a view with which there can be no quarrel, and to single out such comments as 'a pretty Epanorthosis in these two verses, and withall a Paronomasia or playing with the word' (*Poetical Works*, p. 423) as instructions to the reader about how to read the poet. The poems themselves are a difficult, learned text which cannot speak directly to the reader. This view takes account of Spenser's novelty and sees the collection as a document of humanist advance. Undoubtedly the poems are such a document, and E. K. acts as their spokesman, but he can be seen also as a poetic rather than a propagandistic device.

At first, E. K. seems to be garrulous and confidential, filling us in on the identities the pastoral names conceal and highlighting the poet's beauties. He knows what we ought to see and is instructed as to what we are likely to want to know. This chatty, officious helpfulness is a misreading, though. E. K.'s function is to disarm curiosity, which he does very efficiently. This is particularly the case 'Of Rosalend (who knowes not Rosalend?)' (p. 450, l. 141). In its context, a conversation among shepherds, the question might carry a tinge of sarcasm, implying that Colin Clout has made so much fuss about her that nobody can have missed it. This is at best only an undertone, though, beneath the dominant avowal of the poet's power to confer fame. Outside the poem, however, the only possible answer is 'nobody'. E. K. has two notable shots at giving us an answer. 'Rosalinde . . . is . . . a feigned name, which being wel ordered, wil bewray the very name of hys loue and mistresse, whom by that name he coloureth'

(p. 423). 'Ordered' hints that some operation on the name is necessary, but it does not seem to be anagrammatical. E. K. slides away into parallel examples, ending with the information that 'this generally hath bene a common custome of counterfeicting the names of secret Personages', leaving us none the wiser. His second shot is still more equivocal. Spenser

> calleth Rosalind the Widowes daughter of the glenne, that is, of a country Hamlet or borough, which I thinke is rather sayde to coloure and concele the person, then simply spoken. For it is well knowen, euen in spighte of Colin and Hobbinoll, that shee is a Gentle woman of no meane house, nor endewed with anye vulgare and common gifts both of nature and manners: but suche indeede, as neede nether Colin be ashamed to haue her made knowne by his verses, nor Hobbinol be greued, that so she should be commended to immortalitie for her rare and singular Vertues.   (p. 433)

Indeed, she deserves such commendation as much as the women praised by Theocritus, Petrarch and Stesichorus. All of which is very well, but tells us nothing. The tension between 'I thinke' and 'it is well knowen' suggests even that E. K. may not be too sure of his ground. He guesses at the poet's intention, then berates the poet's characters for not sharing in the common knowledge of Rosalind's true identity, then expands on what may be no more than gossip by directing us to literary tradition. Reminding us that Rosalind is the latest in a long line of pseudonymous *inamorate*, E. K. kills our interest in her. Where Shakespeare's Dark Lady provokes speculation to the point of obsession, Rosalind diminishes into a formal device. Shepherds must have girls to sing about, so Colin has his Rosalind.

E. K. acts as a distancing-device consonant with the whole apparatus of pastoral. Spenser achieves a magisterial impersonality. Notes can be ridiculous and pedantic, as E. K. may seem, an effect the Scriblerian annotations to *The Dunciad* guy and those to *The Waste Land* toy with; but Spenser like Pope and Eliot shows that they can form an integral part of the poetic effect, to such good purpose that the life he exploits ceases to have any interest outside the poem (utterly unlike that used by *Epipsychidion*).

Spenser effaces himself by apparently asserting the primacy of literature over life, as though life at its best were only the clumsy, intrusive Calidore. Indeed Sir Calidore, whose quest embodies the extirpation of libels in the form of the Blatant Beast, acts as E. K. in the context of Colin's vision. His conversation with Colin teases us with a knowledge we cannot have, but tails off as Calidore remembers Pastorella and sets off back to her. This sliding-away from the point is strongly reminiscent of E. K.'s habits. During the conversation, we learn of the girl who took the part of a fourth Grace that she was 'certes but a countrey lasse,/Yet she all other countrey lasses farre did passe' (*Faerie Queene*, vi.x.25). She is a human, not a deity, and she belongs in the pastoral world of which this vision is the centre. Colin ends his account of her by saying,

> Sunne of the world, great glory of the sky,
> That all the earth doest lighten with thy rayes,
> Great *Gloriana*, greatest Maiesty,
> Pardon thy shepheard, mongst so many layes,
> As he hath sung of thee in all his dayes,
> To make one minime of thy poore handmayd,
> And vnderneath thy feete to place her prayse,
> That when thy glory shall be farre displayed
> To future age of her this mention may be made.
>
> (st. 28)

The Faerie Queene breaks its banks at this moment, for the mask of Colin suddenly reveals Spenser clearly, and he addresses his Queen. She is asked to forgive Spenser for having made brief 'mention' of the woman he loves, when duty should require him to sing the Queen, and complimented indirectly by being told that this woman will enter eternity only because of Elizabeth's greatness. At first sight, this is straightforwardly eulogistic in a way that might seem to us otiose.

However, the passage does not tell us the beloved's name, which is withheld at all points. The 'mention' is a citation of the source of Spenser's vision rather than of an identifiable woman. Like Rosalind's, her existence is at least partly a formal requirement. It also goes unmentioned that at least possibly greater offence might be given by her having here replaced Elizabeth, who had already appeared as a fourth Grace in *The Shepheardes Calender*. The April argument (*Poetical Works*, p. 431) says that Colin 'taketh occasion, for proofe of his more excellencie and skill in poetrie, to recorde a songe, which the sayd Colin sometime made in honor of her Maiestie, whom abruptely he termeth Elysa'. Again the Queen resists incorporation in the allegorical structure, but there is again an undercurrent towards the poet's greatness, for the song is a test of his own virtuosity. 'Abruptely' tells us that the Queen is named without preparation in a sudden breaking-off from the poet's customary decorum. The incorrigible reality of the political sphere threatens the autotelic nature of the poetic. In *The Faerie Queene*, the abruptness is displaced from the vision to Colin's account of it, because the centre of Spenser's world is not a political fact. Spenser claims an autonomy for poetry which he acknowledges to be menaced by history.[23]

That acknowledgement finds a suitable poetic form in what happens to Pastorella. While Calidore is out hunting, the Brigants destroy the pastoral world and kidnap its inhabitants.[24] They are taken to an island hideaway and then removed from any obvious possibility of rescue.

> For vnderneath the ground their way was made,
>   Through hollow caues, that no man mote discouer
>   For the thicke shrubs, which did them alwaies shade
>   From view of liuing wight, and couered ouer;
>   But darkenesse dred and daily night did houer
>   Through all the inner parts, wherein they dwelt,
>   Ne lightned was with window, nor with louer,
>   But with continuall candlelight, which delt
> A doubtfull sense of things, not so well seene, as felt.
>
> (VI.x.42)

Spenser turns landscape into psychological condition. The darkness is 'dred', but more ominous is the 'daily night', an oxymoron which disrupts all order and the human cycle. The 'inner parts, wherein they dwelt' constitute the Brigants' utmost privacy: they choose to dwell in this permanent, static chaos.[25] It is important that there is no vitality here. The perpetual candlelight, smoky and shadowy, changes vision to feeling. Everybody blunders about in this sepulchral twilight, but the 'doubtfull sense' is mental. The 'things' are not just tables and chairs but take on the wide sense of things in general. Even

mental experience withdraws from the lucidity of consciousness
into a more unstable world of emotional impulse.
The chief Brigant is attracted by

> Faire *Pastorella*, whose sad mournefull hew
> Like the faire Morning clad in misty fog did shew.
>
> (VI.xi.3)

Even when she is sad Pastorella illuminates her surroundings, if
dimly. Her radiance gives the Brigant chief a fixed aim 'in mynde',
and

> From that day forth he kyndnesse to her showed,
> And sought her loue, by all the meanes he mote;
> With looks, with words, with gifts he oft her wowed;
> And mixed threats among, and much vnto her vowed.
>
> (st. 4)

This importunate, incompetent wooer mixes vows and threats, as
we should expect. Pastorella keeps a 'constant mynd' (st. 5) but in
order to prevent him from raping her she has to treat him with
'better tearmes' (st. 7), and so as to hold things at that level she
must feign 'sodaine sickenesse' which makes her incapable of sex
(st. 7).

> By meanes whereof she would not him permit
> Once to approch to her in priutiy,
> But onely mongst the rest by her to sit,
> Mourning the rigour of her malady,
> And seeking all things meete for remedy.
> But she resolu'd no remedy to fynde,
> Nor better cheare to shew in misery,
> Till Fortune would her captiue bonds unbynde,
> Her sickenesse was not of the body but the mynde.
>
> (st. 8)

The hysterical comedy of this stanza conceals its psychological
acumen. Pastorella's role as invalid, with the assembled company
sitting round, anticipates a novelistic world of drawing-rooms and
chaperones, but the pose she adopts feeds into her being, and by
the end of the stanza she is truly sick at heart, sick in mind.

Pastorella's plight worsens. The Brigants propose to sell their captives to some merchants who happen along. The Captain tries to hold her back from sale and the Brigants fall out. The captives are put to the sword

> But *Pastorella*, wofull wretched Elfe,
>   Was by the Captaine all this while defended,
>   Who minding more her safety than himselfe,
>   His target alwayes ouer her pretended.
>
> (st. 19)

Unsurprisingly, his gallantry gets him killed. The parodic novel of manners ends with Pastorella consigned to the custody of one of the Brigants, who treats her cruelly (st. 24).

The cowardly yokel Coridon has slipped away in the confusion, and a sequence of happy chances brings him back with Calidore, who rescues Pastorella, gives Coridon back his sheep and restores all to order. Spenser devotes two stanzas (44–5) to Pastorella's emotional recuperation before dealing with the battle, an emphasis significant in the light of the whole story's psychological drift. The destruction of the pastoral world is not just a question of burned cottages and rustled sheep, for it has a mental implication. As Virginia Woolf put it, Spenser 'impersonated his psychology'[26] throughout the poem: nowhere does he do so more subtly than here.

Pastorella is forced into an uncertain world where she must improvise to preserve her virginity. The world she enters is one of manners, in however travestied and distorted a form. To act is to be corrupted by the role: Pastorella moves from a feigned illness to genuine psychic malady, as we are forewarned by the way the underground retreat is also a state of mind. The possessive world of lust and money undermines her faith in providence to an alarming degree. The erotic peril Pastorella runs reflects that of Serena earlier in the book.[27] When Serena is captured by the savages, her body is seen as architecture:

> Her yuorie necke, her alablaster brest,
>   Her paps, which like white silken pillowes were,
>   For loue in soft delight thereon to rest;
>   Her tender sides, her bellie white and clere,
>   Which like an Altar did it selfe vprere,

To offer sacrifice diuine thereon;
Her goodly thighes, whose glorie did appeare
Like a triumphall Arch, and thereupon
The spoiles of Princes hang'd, which were in battel won.
(vi.viii.42)

Everything is designed for use and the celebration of male power. The altar which is her belly anticipates the altar she is put on for sacrifice. When the priest 'gan aloft t'aduance his arme' (st. 45) we can only understand his action as a symbolic rape. Again, the poem embodies psychological motives. A. C. Hamilton observes of Serena on the altar that the vision 'gathers all the sexual phantasies of woman in love. This ironic vision is broadly comic in tone. . . . What delicious horror she must feel, this reluctant Hellenore among the satyrs.'[28] It seems more likely that what we see here are male fantasies about women's desires, but there is indeed a tremulous excess to the description which engages the reader at more than the didactic level. The comedy of desire has the structural function of preparing us for Pastorella's incarceration. Where the other side of serenity is erotic fury, the other side of pastoral is flirtatious deviousness.

Serena and Pastorella offer two visions of female sexuality in danger. Serena is exposed to the gloating exuberance of bondage, Pastorella to the precariousness of good behaviour. These worldly dangers are averted respectively by Calepine and Calidore, who are 'two sides of the same coin': Calepine represents the gentleman's 'internal disposition . . . and his struggle to maintain a proper balance of wishes within his own soul', Calidore, 'Spenser's ideal gentleman in his daily contacts with other people'.[29] Calepine's business is the suppression of lust, Calidore's the correction of manners.

However, too strictly allegorical a decoding of the sixth book violates its integrity of mood. Alastair Fowler notes in it a 'seeming absence of any complexities of number symbolism',[30] an absence which is telling. Spenser needs less structural elaboration the closer he comes to the heart of his own vision on Mount Acidale. The nature of that vision informs book, poem and poetic career.

We approach the sacred hill with Calidore, and at first see what he sees, the dancing maidens, the three Graces and the damsel in their midst. The central figure 'Was she to whom that shepheard pypt alone' (vi.x.15). The Graces, from whom Venus borrows all

that she 'in her selfe doth vaunt' (st. 15), are set in motion by the
music which expresses the shepherd's particular love.

> She was to weete that iolly Shepheards lasse,
> Which piped there vnto that merry rout,
> That iolly shepheard which there piped, was
> Poore *Colin Clout* (who knowes not *Colin Clout?*)
> He pypt apace, whilest they him daunst about.
> Pype iolly shepheard, pype thou now apace
> Vnto thy loue, that made thee low to lout:
> Thy loue is present there with thee in place,
> Thy loue is there aduaunst to be another Grace.

> (st. 16)

The appearance of Colin Clout is climactic. When Calidore first
woos Pastorella, he discovers that she 'cared more for *Colins*
carolings / Than all that he could doe' (VI.ix.35). The Christian
name by itself alerts us, but it is not until the shepherds agree in
stanza 41 'That *Colin Clout* should pipe as one most fit' that we are
sure of the poet's persona's presence. Colin is chosen to pipe,
'And *Calidore* should lead the ring, as hee / That most in *Pastorellaes*
grace did sit'. The poet's art is at the service of a community, his
song made 'To flatter beauty's ignorant ear'[31] at its most trivial but
at its grandest to express the concord of love. This social function
of art is, though, only a dim reflection of its private source. Colin
must steal away by himself to pipe to his own love and set in
motion the divine powers.

In the last four lines of the stanza Spenser addresses himself.
He does so in the present tense because the objective projection
of himself his poem has created exists in an eternal present. The
vision is of eternity, and that content is embodied in the poem's
formal lastingness. Spenser celebrates his love, his vision and the
poem that celebrates them. In this context, the line 'Poore *Colin
Clout* (who knowes not *Colin Clout?*)' has a peculiar resonance. It
takes up the form of 'Of Rosalend (who knowes not Rosalend?)'
in *The Shepheardes Calender*, which we looked at earlier. That line
celebrated poetry's power to make its subjects famous: now,
Spenser celebrates his own self-creation. The appropriate answer
here is not 'nobody' but 'everybody', for we have grown
accustomed to Colin Clout as the poet's persona over a long
period.

In particular, we may remember the extraordinary *tour de force Colin Clouts Come Home Againe*,[32] which describes Spenser visiting Elizabeth's court from his exile in Ireland and his reactions to what he found. Spenser is disgruntled in both places. Ireland is provincial and boring, while in the court Spenser finds his own power to love (ll. 464–79) mocked by the fact that

>   loue most aboundeth there.
> For all the walls and windows there are writ,
> All full of loue, and loue, and loue my deare,
> And all their talke and studie is of it.
> Ne any there doth braue or valiant seeme,
> Vnlesse that some gay Mistresse badge he beares:
> Ne any one himselfe doth ought esteeme,
> Vnlesse he swim in loue vp to the eares.
> But they loue and of his sacred lere,
> (As it should be) all otherwise deuise,
> Then we poore shepheards are accustomed here . . .
> For with lewd speeches and licentious deeds,
> His mightie mysteries they do prophane . . .
> Ah my dread Lord, that doest liege hearts possesse,
> Auenge thyself on them for their abuses.
>   (ll. 775–85, 787–8, 793–4)

The variety of tone here is remarkable. The passage moves from being very funny to sarcastically moral to passionately vengeful in a masterly sustained escalation. At the beginning, love appears as a casual graffitist, but the leisurely third line has the languishing to which Pastorella is condemned. Even when such languishing is most feigned it corrupts the soul. 'Seeme' is exposed to our scepticism at the end of a line. That nobody can value himself unless he behaves preposterously, swims 'in loue vp to the eares', is a reflection on the sheer triviality of court life. The court's understanding of love is quite unlike that of Spenser and his Irish circle. 'Poore shepheards' is viciously sardonic, for Spenser is truly living in rusticity as well as being a pastoral poet, and the poverty around him is yet preferable to London's vanity. The final prayer to God characteristically breaks the form's bounds, for it names 'abruptly' a power that should not be allegorised. Glad to be saved by Ralegh from 'that waste, where I was quite forgot' (l. 183), a fastness 'Vnmeet for man, in whom was ought regardfull' (l. 185) – sentiments he comically attributes to Ralegh but shares sufficiently to be moved by – Spenser is disillusioned by London and half glad to 'Come Home Againe'. He remains unsettled, snootily reminding the other shepherds that Rosalind 'is not like as the other crew / Of shepheards daughters which emongst you bee' (ll. 931–2), and is still haunted by the beauty he has seen among the members of the court (ll. 40–7).

But where is Colin's 'Home'? On this reading, it would appear to be Ireland. The poem describes Colin's return to his friends and his relation of his travels, but this is not satisfactory in that Ireland is not made to feel homely and Spenser's true home was England. The title can be read the other way round, as a statement that Colin Clout has come back to London, which he does doubly, once as the man Spenser and once as the persona Colin. He comes home to be rejected as a man but to remain as a poet, even as a poem.[33]

It is easy to underestimate Spenser's pride in his own achievement and his sense that he had not had the rewards he could properly have expected. The ambiguous animus of *Colin Clouts Come Home Againe* is pure triumph in the question 'who knowes not *Colin Clout?*' Spenser uses the same verbal form again in Book VII of *The Faerie Queene*, when Nature hears the trial on

> *Arlo-hill* (Who knowes not *Arlo-hill?*)
> That is the highest head (in all mens sights)
> Of my old father *Mole*, whom Shepheards quill
> Renowmed hath with hymnes fit for a rural skill.[34]
>
> (VII.vi.36)

We can find old Father Mole 'renowmed' in *Colin Clouts Come Home Againe*, ll. 103–55, where his children's amorous cavortings are described. The tone of the question here is new, though: it no longer matters whether we know or not. Spenser manages at once to tease and to defy.

Spenser shuts up *The Faerie Queene* with two stanzas that might seem to undermine the whole work.

> When I bethink me on that speech whyleare,
>   Of *Mutability*, and well it way:
>   Me seemes, that though she all vnworthy were
>   Of the Heav'ns Rule; yet very sooth to say,
>   In all things else she beares the greatest sway.

Which makes me loath this state of life so tickle,
And loue of things so vaine to cast away;
Whose flowring pride, so fading and so fickle,
Short *Time* shall soon cut down with his consuming sickle.

Then gin I thinke on that which Nature sayd,
Of that same time when no more *Change* shall be,
But stedfast rest of all things firmely stayd
Upon the pillars of Eternity,
That is contrayr to *Mutabilitie*:
For, all that moueth, doth in *Change* delight:
But thence-forth all shall rest eternally
With Him that is the God of Sabbaoth hight:
O that great Sabbaoth God, graunt me that Sabaoths sight.

                                                    (vii.viii.1–2)

It could be argued that Mutability is the informing spirit of allegory and that, faced by this principle in its pure form, Spenser is nauseated by the shifting, centreless world he has created and turns to a transcendence allegory can, by its nature, not admit. It should be remembered, though, that Mutability speaks of things becoming 'Vnlike in forme, and chang'd by strange disguise' (vii.vii.18) and claims that even the gods in their planetary forms undergo 'alteration plaine' (st. 55). Alteration, according to Aquinas, is a change of 'passions or qualities, with no transmutation in . . . substance'.[35] Mutability's own language evinces a limitation of her powers. Alastair Fowler finds it significant that Mutability's pageants do not include the planetary week, because it is 'the most fundamental of the structural series of the poem' and puts the work on Nature's side against Mutability.[36]

Earlier we are told of Mutability

That all which Nature had establisht first
In good estate, and in meet order ranged,
She did pervert, and all their statutes burst.

                                                    (vii.vi.5)

She has the force of original sin, making 'them all accurst/That God had blest' (st. 5),

> And wrong of right, and bad of good did make,
> And death of life exchanged foolishlie:
> Since which, all liuing wights haue learn'd to die.
>
> (st. 6)

Man is now part of a fallen natural world with which he must
negotiate on equal terms, as we learn from Melibee's

> Sometime the fawne I practise from the Doe,
> Or from the Goat her kidde how to conuay.
>
> (vi.ix.23)

Spenser's allegorical pastoral is not the Jonsonian landscape in
which 'The painted partridge lies in every field, / And for thy mess
is willing to be killed'.[37] Rather, like Milton's, it must be worked,
if for different reasons. The last stanzas of *The Faerie Queene* rebel
against man's fallenness: where for Milton man's fall will be an
historical event to be treated epically, for Spenser it belongs to
mythological time and defines the horizon within which allegory
exists.

Spenser's peculiar achievement is to show us a transcendent
vision which depends on his human experience as a lover and the
celebration of which sets the allegorical machinery dancing. The
vision on Mount Acidale has a suggestive lambency because it is
symbolic rather than allegorical. For Spenser, allegory is the
necessary exfoliation of symbolic experience under the conditions
of our mental life. In the last stanzas of *The Faerie Queene* Spenser
expresses a weariness with poetry, a longing for all-embracing
vision. As a man, he escapes his own artifice, leaving behind him
Colin Clout, who symbolises the poet as poet. Spenser does not
claim to be a demonic, haunted figure, because he has no need to,
being assured of his vision's reality and its artistic permanence.
Mount Acidale is, in this sense, the beginning and the end of his
poetic career. Spenser knows that it is an artistic triumph, but
manages to prevent our even trying to interpret what he sees
there. It is grounded both in religious experience and in a very
private life: Spenser's success is to persuade us that the two are
the same.

Spenser's poetic ambition and his awareness of his own high
achievement should be stressed, because the way in which he

disentangles his person from his art gives the latter more certain authority. Milton learnt much from Spenser, and it may be suggested that he learnt this too. *Paradise Lost* is a poem of overweening ambition which moves in distinctly unSpenserian ways, but its detachment of the poet's personal being from his achievement is very similar to Spenser's in its effect. Where Spenser shows us that allegory is grounded in the symbolic, Milton goes further, and shows that allegory is only a small part of the domain of the symbolic properly understood.

The primary problem of *Paradise Lost*[38] is generic, the poem's troubling relation with epic. Satan is manifestly an epic, tragic hero. His beginnings are alleged to have been dramatic,[39] and certainly his vaunting soliloquies remind us of Jacobean tragedy. This has led one writer to see *Paradise Lost* as an 'encyclopedic drama-epic', and to diagram the poem as an overlapping mixture of dramatic genres.[40] This interesting approach should be extended to cover the question of poetic genre.

When the fallen angels separate in Book II, the 'more mild'

> Retreated in a silent valley, sing
> With notes angelical to many a harp
> Their own heroic deeds and hapless fall
> By doom of battle; and complain that fate
> Free virtue should enthral to force or chance.
> The song was partial, but the harmony
> (What could it less when spirits immortal sing?)
> Suspended hell, and took with ravishment
> The thronging audience.
>
> (ll. 546–55)

Epic is associated with retreat, being the record of heroism rather than heroism itself.[41] The 'fate' which acts through 'force or chance' is not a Boethian providence but tragic necessity. The singers are lost in self-pity. Epic makes grandiose what has happened to them, turning into 'fate' the consequences of their own mistaken free choice. By separating their freedom from its consequences, the devils open an illusory mental space for impotent, self-regarding regret. What they sing is 'partial': polyphonic and prejudiced, but also incomplete.[42] As we shall see, *Paradise Lost* is designed as the completion or fulfilment of epic tradition. This lachrymose poetry is able to make its audiences forget their circumstances, a dishonesty which Milton's poem repudiates by concentrating on our common ancestors.

This association of the epic with the demonic should alert us to the generic versatility of Milton's poem, which is by turns epic, satiric, erotic, pastoral, comic and prophetic. *Paradise Lost* contains an epic, whose hero is Satan, but it contains much else. It gives Adam, for instance, the mental latitude of a novel to explore his feelings. In the meeting of Satan with Sin and Death, it is briefly allegorical. Milton's ambition is to create an encyclopaedia of poetic forms.

His purpose, of course, is more than aesthetic. As T. J. B. Spencer says, 'For Milton, the great poets of former days in Europe were not influences, but rivals; rivals to be surpassed',[43] and they must be overcome to show not merely Milton's pre-eminence but also the supremacy of the religious system he describes. We can see what this means for the poem by looking at the famous description of Eve before the Fall. Breezes harmonise

> The trembling leaves, while universal Pan
> Knit with the Graces and the Hours in dance
> Led on the eternal spring. Not that fair field
> Of Enna, where Proserpine gathering flowers
> Her self a fairer flower by gloomy Dis
> Was gathered, which cost Ceres all that pain
> To seek her through the world . . .
> might with this Paradise
> Of Eden strive

(IV.266–72, 274–5)

Pan here is not an occasional goatish visitor but the permanent presence of the power that informs nature, 'Knit' with the spirits of bounty and the passage of time. This 'eternal spring' is the fountain-head of pastoral, in a setting almost beyond expression. Milton has just expressed a wish to describe, 'if art could tell' (l. 236), the streams and flowers of Paradise, intimating the inadequacy of his expression. The scrupulous, remorseful intelligence with which Proserpine is not introduced is one of the most moving effects in Milton. Typologically, as Alastair Fowler shows, Proserpine is an anticipation of Eve.[44] Further, she classically embodies the evanescent frailty of nature. That she is gathered 'by gloomy Dis' mirrors the way in which she is gathered by gloomy Milton, removed to the status of inadequate forebear. That move turns Ceres, the goddess of harvest, into a weary sufferer. Proserpine is lost and Eve will fall: man will be expelled from the self-renewing fecundity of Eden to an earth he must labour on to make it productive. Proserpine is evoked lyrically but denied, because this poem is not interested in her, as it aspires to a higher, unattainable pastoral which it will itself have to leave in the interests of truth.

The Fall is embodied in a transformation of genre, just as after it 'the Father and the Son enter into a kind of husbandry that did not exist before',[45] as the interceding Son shows that he can bring

> Fruits of more pleasing savour from thy seed
> Sown with contrition in his heart, than those
> Which his own hand manuring all the trees
> Of Paradise could have produced.
>
> (xi.26–9)

'The traditional term for this restoration was "engrafting", or as Milton's God says to the Son, man shall "live in thee transplanted" (iii, 293).'[46] The imagery of gardening turned to bleaker agriculture operates at the literary, the human and the divine levels. Prosperine cannot 'strive' with Eve, and it is to her own good that she should not, because *Paradise Lost* is a poem in which former things are understood in the light of what comes later.

In Book ix, Milton speaks of Urania, who comes to him in

> Her nightly visitation unimplored,
> And dictates to me slumbering, or inspires
> Easy my unpremeditated verse.
>
> (ll. 22–4)

The claim that *Paradise Lost* is 'unpremeditated' is not very plausible. The degree of intellectual organisation shown by the poem is the outcome of a long period of reading, digesting and plotting. Milton's own skill is the outcome of a long period of deliberate training as a poet. The self-consciousness with which Milton set out to become a poem himself[47] can, however, be allied to what he says here if we see that the poem itself comes after the struggle. By the time he starts *Paradise Lost*, Milton has finished his training. Verse is a habit of his fingers.

The claim to be inspired has a further importance, however. If we approach *Paradise Lost* solely from the angle of genre, we risk turning it into the purely aesthetic object it emphatically is not. Milton wants to persuade us that his will has very little to do with how the poem turns out. Man's will is fallible, and this poem claims an absolute authority. We must take not Milton's word but the Word of God.

Donald F. Bouchard argues that God's creation is reflected in an 'original and perfect etymology'.[48] This helps point us to the extraordinary nature of Milton's language, which is, as J. B. Broadbent says, aprioristic, expecting a 'conceptual rather than sensory' response.[49] When Satan says, 'Evil be thou my good' (IV.110), the words rebel in his mouth.

> So farewell hope, and with hope farewell fear,
> Farewell remorse: all good to me is lost;
> Evil be thou my good.
>
> (IV.108–10)

Satan significantly picks up the intonation of 'Farewell the tranquil mind; farewell content' (*Othello*, III.iii.349). Like Shakespeare, Milton sets this languishing tone of renunciation in a context that makes it absurd. Satan tries to remove the future (hope and fear being the emotions which most powerfully anticipate) and turn himself into an object. Although he claims to be the existential hero who chooses his own values, in fact he denies himself choice and commits himself to the logic of his fall. The locution 'my good' is patently self-contradictory. Satan is less powerful than the words he uses, and their logocentrism is focused on the Word.

Milton's words are morally charged throughout the poem. The poet shows that their ultimate orientation is toward God, and that is why he can claim his work to be 'unpremeditated'. Milton takes the language as he finds it, still impregnated with divine truths he can disclose by setting it in meaningful order. *Paradise Lost* is a poem that has already been written, because it is simply the reflection of truth. The poem is a symbol, a synechdochic encapsulation of the order of the universe.

It is also a type, the fulfilment of prediction and the completion of a figural cycle. Throughout his career, in 'Lycidas', in *Comus*, in *Paradise Lost* and in *Samson Agonistes*, Milton sets out to redeem the fallen world of literature.[50] 'Lycidas' takes up the pastoral elegy and turns it into Christian celebration. In *Comus* the showy, erotic masque is chastened into philosophic disquisition.[51] *Samson Agonistes* takes Greek tragedy and presents it to God. The implication is that only in Milton's hands are the true meanings of the forms disclosed. Where man's fallen writings are aesthetic celebrations of man's own being, blind to his true condition, Milton's show that the inner logic of genre is Christian. This is why Satan is so attractive. Milton and his readers must be drawn to him because they, we, are fallen. We would have eaten the apple, and must experience Eve's seduction with complete sympathy. The poem should end by driving us to prayer. Its extremism finds the aesthetic fulfilled in the religious.

Wordsworth wrote,

> Jehovah – with his thunder, and the choir
> Of shouting Angels, and the empyreal thrones –
> I pass them unalarmed.
>   (Prospectus to *The Recluse*, ll. 33–5)[52]

He had to do so in order to write an epic himself. *Paradise Lost* takes up the classical epic and destroys the possibility of its being done again. 'Shouting' impudently mocks what Wordsworth cannot ignore. To make epic possible for himself he must turn inward, away from all power 'That ever was put forth in personal form' (Prospectus to *The Recluse*, l. 32) 'Into our Minds, into the Mind of Man' (l. 40). The catholicity of Milton's poem is such that all successor epical writers find themselves compelled to a Protestantism of personal piety. Spenser could identify religious vision with private life by showing that the symbolic centre of his vision was necessarily incommunicable. Platonised Christianity gave him that freedom. Ezra Pound failed in such an effort, which is why the *Cantos* come unravelled with the questioning

> M'amour, m'amour
>   what do I love and
>   where are you?

That I lost my center
        fighting the world.
The dreams clash
        and are shattered –
and that I tried to make a paradiso
               terrestre.[53]

Pound's symbolist vision seeks the political correlates which necessarily threaten it. It might be said that Mussolini was his Sir Calidore. His 'center' is lost, and his romance loses Spenserian coherence for a series of Olympian personifications of vision which do not marry with the political and economic matter. For Milton, history was the present threat of royalist revenge: 'In darkness, and with dangers compassed round' (*Paradise Lost*, VII.27) he knows that his poem has only one way of achieving 'heroic name' (IX.40). Abandoning traditional epic topics,

              higher argument
Remains, sufficient of it self to raise
That name, unless an age too late, or cold
Climate, or years damp my intended wing
Depressed, and much they may, if all be mine,
Not hers who brings it nightly to my ear.
                    (ll. 42–7)

Paradise Lost replaces the transitory, tragic world of epic with the stable one of Christian revelation. To ensure that it does so, Milton saves it from the accidents contingent on human life, of which history in the present is one, and attributes it to the Muse.

The Muse, whether Milton's (and Wordsworth's[54]) Urania or Spenser's fourth Grace, lovingly grants the poet inspiration beyond his unaided powers. She is a figure for access to the numinous to which the symbolic points and on which, therefore, allegory is ultimately dependent. Spenser shows us that his allegory proceeds from a symbolic core: Milton shows that allegory, whether the crude one of Sin and Death or the more subtle form which is classical personification, is entirely subsumed by the symbolic order of his poem. *Paradise Lost* is both symbolic and a symbol. Internally, it uses genre and classical or historical characters as symbolic anticipations or alternatives for what it can often only describe by negation. Externally, the poem embodies the truth it proclaims by manifesting the organisation of the universe within which our free will has meaning.

And its centre is pastoral, which has two forms. One is Eden, the garden whose luxuriance must be restrained. The other is the earth on which fallen man must labour.

> The cherubim descended; on the ground
> Gliding meteorous, as evening mist
> Risen from a river o'er the marish glides,
> And gathers ground fast at the labourer's heel
> Homeward returning.

(XII.628–32)

We are reminded of God's vengeance by every English November. We live among 'A doubtfull sense of things' (*The Faerie Queene*, VI.x.42) in which the personifications of allegory take on a menacing reality, effacing their symbolic origin.

What for Milton is intensely serious is for his friend Andrew Marvell partly comic. Marvell's work contains examples both of the pastoral leisure of Spenser and the typological intensity of Milton, and I propose to look at an example of each, beginning with 'The Garden'.[55] In this celebration of contemplative withdrawal, Marvell's relaxed mind is permitted to assimilate itself to nature, becoming 'a green thought in a green shade'. Lorca tries to celebrate a landscape 'Green as I would have you be',[56] but his verdure is a rhetorical fiat. The gipsy girl with 'Green flesh, green hair' is menaced by 'Things she cannot see'. Her self-certainty is threatened by a combative world in which an old man says, 'I hardly know who I am.'

Lorca, unlike Marvell, fails to persuade us that green is the colour of both beginning and permanence, 'eternal spring' (*Paradise Lost*, IV.268). Marvell renounces the historical world of 'the palm, the oak, or bays' for 'the garlands of repose'.

> What wondrous life is this I lead!
> Ripe apples drop about my head;
> The luscious clusters of the vine
> Upon my mouth do crush their wine;
> The nectarine, and curious peach,
> Into my hands themselves do reach;
> Stumbling on melons, as I pass,
> Ensnared with flowers, I fall on grass.

This happy fall may have a theological content, as Empson points out,[57] but that coding seems beside the point. The poem must have such seriousness but leave it in abeyance, forcing us rather to contemplate the reality of rind and pulp. This is Jonson's compliant natural world run riot, answering Marvell's wish in the woods at Appleton House that the woodbines should bind him and, 'lest your fetters prove too weak',

> Do you, O brambles, chain me too,
> And, courteous briars, nail me through.[58]

Marvell jokes his way out of history and theology with insouciant ease.

Empson remarked that the stanza I have quoted from 'The Garden' is Keatsian in style.[59] It is, but there is an important difference between the two poets which we can see if we turn to 'Ode to a Nightingale'.[60]

> I cannot see what flowers are at my feet,
>   Nor what soft incense hangs upon the boughs,
> But, in embalmèd darkness, guess each sweet
>   Wherewith the seasonable month endows
> The grass, the thicket, and the fruit-tree wild –
>   White hawthorn, and the pastoral eglantine;
>   Fast fading violets covered up in leaves;
>   And mid-May's eldest child,
>   The coming musk-rose, full of dewy wine,
>   The murmurous haunt of flies on summer eves.

Keats' visionary trance happens at twilight, and he 'cannot see', unlike Marvell, who enters a tangible and visible world of apples and melons. 'Embalmèd', saved from corruption, Keats must 'guess' what is around him. 'Soft incense' shows flowers at the moment of becoming scent. They exist for and by their least concrete appearance. Keats knows that there is a bare world around him of grass, thicket and wild fruit-trees, but these are only the bones of a world, things in themselves, substances without accidents. Nature 'endows' them with more sensuous manifestations of her own creativity, and in guessing what they are Keats hopes that he will be right, that the expansive imagination of the last five lines parallels nature's imagination exactly.

Both poems have birds in them. Marvell's soul flies into a tree:

> There like a bird it sits, and sings,
> Then whets, and combs its silver wings;
> And, till prepared for longer flight,
> Waves in its plumes the various light.

This birdlike soul resembles remarkably Wallace Stevens' figure 'Of Mere Being',[61] where 'A gold-feathered bird/Sings . . . without human meaning,/Without human feeling, a foreign song'. The difference is that Stevens' bird has gone as far as it can, to 'the end of the mind', Marvell's as far as it wants to. Marvell's universe is opener that Stevens' fictive, Cartesian enclosure. Keats' bird is different again, for it has the Grecian Urn's ability to 'tease us out of thought'.[62] We are teased out like knots in wool: either the Urn discloses a cold world of pure impersonal thought or it raises us to a contemplation beyond our thought. 'Tease' suggests also our cerebral convolutions. The nightingale departs, though, and Keats realises that 'the fancy cannot cheat so well/As she is famed to do'. Marvell shimmers on the edge of eternity, while Keats' aspirations are dashed down.

Keats is subject to time, where Marvell finds a way round it.

> How well the skilful gardener drew
> Of flowers and herbs this dial new,
> Where from above the milder sun
> Does through a fragrant zodiac run;
> And, as it works, the industrious bee
> Computes its time as well as we.
> How could such sweet and wholesome hours
> Be reckoned but with herbs and flowers!

'So far he becomes Nature, he becomes permanent', says Empson.[63] The garden is a floral clock.[64] 'Herbs and flowers' reverses 'flowers and herbs', making a little circle within the stanza. Turning time into landscape, Marvell discovers eternity, just as Wordsworth will explore 'general Truths' (*The Prelude*, 1.162)[65] by turning his autobiography into a landscape. 'The earth is all before me' (l. 15) he writes, identifying himself as fallen:[66]

> whither shall I turn,
> By road or pathway, or through open field,
> Or shall a twig or any floating thing
> Upon the river point me out my course?
>
> (ll. 29–32)

The paradox, to which I shall return, is that what for Marvell is half jocular is for Wordsworth wholly serious.

Richard Hurd described *The Faerie Queene* as a garden down whose alleys the reader might wander.[67] Spenser's narrative is strangely atemporal: it is often unclear how much time is passing, and narrative compels the simultaneous into sequentiality, which delights Spenser because it separates stories and denies the power of time over them. In 'The Garden', Marvell is a Spenserian without a conscience. Where Spenser's vision unfolds itself as allegory and teaches us how to live,[68] Marvell's offers the pictures of hedonistic salvation. Marvell enjoys his vision enough to find it funny as well as compelling, but is too little awed by it to build a long work on it.[69]

Keats remarks in a letter that 'What the imagination seizes as Beauty must be truth – whether it existed before or not' (22 November 1817).[70] As a seizure of imagination, the dream is especially important, because it contains rather than expounds its meaning. In *The Eve of St Agnes*,[71] Madeline wakes from dreaming of Porphyro to find him by her bed. 'How changed thou art! How pallid, chill and drear!' (l. 311) she exclaims. No longer giving his 'looks immortal' (l. 313), Porphyro seems unable to live up to her idea of him. For a moment, Keats has the brutal realism about love of

> Love in a hut, with water and a crust,
> Is – Love, forgive us! – cinder, ashes, dust.
>
> (*Lamia*, ii.1–2)[72]

Porphyro is able to change because of his passion. 'Beyond a mortal man impassioned far' (l. 316), entering the immortality of her dream, 'Into her dream he melted' (l. 320). The 'solution sweet' (l. 322) is both sexual intercourse and the dissolving of Porphyro into Madeline's imaginative projection.[73]

Keats finds the translation into symbolic truth through private experience. His Titans serve to exemplify the law 'That first in beauty should be first in might' (*Hyperion*, II.229).[74] This undynamic role of yielding to succession prevents their epic, *Hyperion*, from being completed, as it renounces narrative complexity for symbolic truth; *The Fall of Hyperion*[75] offers a Disneyland of the supernatural, where the Titans form a sculpture park round which Moneta guides the poet. It may be objected that Moneta has the function Virgil and Beatrice filled for Dante, but the objection is ill-founded. Virgil and Beatrice exist outside Dante's poem, and the journey on which they take the poet is structured by theological truth. Dante's visionary exploration is organised hierarchically in a way that Keats' cannot be.

Indeed, thinking of Dante reminds us how curious Keats' career was. In 'Sleep and Poetry',[76] Keats commits himself to a version of the traditional poetic *curriculum vitae*, which rises from pastoral and romance to epic, the career Spenser and Milton followed and for which Virgil is the model. The 'ten years' of 'poesy' (ll. 96–7) Keats wishes for are essentially pastoral and erotic:

> First the realm I'll pass
> Of Flora, and old Pan: sleep in the grass,
> Feed upon apples red, and strawberries,
> And choose each pleasure that my fancy sees;
> Catch the white-handed nymphs in shady places,
> To woo sweet kisses from averted faces –
> Play with their fingers, touch their shoulders white
> Into a pretty shrinking with a bite
> As hard as lips can make it, till, agreed,
> A lovely tale of human life we'll read.
>
> (ll. 101–10)

Nature burgeons round the drowsy poet, and he becomes passive in choice, opting for what his 'fancy' has noticed. The 'lovely tale of human life' is precisely not a tale but sexual intercourse. Literature was a physical pleasure for Keats, as we remember from his response to Spenser's whales,[77] and consequently a natural image for any pleasure. Paolo and Francesca 'read no more'[78] because Dante knows literature and sex as distinct things, however inflaming words may be.

> And can I ever bid these joys farewell?
> Yes, I must pass them for a nobler life,

> Where I may find the agonies, the strife
> Of human hearts.
>
> ('Sleep and Poetry', ll. 122–5)

The surmounting of pastoral by epic isolates and dignifies the poet's soul, which depends on vision for its elevation. When the mysterious charioteer whose passage embodies epic dignity vanishes,

> A sense of real things comes doubly strong,
> And, like a muddy stream, would bear along
> My soul to nothingness.
>
> (ll. 157–9)

The 'sense of real things' is, of course, the life of Keats' poetry as we know it, but it was a life which by indulging his senses imperilled what he saw as the single-mindedness needed for poetic greatness. Seeing a lock of Milton's hair,[79] Keats felt he must become 'mad with glimpses of futurity' before he could do his predecessor justice, but he was already so maddened. Inspiration flushes his brow when he sees the lock, and we find in this poem Keats' sense of poetry as individual vocation. The 'real things' that threaten him he wants always to still and to subdue, which is why he is drawn to figures such as the Grecian Urn, which immobilises and preserves in the ironically 'Cold Pastoral'[80] what would, warm and living, distract him from higher things.

Keats' aspiration to the symbolic vision of higher truth makes of the poetic career a private joy. Where Spenser and Milton train for greatness, reading and practising, Keats hopes to force his way there by passion. The slightness of such a base for symbolism perhaps explains a hostility to it which some critics have recently expressed. Paul de Man, for instance, finds Wordsworth's lines 'The immeasurable height/Of woods decaying, never to be decayed,/The stationary blast of waterfalls' exemplary of 'paradoxical assertions of eternity in motion' which 'can be applied to nature but not to a self caught up entirely within mutability'.[81] De Man sees in Romantic symbolism the urge of a mankind trapped in temporality (the pervasive, barely examined notion which haunts his work[82]) to transcend itself, and by denying this possibility as a truth finds all symbolism turned into allegory.[83]

The Romantic devaluation of allegory is, he argues, a mask for Romantic irony's awareness that certainties are only provisional assertions of selfhood.[84] Such a reading misunderstands the real distance between Keats and Spenser, which is simply that Spenser can refer to a common code of Christianity where Keats must rely wholly on private experience. The Romantic symbol must impose on us by its magnificence because the vehicles of allegory have been withdrawn, but the symbolic mode is not a Romantic discovery.

Angus Fletcher is as strongly mistrustful of the claims of the symbolic as Paul de Man. He argues that allegory must necessarily have a message,[85] and that such messages are characteristic even of the sublime, a Romantic notion which he argues should not be seen as wholly personal in origin, because behind it stand the categories of idealist philosophy.[86] The sublime, he writes against Kant, is not disinterested: 'The sublime is not a medium for tragedy or comedy, both of which tend not to judge the hero, nor to reward him with "poetic justice", but rather to show him for what he is, failing or triumphing over evil.'[87] This view of sublimity is of a piece with Fletcher's view of *The Faerie Queene* as sublime. *The Faerie Queene* is not, he contends, a disinterested work, and therefore breaks the Kantian precept.[88] Spenser is a writer in whom, however, allegory presses towards myth, towards claiming an autonomous, originary truth.[89] So far I agree, but when Fletcher calls the vision on Mount Acidale an 'allegory' which he qualifies as 'apocalyptic'[90] the term 'allegory' has taken too wide a significance. The apocalypse is an ending beyond which all is changed, and this power of transformation inheres in the apocalyptic by its nature rather than because of what it signifies. Where allegory is, as Fletcher recognises, potentially infinite and unstoppable,[91] the vision of Mount Acidale cannot be gone beyond. It is presented for contemplation rather than as a text for analysis.

The critical impulse to elevate allegory over the symbolic is a profoundly principled attempt to relate our reading of literature to a pervasive view of the human condition. Paradoxically, though, Fletcher concedes that allegory must be believed in to work, and that once faith in its procedures has died it dwindles to the merely decorative.[92] This seems to be true historically of poetic practice, but it is not the case that *The Faerie Queene* is now merely wallpaper: its power to signify survives, and I would argue that this is precisely because the numinous quality of its central and informing vision is still accessible to us.

The point is made more forcefully by *Paradise Lost*, where allegory only appears baldly once, when Sin and Death are presented as characters. Addison objected that such figures 'are not agreeable to the Nature of an Heroic Poem' (in that 'Nature' we hear the full force of a prescriptive theory): they may be admitted 'to convey particular Circumstances . . . after an unusual and entertaining Manner', but when they act 'they take too much upon them' and are improper in 'an Heroic Poem, which ought to appear credible in its principal Parts'.[93] Addison's judgements are not as dictatorial as they may at first seem. His 'appear credible' acknowledges art's imaginative autonomy as being nothing to do with fact, and what primarily worries him is that these allegorical personages belong to a lower class of poetry, that they bring down the tone.

In a sense Addison is right, but it may be supposed that this is precisely the effect Milton intended. Death's genesis is, as Alastair Fowler says, a 'parody of divine generation':[94] the Fall sets Sin and Death free to roam through the world. 'Thou hast achieved our liberty' (x.368), Sin tells Satan as he returns from Eden, and the allegorical figures prove more durable than their sire, who is speedily transformed into a serpent. Fallen man only encounters Satan in allegorical form, and must learn to read his emissaries in the light of their origin. The language of *Paradise Lost* is purged by its continual pointing to God, but what the poem accomplishes aesthetically we must learn to do in life. Allegory is used in *Paradise Lost* to place and judge its subject-matter, Milton using every means available to that end.

Indeed, it is Milton's capacity to pick up and use ostensibly lower literary forms which makes for some of his most disconcerting effects. Dr Johnson found 'indecent' the commingling of pastoral and Christianity in 'Lycidas'[95] because he did not appreciate how far Milton was deliberately completing the genre of pastoral elegy and fulfilling its typological role, a failure of appreciation perhaps caused by his being nearer to pastoral than we are and more strongly responsive a reader. For Milton the completion of pastoral is a wrestling with something deeply important and moving, just as it is for Johnson: we do neither justice if we think of the progress of Milton's career as a series of literary moves devoid of personal moral import. Johnson may be said to have believed it impossible that pastoral could be sufficiently chastened to become Christian.

One way of chastening pastoral is to make its labour serious. After the Fall, man's soul is turned into a landscape God works, just as the earth itself is changed from the superabundace of Eden to a parched landscape in which man must labour for his bread.[96] Where Keats is menaced by pastoral and the 'sense of real things', Milton returns to it at the end of *Paradise Lost*, 'sceptically', as Peter Conrad puts it.[97]

Conrad observes that there is a parallel between this and the sixth book of *The Faerie Queene*, where 'Spenser abandons the courtly and hierarchical scheme outlined to Raleigh to lose himself in the varieties of love and to remove courtesy from polite society to nature, among salvage men and penurious peasant farmers.'[98] He goes on to relate this to *The Prelude*, which 'inverts epic so as to make it pastoral, neglecting the French Revolution to retire into the fortitude of the mind and the settled low content of the poet's native landscape'.[99] So doing, he brings out the relationship pastoral may have with the symbolic when it is experienced as private truth rather than the universal divine revelation of scripture. The landscape of pastoral turns out to be an internal, mental space. For Milton, as we saw, epic itself entered that condition, which was why the fallen angels could retreat into it. In both cases, the withdrawn figure seeks an end to his mutability, and that end is expressed in symbolic form. The private symbol does for its witness something external experience cannot offer.

It may be that there is an historical explanation for such withdrawals, but such an explanation would have to do rather with how history feels as it is lived than with any historical change. Marvell's picture of Cromwell is, in the 'Horatian Ode',[100] typological. Cromwell has set the example to be fulfilled by 'The forward youth that would appear'. History menaces withdrawal, and offers the theatrical delights of appearance. To enter history is to gain reckless momentum: Cromwell may not 'yet' be 'grown stiffer with command,/But still in the Republic's hand', but, as C. A. Patrides points out, 'yet' and 'still' carry ominous overtones if we observe the metrical stresses applied to them.[101]

> The same arts that did gain
> A power, must it maintain.

History enforces a grim necessity, and all the poet can do is to record that that is the case by turning contemporary figures into types. For Marvell, Cromwell is a living symbol calling for typological fulfilment.

What distinguishes Cromwell from Kubla Khan is that he can be described in a public vocabulary. Kubla 'decreed': the Jehovan overtones make him more than human, while Cromwell is a figure of verifiable 'courage'. The same distinction applies to the kinds of response the two poems seem to look for. Marvell's poem begins by appearing to be a panegyric, but its equivocations force us to read closely and invite us to discuss the pros and cons of the Protector's career. We are led to think on public matters, rather than to withdraw into a rapt contemplation of the powers of the human mind, which is what Coleridge invites us to do and what his own critical close readings attempt in their tracing the lineaments of imagination.[102] Marvell says something about the world, but 'Kubla Khan' tells us to look within ourselves, even if its ambition is to produce an object of knowledge.[103]

Marvell 'seems' to say something, that is, but this is largely an illusion. Whether or not we assent to his view of Cromwell depends at least as much on what we know from outside the text as on what we know within it. The subject of this discussion so far, the relation of symbolism to allegory, is closely related to that distinction. Allegory depends on a symbolic centre to be credible, for it is in the symbol that truth seems to inhere. I say 'seems' because, as Kant argued, the symbol defines the horizon of mental possibility. For instance, Kant says that 'All our knowledge of God is merely symbolic',[104] and anyone who takes it to be 'schematic' – that is, to present the concept directly[105] – 'falls into anthropomorphism', but if he abandons all appeal to the senses 'he falls into Deism which furnishes no knowledge whatsoever'.[106] In the Romantic symbol we recognise the limits of understanding, and thereby grasp something of what we are. To interpret it is to falsify its nature, for the symbol begins where interpretation ends.

We can see changes in the valuation of symbolism and allegory, then, as changes in perception of man's place in the world. For de Man, man's tragedy is to be able to interpret endlessly and find nothing adequate to embody and stabilise the source of that activity, a view which is recognisably current and pervasive. Poetry is rebuked for not yielding the knowledge it cannot. Spenser's vision on Mount Acidale is related to a cosmos[107] in

which man's place is known and the constellations are stable, so
that the beauty of the dancing girls can safely be compared with
Ariadne's crown, which,

> Being now placed in the firmament,
> Through the bright heauen doth her beams display,
> And is vnto the starres an ornament,
> Which round about her moue in order excellent.
>
> (*Faerie Queene*, vi.x.13)

Spenser presents his symbolic vision as ultimately private, but is
able to set it in a shared context, both religious and scientific,
which makes it public and enables it to breed allegory. Although
pastoral is a sceptical retirement, Spenser's world is such that we
can all enter it. It is the lack of such a shared world which
prevents Shelley from reading the allegorical signs hidden by
foliage in the pleasure-house, because for the Romantics symbolic
vision is only private and, shared belief having died, the allegorical
has, as Angus Fletcher leads us to believe, become merely
decorative.

It may be said that the Romantic quest for the symbolic aims to
make a world fit for allegory. The two modes of vision necessarily
coexist. Romanticism leads us to overvalue the private symbol,
but to repudiate this entirely is to repudiate the possibility of
meaning. True idealism sees the symbol as giving out onto a
world of things as they really are,[108] beyond our comprehension.
Romanticism secretly fears that there may be nothing beyond,
forced as it is by scientific progress to accept the mutability of
natural forms. The poet of 'Kubla Khan' does not speak. Spenser's
astronomy is unevolving, where Shelley goes to considerable
lengths to gather the material for his footnote to *Queen Mab* where
he defines the 'red and baleful sun' as

> The north polar star, to which the axis of the earth, in its
> present state of obliquity, points. It is exceedingly probable,
> from many considerations, that this obliquity will gradually
> diminish, until the equator coincides with the ecliptic: the
> nights and days will then become equal on the earth throughout
> the year, and probably the seasons also.[109]

Shelley's concern for scientific accuracy is part of his radicalism.

He does not, as he might well, point out that the future state he anticipates is that of Milton's cosmology before the Fall,[110] and that the revolution of the skies is a revolution against the order of the God he hated. Impersonal nature now brings about what man once aspired to do, and in that diminution of man's possibilities lies the retreat from sharable to incommunicable symbols.

We may not read Spenser as we should inasmuch as we do not share his beliefs about the universe and are in danger of seeing as literary what was for him also true: the same is the case for Milton and Marvell. The Romantics pose a different problem for reading in that their work acknowledges the privacy of the symbols to which they responded, and indeed gives to their predicament a tragic grandeur. We should not, however, mistake their ambition for poetry to create objects of knowledge for its having done so: as Angus Fletcher says, idealist philosophy lies behind them, and it insists that the symbol expresses precisely the limit of knowledge. It is this confusion which bedevils much recent criticism. Spenser's stars are set adrift by modern astronomy, and we should perhaps remember that the cautionary tale of Frankenstein was originally told to a man who had set out on an expedition viewed by his sister with 'evil forebodings' to a polar region where he 'may regulate a thousand celestial observations, that require only this voyage to render their seeming eccentricities consistent forever'.[111]

II

It may well be wondered, whether or not my arguments are accepted, what possible connection there is between changing ideas of the source of poetic authority and the work of a dramatist. The answer has to do with the nature of our responses to literature, and with what we understand by 'poetic truth'. Symbolism and allegory are both kinds of formal organisation, by which disparate material is shaped into artistic wholes, and this is as much a problem for the dramatist as for the poet. The ideas we have examined turn out to bear importantly on Shakespeare's work.

A good place to begin examining why this is so is at the end of *Measure for Measure*, a scene which has aroused considerable critical controversy and a particular kind of response on which I want to focus. E. M. W. Tillyard proposes of the play as a whole that after Act III Scene i, in which the Duke proposes the Mariana substitution to Isabella, Isabella's role in the play diminishes, and as the Duke comes to predominate so the play becomes less human and more allegorical.[112] Shakespeare is implicitly seen here as deliberately taking on intractable material and then resolving it by use of a quasi-divine intervention, whose purpose is to show the nature and appearance of moral order in the world.

This view receives some endorsement from Philip Edwards, who writes that 'Modern criticism has established beyond disproof that there is in these plays [*All's Well* and *Measure for Measure*], intertwining with the far-fetched plots of comedy, a Christian or near-Christian pattern of providence and redemption'[113] In *Measure for Measure*, Shakespeare 'chose to alter the whole spirit of the dramatic movement from lonely human choice to the devices and intrigue of a controlling superhuman figure'.[114] Unfortunately, Shakespeare

> seems not to be able to convince himself, and he does not convince us, that the Christian idea can fully come alive within the tragicomic form. The plays can only be kept heartwhole by methodical criticism which treats them as allegories, which they certainly are not.[115]

Edwards says that 'The distance between the contrivances necessary for the fulfilment of the comedy and the workings of God which they are meant to suggest is impossibly great'.[116] However, despite the artistic failure, the muted and restrained happy ending is in itself successful.[117]

Edwards finds Shakespeare ultimately failing to achieve what Tillyard agrees is his aim: both are related to a tradition deriving from G. Wilson Knight 'in which *Measure for Measure* became an allegory of the Divine Atonement. The disguised Duke was taken to symbolize the Incarnate Lord; Lucio was seen as the eternal Adversary; Isabella represented the soul of man, elected to be the Bride of God'.[118] Tillyard and Edwards represent less extreme statements of this now commonplace view, but exemplify its faults the more clearly for that.

It is important to note how crowded the stage is at the end of *Measure for Measure*. What takes place is deliberately publicised – the Duke chooses that it should be so – and this is in flagrant contrast with the manner of the Duke's departure.

> I'll privily away. I love the people,
> But do not like to stage me to their eyes:
> Though it do well, I do not relish well
> Their loud applause and *Aves* vehement;
> Nor do I think the man of safe discretion
> That does affect it.
>
> (I.i.67–72)

The Duke is reluctant to perform, to 'stage' his disappearance, and makes of his distaste for publicity-seeking a moral principle. The search for applause betokens unsound judgement.

On his return, the Duke tells Escalus and Angelo that he hears such good of them that he must give 'public thanks' (v.i.7), for

> your desert speaks loud, and I should wrong it
> To lock it in the wards of covert bosom,
> When it deserves with characters of brass
> A forted residence 'gainst the tooth of time
> And razure of oblivion. Give we our hand,
> And let the subject see, to make them know
> That outward courtesies would fain proclaim
> Favours that keep within.
>
> (ll. 10–17)

Merit deserves to be honoured at large, rather than being treasured in private. To publish it is to give it an enduring memorial. 'The subject' are here not to applaud but to 'see', to be made know, what the Duke feels, and to learn that his 'outward' speaks of what is 'within'. The Duke's seeming is a true one (implicity, unlike Angelo's) and the function of this public appearance is to act as an object-lesson. The man the Duke mistrusts is one who revels in popular acclaim, and his own attitude to 'the subject' is moralistic and didactic. It is fair before thinking too hardly of the Duke at this point to remember that what we have seen of the low life of Vienna is remarkably unattractive, and that his apparent dislike of his people is not altogether unreasonable.

What turns out to happen is another kind of object-lesson, but one well prepared. The Duke has already instructed Friar Peter that 'The Provost knows our purpose and our plot' (IV.v.2), the word 'plot' stressing the dramatic nature of what he is doing. The

Friar must stick to 'our special drift' (l. 4), 'Though sometimes you do blench from this to that / As cause doth minister' (ll. 5–6). Equally, Isabella, though unwilling to speak 'indirectly' (v.vi.1) is 'advis'd to do it . . . to veil full purpose' (ll. 3–4). If contradicted by the Duke at any point, 'I should not think it strange, for 'tis a physic / That's bitter to sweet end' (ll. 7–8). The medicinal image is appropriate here to the ruler whose moralism ignores pain caused by the pursuit of good. The Duke keeps the news of Claudio's survival from Isabella 'To make her heavenly comforts of despair / When it is least expected' (iv.iii.109–10). It is this which provokes Philip Edwards' dissatisfaction: 'God works in mysterious ways, but this beats all – willingly to cause despair in order to show the beauty of divine consolation.'[119] Indeed so, and perhaps the Duke's repulsive glee over his own contrivance should alert us to the possibility that he is not a divine agent at all.

The purpose of the Duke's temporary absence has been twofold: first, to let Angelo enforce the law that he (the Duke) has been too lax to apply (i.iii.19–43), and, secondly (if we assume that the 'more reasons' of l. 48 are like it, which is in the context reasonable), to test Angelo:

> Lord Angelo is precise;
> Stands at a guard with Envy; scarce confesses
> That his blood flows; or that his appetite
> Is more to bread than stone. Hence shall we see
> If power change purpose, what our seemers be.
>
> (ll. 50–4)

The Duke has 'ever lov'd the life remov'd' (l. 8) and kept away from 'assemblies' (l. 9), but shows here a fascination with what people are really like that can only be satisfied by observation. The 'seemers' number more than Angelo: indeed, because he is the Duke, everyone acts in front of him. The Duke is particularly intrigued by Angelo's character, which he plainly though not explicitly mistrusts. At the start of the play, then, the Duke proposes a disinterested curiosity about human nature, a passion for truth, as one of his motives.

However, by the final scene these motives have become vindictive and self-regarding. This is not to dispute that justice is done, and seen to be done, but to question the view of the Duke as a divine agent. It should be noticed in particular that Angelo

fears exposure more than anything. His last speech is a wish for
death (v.i.472–5) because his repentance wounds him so deeply,
but it is a wish that ultimately the Duke will not grant. Angelo has
shifted from his first response to disgrace, which was

> O my dread lord,
> I should be guiltier than my guiltiness
> To think I can be undiscernible,
> When I perceive your Grace, like power divine,
> Hath looked upon my passes. Then, good prince,
> No longer session hold upon my shame,
> But let my trial be mine own confession.
> Immediate sentence, then, and sequent death
> Is all the grace I beg.
>
> (ii. 364–72)

Angelo credits the Duke with semi-divine powers, although it
may be that he has in mind as well the Duke's disguise as a friar.
He emphasises his own 'shame', an emotion which depends on
being observed by others, and pleads to die. What hurts him is
not so much the discovery he has made of his own nature but
that this should now be disclosed to others (he is not yet
repentant), which is not surprising in view of his earlier reference
to 'my gravity, / Wherein – let no man hear me – I take pride'
(II.iv.9–10). Angelo has been conscious before his temptation that
his coldness is a seeming, and has been happy to enjoy his own
performance.

Isabella remarks on authority as performance when she tells
Angelo that

> man, proud man,
> Dress'd in a little brief authority,
> Most ignorant of what he's most assur'd –
> His glassy essence – like an angry ape
> Plays such fantastic tricks before high heaven
> As makes the angels weep; who, with our spleens,
> Would all laugh themselves mortal.
>
> (II.ii.118–24)

Lucio immediately sees this as an effective ploy to win Angelo (ll.
125–6) because for him all intercourse is performance, but it is
more than that.

Wallace Stevens describes

> The impossible possible philosophers' man . . .
> The central man, the human globe, responsive
> As a mirror with a voice, the man of glass,
> Who in a million diamonds sums us up

and says of him that

> He is the transparence of the place in which
> He is and in his poems we find peace.[120]

This man is presented as imaginative self-sufficiency, a being who both reflects light and allows it to pass through him. Stevens plays on glass as a clear substance, something which can be as though it were not there, and Isabella treats the same idea. Where Stevens hopes that 'The central man' can again be recognised as he has been in the past,[121] Isabella declares man to be 'most ignorant' of his inner nature, which is both to reflect the world and to let its true nature appear through him.[122] She sees performance as a denial of reality, authority as inhuman. This idea is of central importance to the play because if the Duke is 'The impossible possible philosophers' man' he is so in a quite unexpected and moving way.

By exposing Angelo to public shame, the Duke flays him inwardly. The whole final scene of *Measure for Measure* is concerned with the revelation and judgement of deep feeling, which can be seen at its finest in Mariana. When the Duke threatens to have Angelo executed, he tells Mariana that she will be given his goods 'To buy you a better husband' (v.i.423). Mariana replies, 'O my dear lord, / I crave no other, nor no better man' (ll. 423–4). 'Crave' is brutally physical, an expression of naked desire. In its indigent demand it moves us by its strength, while showing the power of the emotions to survive the withdrawal to the moated grange, the one place in the play where we hear music.

When we first see Mariana she is alone on stage with a boy who is singing a beautiful song of romantic regret (iv.i.1–6). When the Duke enters, she says,

> Break off thy song, and haste thee quick away;
> Here comes a man of comfort, whose advice
> Hath often still'd my brawling discontent.
>
> (ll. 7–9)

What we are seeing is the re-enactment of a habit: Mariana luxuriates in the weepy indulgence of music, which exacerbates and prolongs her 'discontent', and the Duke acts to appease her disquiet. The sense of indulgence here is made little of, but was seized on by Tennyson, who in 'Mariana' and 'Mariana in the South' turns her into another of his imprisoned women, figures for the imagination out of touch with reality and, as 'The Lady of Shalott' shows, afraid of what they desire. Some of the details Tennyson uses, the brick wall and latch, seem to be lifted from the description Isabella gives of Angelo's plotting her coming to him by night (*Measure for Measure*, IV.i.28–36) in 'a garden circummur'd with brick' (l. 28). Mariana's rural retreat is unnamed and tearful, while Angelo's pleasure-garden has become the scene of furtive crime. In a sense, the grange and Angelo's garden can be seen as two parts of the landscape of good, severed.

Mariana is incapable of action on her own account, and has to be manoeuvred into it by the Duke. Once the plot is completed, she has nothing to say but to 'crave', to beg Isabella to help her, and to argue that

> They say best men are moulded out of faults,
> And, for the most, become much more the better
> For being a little bad. So may my husband.
> (v.i.437–9)

'They say': Mariana appeals to a proverbial sense of man's intrinsic imperfection, a realism about life which undercuts the idealism we have heard from both Isabella and Angelo. The 'glassy essence' is irremediably cracked.

Mariana's view expresses the chastening wisdom of tragicomedy, which denies man the self-satisfaction of a tragic pose. This is what the Duke denies Angelo, who must live on shamed and contrite into the human complexities of marriage. However, the Duke is in his turn denied the complete power he seeks by the seemingly irrepressible Lucio. G. Wilson Knight, who started the hare of symbolic or allegorical interpretation, says of what the Duke finally does that 'Idleness, triviality, thoughtlessness receive the Duke's strongest condemnation'.[123] If, though, we look at what the Duke actually does and Lucio's response to it, the position turns out to be rather more complicated. When Lucio unmasks the Duke, he tries to creep away. 'Sneak not away, sir'

(l. 356) the Duke says. Lucio is laid hold on, and mutters aside that 'This may prove worse than hanging' (l. 358). He must have the last word, but is afraid of what is to happen. His aside is an involuntary reflex of his personality. The action passes away from him, and returns with the Duke's 'And yet here's one in place I cannot pardon' (l. 497). Lucio is a thing of darkness he will not acknowledge as his own, who escapes his moral control.

Lucio excuses his slanders by reference to 'the trick', social custom,[124] and says that, 'if you will hang me for it, you may: but I had rather it would please you I might be whipped' (ll. 503–4). Lucio is unable simply to throw himself on the Duke's mercy, but must intrude the note of personal preference. 'Whipp'd first, sir, and hang'd after' (l. 505) is the Duke's response, but he then says that Lucio must first be married to any woman he may have made pregnant. Lucio responds, 'I beseech your Highness, do not marry me to a whore. Your Highness said even now, I made you a duke; good my lord, do not recompense me in making me a cuckold' (ll. 512–15). The reiterated 'your Highness' is the obsequiousness of a nervous inferior, an appeal to the Duke's vanity, but Lucio remains capable of witty antithesis. The fear of being made 'a cuckold' is not a concern that he may be betrayed – he will, after all, be dead – but a terror of being laughed at. 'Upon mine honour, thou shalt marry her' (l. 516), the Duke avows, remitting all other penalties, and Lucio responds that 'Marrying a punk, my lord, is pressing to death, / Whipping, and hanging' (ll. 520–1). The Duke tells him of this comic agony that 'Slandering a prince deserves it' (l. 521). He who mocks authority must expect to be made a butt himself. Angelo told Isabella that 'It is the law, not I, condemn your brother' (ii.ii.80); the Duke implicitly makes the same claim here, but in both cases we are led (by the Duke's detailed memory of Lucio's insults and Angelo's forceful 'I will not do't' (ii.ii.51)) to suppose that personal interest is involved. Angelo is fighting for an image of himself, but the Duke also seeks to be seen as a benevolent despot.

This is clear in his final speech. Claudio is told to look after Juliet, Escalus and the Provost are thanked, and the match the Duke has made is sealed with 'Joy to you, Mariana; love her, Angelo: / I have confess'd her, and I know her virtue' (v.i.523–4). The first line raises no problems, but the second must make us uneasy. The Duke has after all, no right to hear confessions, let alone to reveal their import as he does here.[125] His omniscience is gained by ruse rather than providential illumination, and this intrusive claim denies Angelo the last vestiges of privacy. Neither he nor his wife has any secrets left. Lucio saw his penalty in physical terms ('pressing to death'), as the exercise of force, and Angelo might be excused for feeling that his life had been directed beyond what was necessary. Wilson Knight says of the Duke's withdrawal from office that 'The scheme is a plot, or trap: a scientific experiment to see if extreme ascetic righteousness can stand the test of power',[126] a description which does the Duke little moral credit and throws considerable doubt on his role as a Christian figure. Christ does not usually act as a tempter, and when God leaves man to the devil's devices what we get is not the New Testament but the embittering arbitrariness of the Book of Job. The bleakness of a moral universe is revealed as starkly through the Duke as through Angelo.

'Dear Isabel', the Duke continues,

> I have a motion much imports your good;
> Whereto if you'll a willing ear incline,
> What's mine is yours, and what is yours is mine.
> So bring us to our palace, where we'll show
> What's yet behind that's meet you all should know.
>
> (ll. 531–6)

In that 'meet' we may detect the Duke holding on to his monopoly of the supply of information, but it is the apparent proposal of marriage to Isabella which causes the greatest confusion. Wilson Knight is sure that it 'may be understood symbolically. It is to be the marriage of understanding with purity; of tolerance with moral fervour.'[127] Philip Edwards introduces a note of tentativeness when he explains that Isabella remains silent because

> The suggestion of betrothal is as far as Shakespeare wished to go, and it is a much richer thing to leave it there, half earthly and half unearthly, than to take it further and make this novice nun agree at the first beckon from the Duke to surrender that virginity she has so insisted on preserving.[128]

Edwards invests the scene with extraordinary poetic charm, 'half earthly and half unearthly', and, by proposing that the play hints at a cosmic reconciliation the dramatist chooses not to make explicit, turns the scene into a symbolic statement of great power. I find this reading deeply sympathetic and wrong. Isabella's silence does not of itself give her symbolic status. John Bayley points out that Cordelia's silence in *King Lear* is a refusal to take part in the play-acting her father demands, and that her muteness renders her unfit for drama.[129] When Lear proposes that they pass imprisonment together 'like birds i'the cage' (v.iii.9) he ignores the reality of her life elsewhere, her marriage to France and the cares it entails.[130] Saying that 'When thou dost ask me blessing, I'll kneel down' (l. 10), Lear invests gesture with the same importance as he did with his first demands for affirmations of love: the claim that he and Cordelia can live 'As if we were God's spies' (l. 17) is a self-aggrandisement to which nothing he has said or done gives him any right.[131] Imprisonment is a seclusion from the world in which, as Browning reminds us, God's spy must at least 'go up and down'.[132] As Bayley shows, Lear's speech is peculiarly discordant and evasive following, as it does, Cordelia's blunt statement of the facts in the question 'Shall we not see these daughters and these sisters?' (l. 7).[133] Far from having symbolic significance as an incarnation of goodness, Cordelia has a sensible practicality which wants nothing to do with the poetry of illusion.

This is not to say that silence cannot play a symbolic function on stage. A clear instance of this is John Ford's *The Broken Heart*.[134] In Act v Scene ii, the news of the drama's deaths is reported to Calantha while she dances with the nobles. 'To the other change' (l. 13), 'Lead to the next' (l. 15) and 'How dull this music sounds! Strike up more sprightly;/Our footings are not active like our heart,/Which treads the nimbler measure' (ll. 17–19) are her responses to the deaths of her father, her lover's sister and her lover. It is hardly surprising that her interlocutors wonder, 'Is't possible?' (l. 13), and exclaim, 'Amazement dulls my senses' (l. 15) and 'I am thunderstruck' (l. 19).

The dance persisted in despite disastrous news invites us to perceive symbolically. Clifford Leech describes Ford's attraction to an 'aristocratic code of endurance', and argues that Ford's tragedies are analogous to the Grecian Urn in that, 'Defying the natural limitations of drama, Ford aims at a form of spatial perception'.[135] Dorothy M. Farr finds in this play a 'fundamental affinity with the attitudes of Greek tragedy', sees in its conclusion a 'circle closed and order restored', and attributes 'deliberate exaggeration' to the dance scene.[136] Una Ellis-Fermor thinks that the play, 'for simplicity and compactness of line, for dignity and for compression of emotion, thought and phrase is unsurpassed in Jacobean drama',[137] and T. S. Eliot was moved to observe of the dance scene that it 'must have been very effective on the stage'.[138] What these diverse responses share is a sense of the play as aspiring to poetic, symbolic form, and an almost universal acknowledgement that this is achieved.

Una Ellis-Fermor says that in Ford's work generally 'Rhetoric is crushed by the presence of inexpressible grief, the silent griefs that stifle and extinguish.'[139] This is what *The Broken Heart* has in common with Greek tragedy, a sense that the tragic is of the nature of the universe, both unbearable and inexplicable. Calantha maintains her heroic poise, arranging the fate of the kingdom and speaking for herself only in her penultimate speech.

> Oh, my lords,
> I but deceived your eyes with antic gesture,
> When one news straight came huddling on another
> Of death, and death, and death. Still I danced forward;
> But it struck home, and here, and in an instant.
> Be such mere women, who with shrieks and outcries
> Can vow a present end to all their sorrows,
> Yet live to vow new pleasures, and outlive them.
> They are the silent griefs which cut the heart-strings;
> Let me die smiling.
>
> (v.iii.67–76)

Calantha confesses that her dancing was one kind of performance, but stresses its superiority to feminine hysteria, ostentatious and brief as 'shrieks and outcries'. This declaration of principle leads to the almost contradictory wish to 'die smiling', which is not a contradiction, because Calantha herself aspires to symbolic status and is therefore, like the poet who so aspires, 'half in love with easeful Death'.[140] Calantha places 'One kiss' (l. 77) on Ithocles' dead mouth, renounces the kingdom, and bids, 'Command the voices/Which wait at th'altar now to sing the song/I fitted for my end' (ll. 78–80). She has prepared her own musical apotheosis to mark her transition to a symbolic and typological level. As Armestes says, Tecnicus' prophecy is 'here fulfilled' (l. 101). The song tells of the mutability of worldly things and ends with the dictum that

> *Love only reigns in death; though art*
> *Can find no comfort for a broken heart.*
> (ll. 93–4)

Calantha becomes the embodiment of a truth which divorces symbolic status from the worldly tribulations of 'a broken heart', and in plotting her death recognises that her triumph is aesthetic. It is characteristic of Shakespeare that Cleopatra, who plans a similar apotheosis for herself, achieves it in the teeth of the comic subversion of the clown and the serpents who emblemise her carnality. Ford presents us with no such ambiguity, which makes his play easier to describe as an aesthetic unity.

Aesthetic unity is appropriate to a work which is both in itself and in its characters directed towards a symbolic expression. More potentially troubling for drama, it may be suspected, is allegory, whose continual flow seems to fight against the requirements of the theatre. This might particularly appear to be so in the case of Ben Jonson, whose work exhibits a natural tendency towards allegory.[141]

Ford finds an appropriately laconic setting for Calantha's meaningful and exemplary silence in Sparta. Jonson places his *Epicoene, or The Silent Woman*[142] in London. It is a comedy rather than a tragedy, and appears at first sight to be one praising the virtues of sociability over the morose withdrawal of silence. However, there are a few points in it which trouble such a reading, and suggest that the play has more threatening implications.

In Act II Scene i, Morose complains that 'all discourses, but mine owne, afflict mee, they seeme harsh, impertinent, and irksome' (ll. 4–5). This ostensibly signals to us his egotistical vanity, and the hopping up and down of the mute who must signal by making legs suggests that this vanity mechanises those around him. When we consider some of the discourses to which Morose is subjected, though, we come to feel an alarming sympathy for him. His love of silence may seem hostile to life itself, as when the discovery that Epicoene can speak provokes him to call her a 'manifest woman' (III.iv.42), and Morose is tellingly incapable of the 'martyrs resolution' (III.vii.11) recommended by True-wit, the heroic patience of the Duchess of Malfi when she is tormented, but the object of his tormentors is material gain rather than his moral reform. Indeed, the young fops of the play so enjoy the peculiarity of characters trapped in modes of behaviour that Dauphine tries to prevent True-wit and Cleremont from engineering a '*catastrophe*' (IV.v.241) in the plot against La-Foole and Jack Daw thus: 'Let them continue in the state of ignorance, and erre still: thinke 'hem wits, and fine fellowes, as they haue done. 'Twere sinne to reforme them' (ll. 243–6). Morose must be persuaded to maintain Dauphine as his heir, but the characters who tease him do not seek any transformation in his character. Morality is not eminently noticeable in the play's motives.

When Otter and Cutberd are presented to Morose as Parson and Doctor, True-wit enjoins them to

> looke to your parts now, and discharge 'hem brauely: you are well set forth, performe it as well. If you chance to be out, doe not confesse it with standing still, or humming, or gaping one at another: but goe on, and talke alowd, and eagerly, vse vehement actions, and onely remember your termes, and you are safe. Let the matter goe where it will: you haue many will doe so. (v.iii.13–18)

To be a priest or a lawyer is to be an actor. The man who pretends cannot be told from the genuine article, because, even of those who are truly what they claim, 'many' rely on the rhetoric of their callings to tide them over gaps in thought. The audience cannot tell the actor who is improvising confidently from the one who is sticking to the script. Significantly, Jonson sets against this degraded analysis of high vocation Morose's touching recollection that

> My father, in my education, was wont to aduise mee, that I should alwayes collect, and contayne my mind, not suffring it to flow loosely; that I should looke to what things were necessary to the carriage of my life, and what not: embracing the one, and eschewing the other. In short, that I should endeare my selfe to rest, and auoid turmoile: which now is growne to be another nature to me. So that I come not to your publike pleadings, or your places of noise; not that I neglect

those things, that make for the dignitie of the common-wealth:
but for the meere auoiding of clamors, & impertinencies of
Orators, that know not how to be silent.   (ll. 48–59)

Morose's oddity is the result of upbringing and filial loyalty. His
father's advice to 'collect, and contayne' his mind is not in itself
bad, likewise the recommendation to study what is necessary.
Morose has been educated by a cautious, provident man but has
exaggerated these traits into a linguistic miserliness.[143] His imagery
embraces economic as well as mental necessity, and suggests how
meannesses of all kinds cohere. Morose is aware that what he is is
distorted, that he has had wilfully to 'endeare' himself to the
condition which is now 'another nature'. He excuses himself for
not normally going among priests and lawyers, but argues that
this is not a social or political danger. Orators who 'know not how
to be silent' are the 'many' True-wit spoke of: Morose is about to
hear speaking two impostors who will be indistinguishable from
the types they enact. It may be argued that Morose is here
seeking to ingratiate himself, that this voice is not the one we
have heard in his domestic altercations, but it may be replied that
he rises here to the gravity of the occasion as he conceives it. It is
True-wit rather than Morose who reminds us of the vanity of
experts with his 'Nay, good sir, attend the learned men, they'll
thinke you neglect 'hem else' (ll. 214–15). What Morose hears is
entirely impertinent or irrelevant, and his worst fears are realised.
  Although *Epicoene* appears to be a play about sociability, then, it
turns out that it opposes to the costiveness of silence a world of
trickery and adultery. The world of this play is without a stable
centre, for the figure Morose wishes to instate at its centre is
duplicitous, his bride a boy. The effect of this in a theatre where
women were played by boys is very complex, because in one
sense we have known this all along. We must now see the boy as
distinct from the other women on stage, submitting to two
different kinds of illusion at the same time: the boy might as well
be played by a girl in this flickering world of dualities. The play
brings out the problematic nature of theatrical reality and suggests
that such is the nature of the world. The emotion we are left with
is one of mistrust, because, although the comic plot formally
expects us to sympathise with Dauphine, he and his friends are
remarkably unlikeable in their bullying superiority.
  The ambiguities in the play are most apparent in its central

figure, the silent woman who, capable of symbolic function as an incarnation of value, is here shown to be an expoundable allegorical sign. The play is ultimately centreless and amoral, a portrayal of neurotic energy rather than ethical purpose, an effect which is frequently felt in Jonsonian comedy. Edmund Wilson points out the interesting relation between Jonson's fascination with misers and his methods of plot and characterisation, which allow no room for human development.[144] Jonson's language is not the promiscuous metaphorical liquidity of Shakespeare but often a collection of professional jargons, as in *The Alchemist*, part of whose effect is simply to show how well Jonson has got the subject up. Jonas A. Barish finds that Jonson like Beckett and Ionesco is 'fascinated by the kind of talk that at first sounds normal, and then on closer range proves to be a series of mechanistic twitches that express the emptiness and desperation of the speakers' lives'.[145] That emphasis comes from the fact that Jonson's mode of characterisation is external, the exaggerated reproduction of neurotic traits and motivations which is only rarely, as in Morose's self-explanation, touched with emotional inwardness.

Jonson's attraction to allegory and the picturesque means that his drama risks becoming a series of scenes rather than an organic development. Sir Politic Would-be in the tortoise-shell, for instance, is an emblem of policy detached from the plot and presented for our amusement. This kind of performance might degenerate into pageant – in Spenser, its equivalent would be the procession of the months (*Faerie Queen*, VII.32–43). His answer to the problem is stringent and deterministic plotting. The theatrical brilliance of Jonson's art is achieved at the characters' expense: imprisoned in their names, they are helpless butts of circumstance, emblems of folly in whose world no value can be fixed.

The figure of the silent woman can have symbolic or allegorical potential. Isabella has neither of those qualities, and her exposure and isolation at the end of the play are also interestingly different from similar moments in Webster. On the one hand, Webster uses the exposure of female characters to the manipulation of others as an opportunity for the tragic stoicism which says, 'I am Duchess of Malfi still' (*The Duchess of Malfi*, IV.ii.141)[146] and is informed that

That makes thy sleeps so broken:
Glories, like glow-worms, afar off shine bright,
But look'd to near, have neither heat nor light.

(ll. 142–4)

Here, the determination to persist in an identity is seen as necessarily painful, where in Act III Scene i of *The White Devil* it is the occasion of virtuoso histrionic display.[147] Vittoria ends the trial-scene, banished to a home for reforming prostitutes, with the claim that 'My mind shall make it honester to me/Than the Pope's palace' (ll. 289–90). Her heroic self-determination weakens only when dying, when 'My soul, like to a ship in a black storm,/Is driven I know not whither' (v.vi.246–7) and she is reclaimed in her last speech (ll. 259–60) for the world of prudential maxims against which her career has been a brilliant struggle.

Webster's women preserve an inviolable core which nothing short of death can assail. The sense we get from them is that of Parolles' simple thinghood, and is comparable with Isabella's silence. What transforms it into tragic greatness is the rhetoric, often very simple, with which Webster invests it. *Measure for Measure* might partly be described as a revenge drama without deaths, with the Duke avenging the honour of the slighted Mariana and exposing the corruption of the state. This description is inadequate, though, because in a play genuinely of this kind, *The Malcontent*,[148] Malevole's kicking Mendoza ('an eagle takes not flies' – v.iv.155) suggests a futility in the whole idea of revenge and makes the play acridly unpleasing. Where pure revenge drama turns into tragicomedy, the effect is to trivialise vice, and this is not quite the effect of *Measure for Measure*.

It is not in their deaths but in their lives that Webster's women show the 'glassy essence' of which Isabella speaks. Her silence at the end of *Measure for Measure* is not a symbolic expression of her virtue, neither does it turn her into an allegorical figure, as so many critics believe: rather, it emphasises her humanity. Nothing in the play goes quite as it should, in that each of the characters breaks away from the role he is given. Angelo is not angelic, the Duke is sadistically manipulative, Mariana is a creature of physical yearning as well as musical nostalgia, Claudio is prepared to sacrifice his sister's honour, and so forth. The characters are all moved around by the Duke's machinations, but just as we find something off-putting in his moral certainty so Isabella cannot at once accede to the Duke's proposal. Equally, this solid core of human resistance to manipulation prevents her becoming a movable allegorical sign. Philip Edwards' view of her is of a Romantic greatness, something evermore about to be, while Wilson Knight turns her into a piece in an intellectual chess-game, a pawn about to be queened.

Isabella's silence answers to our mistrust of the Duke's motives. As far as he is an exposer of society's vices, he has the external superiority of Jaques, whose power is to 'moralize . . . spectacle' (*As You Like It*, II.i.44). When Jaques asks for leave to 'speak my mind' and 'Cleanse the foul body of th'infected world' (II.vii.59, 60), Duke Senior tells him he commits

> Most mischievous foul sin, in chiding sin:
> For thou thyself hast been a libertine,
> As sensual as the brutish sting itself;
> And all the embossed sores and headed evils,
> That thou with licence of free foot hast caught,
> Wouldst thou disgorge into the general world.
>
> (ll. 64–9)

Jaques' contempt for mankind is the consequence of self-knowledge without humility. His disclaimer of individual animus in the lines that follow rings hollowly against this charge.[149] Jaques is not, of course, the only social critic to reprehend in others his own greatest failings: there is a touching instance in Marston's *Antonio and Mellida*,[150] where Feliche derides the court, 'tossing up / A grateful spirit to omnipotence' (III.ii.59–60). Castilio replies by boasting of his amorous successes, and Feliche's dander is roused. 'I am as like a man' (l. 70), he protests; you all do lie' (l. 82). He has

> Courted in all sorts, blunt and passionate,
> Had opportunities, put them to the 'ah';
> And by this light, I find them wondrous chaste,
> Impregnable – perchance a kiss or so;
> But for the rest, O most inexorable.
>
> (ll. 85–9)

In a play whose induction seems to propose that the actors burlesque the action,[151] it is perhaps fitting the worldly wisdom should be so rapidly deflated, but there is a serious point. Here, the cynic's view springs from personal failure. Knowledge of the world comes from personal experience, but can easily turn to grandiose generalisations which do not touch the person of their speaker.

The Duke is seen early in *Measure for Measure* as a man who believes he knows himself. He has passed his time in quiet and thought as opposed to social display (i.iii.8–10) and now has 'a purpose/More grave and wrinkled than the aims and ends/Of burning youth' (ll. 4–6). It is remarkable that Friar Thomas' first supposition is that the Duke must be in love, and that the Duke tells him to 'Believe not that the dribbling dart of love/Can pierce a complete bosom' (ll. 2–3), for if we are to take his proposal to Isabella at all seriously he must have fallen in love with her.

Isabella's sexiness has perhaps been too little remarked on. The rhetoric of her novitiate, her desire for 'a more strict restraint' (i.iv.4) and determination that

> Th'impression of keen whips I'd wear as rubies,
> And strip myself to death as to bed
> That longing have been sick for, ere I'd yield
> My body up to shame
>
> (ii.iv.101–4)

are familiarly seen as evincing powerful erotic energies. Her imagery for the death of martyrdom is itself sexual. She is not simply a creature of repressed energies, though, for she has the power to release such energies in others. Those to whom she appeals most strongly are apparently good men, Angelo and the Duke, and they are told apart by the manner of their advances to her. Where Angelo blackmails her into submission, the Duke offers marriage. Each seeks domination over her, though, and in both cases her response is similar. From Angelo she withdraws; from the Duke she keeps her silence. Isabella's relative passivity in the plot should not be taken to indicate an essential passivity. It is, rather, that the world she inhabits gives her no room to act for herself – the only free choice she can make is to enter a nunnery – because of its tumultuous sexual demands. Even in the nunnery, she suspects Lucio of 'mocking' (i.iv.38) when he calls her 'a thing enskied and sainted' (l. 34). Her full reply, that 'You do blaspheme the good, in mocking me', shows that she aspires to a symbolic role, to put the world and its mobility behind her. Her imagery of death suggests that she is half in love with it. This erroneous sublimation is denied her by the play's narrative momentum. Isabella must return to the world, and in doing so assume her being as a sexual agent.

Falling in love with Isabella, the Duke is humanised, but the speed and brevity of his proposal are shocking. It is as though he were struggling to hold himself in, as though afraid that the release of passion would turn him into Lucio's profligate caricature. In Vienna, morality and sexuality have come apart, so that sexual life is conducted at the level of the brothel while morality is as icy as Angelo. The real, if flawed, love of Claudio and Juliet forces the two worlds together, and turns the Duke's detached operation on Angelo into a discovery about himself.

The Duke is as potentially unstable as any other character in the play, for all his protestations to the contrary. The form of the play requires him to be an agent of goodness, but its content challenges his right to that station. It is in the tension between form and content that the play finds its dramatic life.[152]

It is entirely understandable that critics should want to see the play as symbolic. Its moral language and shape do indeed suggest such a reading. As we have seen, though, Isabella herself resists such interpretation. She does not have the rhetoric of Ford's or Webster's women, creatures who possess their integrity in the teeth of sceptical inquiry. The abrasive quality of city comedy[153] cuts against the patterning imposed by symbolism that Calantha's dance embodies, but Isabella is not revealed by its lack of certain values to be merely an epicene actor. Herman Melville, one of whose poems describes Shakespeare as driving to the core of human reality,[154] shows what this might mean in his story 'Bartleby'.[155]

Bartleby himself is a presence and a sentence, 'I would prefer not.'[156] He refuses to take part in any shared human life, and has in a sense no story. Like Cordelia, he must be dragged into action by others. The difference from Cordelia is that Bartleby exists for us only as seen by a narrator, and the story is really the exposition of the narrator's responses. Bartleby's own existence is so nebulous that only a 'vague report' of his past is ever heard, that he 'had been a subordinate clerk in the Dead Letter Office at Washington, from which he had been suddenly removed by a change in the administration'.[157] That Bartleby should be a victim of political and bureaucratic manoeuvring ties in with the story's setting in business Manhattan, but the narrator draws no attention to this. He is instead transfixed by the idea of letters which 'On errands of life . . . speed to death'.[158] 'Ah, Bartleby! Ah, humanity!'[159] he ends. In Bartleby he has met a baffling embodiment of something central to human being, a symbol of will, self-possession and tragic destiny. 'Bartleby' is essentially Romantic in its focus on perceptual responses, but Shakespearean in the enigmatic simplicity with which it leaves us. In *Measure for Measure* Shakespeare leaves us with a similar baffled wonder, but one incomparably more poignant.

The title *Measure for Measure* appears programmatic, leading us to suppose that the play will expound for us the meaning of justice. Tragicomic form was defended by its first great employer, Guarini, as moral and potentially allegorical.[160] It is interesting to note in passing that Guarini's readers have been deeply divided over whether the form is in fact used in *Il Pastor Fido* as an excuse for langorous sensuality, whether the play is not simply cynical pornography. It might similarly be wondered whether, if the Duke's status as divine agent is impugned, we do not have to see this play as a seamy farce, an excuse for pornography of a rather different kind. This latter reading is indeed possible, but does the play as much injustice as symbolic or allegorial exegesis.

Wilson Knight's view of *Measure for Measure* is palpably simplistic in its insistence on symbolic Christianity. Philip Edwards' remarks show a deeper engagement with the text, but an undue respect for the criticism which he says has 'established beyond disproof' the case for the play's moral meaning. Believing that the play moves towards a symbolic adumbration of wholeness, he finds it flawed because the distance is too great between the plot's actuality and what it is 'meant to suggest'. That last phrase reveals the source of his problem, a belief that Shakespeare 'meant to suggest' something in particular. This view of the artist as concerned above all with a single meaning falsifies our whole appreciation of Shakespeare's greatness.

Isabella at the end of *Measure for Measure* is lonely, lost, lovable. Her being refuses assimilation to the Duke's moral scheme and to the intentions ostensibly embodied by tragicomedy on behalf of something truer to life and more artistically satisfactory. We want to believe that at the end of the play moral order has been restored to the world we have seen, but Isabella's reticence and

Lucio's having to be harshly punished remind us that human beings do not naturally fall into symbolic patterns. Calantha, we should remember, does so by knowingly violating her own humanity. Shakespeare powerfully proposes a moral vision in *Measure for Measure* to which the characters in their human loneliness do not wholeheartedly assent. He opposes to this order another picture of the world, which is one of disorder, desire raging unchecked and morality all forgotten. We can see in Mariana's fidelity, Isabella's courage, the Duke's restraint and Angelo's better side that this picture too is too simple. The play hangs between them, bringing together a world of order and a world of chaos but not permitting them to merge. For them to become one, the characters would have to yield up their own natures, which they are unable to do. Chaos threatens them too closely to allow the good to do more than hug their integrity and hope for the best, while the active forces of order prevent the licentious from running completely amok. The play's tragic hero is Angelo, as Pushkin recognised,[161] because his nature does change. He is tempted and falls. His punishment is to have to live with that knowledge: ironically, tragic wisdom is shown as having to remain in the world rather than escaping, stoically or gloriously, from it.

Shakespeare's art is one of showing rather than telling, and its centre is the question what it is to be human. At the end of *Measure for Measure* we are left with an image of humanity, a girl proposed to unexpectedly by a man she hardly knows but whom she must, we feel, marry almost whatever her will, which we cannot penetrate. I use the word deliberately, because in this play Isabella's sexual integrity becomes emblematic of her inscrutability. Virgin, she is an unknown quantity, and the play's ending invites her to submit to knowledge, which can, as Angelo's exposure has shown, be a painful and unremitting process. Symbolically minded critics evade the question of her human knowability by translating her to a higher register, a move which is sympathetic because it respects her vulnerability. However, it also denies her humanity. The bitterness of the play is that it does not make being human seem very exciting. We feel at once that Isabella deserves better but that to choose the apparently better, to return to her nunnery, would be a diminution. Isabella is both inside the play and from an external point of view too complicated a character to be simplified so. The aesthetic triumph Shakespeare achieves is that the demands of the form require her to marry, our sense of her humanity wishes her not to, and we are left on the brink of a decision. Either choice would tie down the play's meaning – if she marries, the symbolists are right; if not, those who see the play as a farce from which she makes a lucky escape – so neither is shown.

III

A resistance to aesthetic closure is the hallmark of not just the problem plays but of Shakespeare's whole dramatic work. This is not simply to say that he opposes art to life, for what is lifelike in his work is itself an aesthetic construct. We are dealing with two different ways of treating dramatic material and the way in which their juxtaposition creates a finally elusive but compelling and satisfying effect.

In W. H. Auden's *The Sea and The Mirror*,[162] Antonio is amused by Prospero's professed renunciation of power. He tells him beneath his breath that as long as he prefers

> To wear my fashion, whatever you wear
> Is a magic robe; while I stand outside
> Your circle, the will to charm is still there.[163]

Prospero is a 'melancholy mentor',[164] unable to renounce his power because Antonio's obduracy, shown by his silence at the end of *The Tempest*, will always provoke him to use it. Prospero's determination to commit himself to reality rather than artifice, 'to suffer / Without saying something ironic or funny / On suffering',[165] is rebuked. Antonio's refusal to be cowed by the plot Prospero has engineered challenges all Prospero's assertions of independence and turns them into role-playing.

This is of a piece with the remarkable reversal of what might be allegorical in *The Tempest* itself. Auden's Prospero calls Ariel an '*Unfeeling god*',[166] which picks up the Shakespearean Ariel's confession that he has no feelings. Shakespeare's Ariel tells Prospero of the royal party that 'your charm so strongly works them, / That if you now beheld them, your affections / Would become tender' (v.i.17–19). 'Dost thou think so, spirit?' (l. 19) Prospero asks. 'Mine would, sir, were I human' (l. 20). Ariel, the spirit of lightness and air, is not human, emotionally insensible. In this he contrasts with the earthy Caliban, a creature who is externally disgusting but has a sympathetic emotional interior from his very first off-stage utterance. 'There's wood enough within' (I.ii.314). We already know that Caliban hews and carries for Prospero and Miranda: the voice here is that of a recalcitrant, put-upon servitor. When Caliban appears, cursing (ll. 321–4), Prospero responds by promising him physical torments (ll. 325–30). That Caliban has been tempted by Miranda's beauty (ll. 347–8) has a more touching side in its explanation that, if not stopped, 'I had peopled else/This isle with Calibans' (ll. 350–1). In however distorted a form, Caliban has a generous creativity denied to Ariel. His wish to fill the world with images of himself is not unlike Falstaff's boast that his own image is propagated in others, for he is 'not only witty in myself, but the cause that wit is in other men' (*Henry IV, Part II*, I.ii.10–11). Caliban's generative urge sets him up as a centre of comic sympathy by which Prospero is placed more exactly than as Shakespeare's self-image as magus. Where we might expect Ariel to represent sublime spirituality and Caliban the self-centred flesh, we are offered instead the spirit as lucidity without feeling, the flesh as the seat of the heart.

That the potentially allegorical pairing is reversed conforms with the play's refusal to be controlled entirely by Prospero's dictates: at the end, the formal unities are breached by Prospero's appeal to the audience for future help. When Ariel tells Prospero that his affections should be moved, Prospero concurs.

> Hast thou, which art but air, a touch, a feeling
> Of their afflictions, and shall not myself,
> One of their kind, that relish all as sharply,
> Passion as they, be kindlier mov'd than thou art?
> (*The Tempest*, v.i.21–4)

Prospero stands on his human dignity. He is 'one of their kind' – the wicked are held at a distance by the kind person – and should be 'kindlier mov'd', both towards kindness and by nature. Ariel seems to shock Prospero into consciousness of common humanity, but Prospero does not completely accede to this.

> Though with their high wrongs I am struck to the quick,
> Yet with my nobler reason 'gainst my fury

Do I take part: the rarer action is
In virtue than in vengeance: they being penitent,
The sole drift of my purpose doth extend
Not a frown further.

(ll. 25–30)

Prospero chooses what is 'nobler', the 'rarer action'. His decision to release his captives comes not from a feeling of solidarity but from pride. He will do no more to them, given that they are 'penitent'. Prospero's humanity makes him give up his aim to punish, but does not bend him immediately to compassion or forgiveness. Without 'Spirits to enforce, art to enchant' (Epilogue, l. 14) his 'ending is despair' (l. 15) unless the audience's 'prayer' (l. 16) releases him from the island into the future.

Prospero's use of masque and magic, his pairing of Ferdinand and Miranda, tempt us to see him as a wise ruler who has been unjustly expelled and who exercises due temperance in claiming his own. However, his speech when examined closely shows this to be wrong. Prospero comes late to self-knowledge, if indeed he comes there at all. His acceptance of his own humanity is grudging and disdainful, and he now invites the assembled company to see him as a wise old man whose 'Every third thought shall be my grave' (v.i.311). His last speech to those on stage is a final 'promise' (l. 314) of magic. The portrayal of Prospero has an ambiguity which prevents our taking him altogether seriously as the voice of good.[167]

It could be argued that this is because Prospero's plot is the contrived ending of a romance. In *The Winter's Tale*, such an argument runs, we see Time as a character, and see regeneration take place over time because of the play's amplitude. *The Tempest*, confined by the unities, shows a man promising to bring such an ending about, and inevitably failing, no matter how good his intentions. Prospero's intentions are clearly vengeful, though, until very late in the play, so that the transition to romance is itself a late development. Prospero's change of purpose makes aesthetic sense of what has happened both within the play and in the time before, and the ending is of a kind which is formally moving, which by its nature tends to console and appease our fears by manifesting reconciliation and harmony. The tension between that aesthetic gratification and Antonio's silence is the play's true aim. Auden has Antonio say, 'What a lot a little music can do',[168] and this cynical mistrust of the play's formal device strikes accurately at Prospero. Antonio remains a villain, not an authoritative voice, but he prevents Prospero from monopolising our admiration.

Antonio's silence obviously resembles Isabella's. In each case, the tragicomic conclusion brought about by a ruler whose motives we have good reason to mistrust reaches out for and misses their silent particularity. The same refusal to be incorporated in the drama's formal requirements is shown by Parolles, who when reduced to extremity discovers in himself a source of new contrivance and unrepentant survival. Ajax, the bonehead who is at first the butt of comedy, gains a dignity nobody else in *Troilus and Cressida* reaches.

In Shakespearean comedy, the famous instances of this are Shylock and Malvolio. Shylock is broken at the end of the trial, and his wretchedness makes us feel that Portia's justice has overstepped the mark and become racial spite. Malvolio's name suggests that he is an allegorical, Jonsonian character, but his tormenting by Feste becomes ultimately shocking as what he takes to be different people visiting him in confinement are known by us to be the same and we see him as a helpless victim. Malvolio says that 'there was never man so notoriously abused' (*Twelfth Night*, IV.ii.95–6), and at the end of the play Olivia agrees that 'He hath been most notoriously abused' (v.i.392). Feste argues that 'thus the whirligig of time brings in his revenges' (ll. 388–9), claiming to represent the healing force of comedy, but Malvolio leaves vowing revenge (l. 390). His refusal to participate in the comic conclusion is a haughty refusal simply to admit defeat, not entirely admirable but not wholly reprehensible. We have already sensed that Feste's teasing has turned into bullying: left to Feste's wisdom that 'the rain it raineth every day' (l. 404) the world would be a humbler but static place. Malvolio's puritan ambition may be funny but is also necessary. A house run by Sir Toby Belch would soon be a poor one.

The women in *Love's Labour's Lost* refuse to be swept up in the courtiers' revels in exactly the same way. The effect is slightly different in every case, of course: in *Twelfth Night* the comedians must learn that they can be cruel, in *Love's Labour's Lost* they must learn to be serious, but in both cases the recognition of the existence of other people is the main thing. Again, though, it must be emphasised that this is itself an effect achieved by aesthetic means.

It has often been felt that Shakespeare's last plays are the expression of a completed philosophy. *The Tempest* turns out on inspection to re-examine preoccupations which go much further back in Shakespeare's career. Part of his greatness is his ability to bring his concerns to new forms, to remain recognisably the same while working through the whole generic spectrum available to Elizabethan and Jacobean drama. He is by no means alone in generic self-conciousness: it is perfectly possible, if somewhat reductive, to read all the drama of the period as a meditation on dramatic form.[169] In his particular case this artistic reflectiveness reaches unusually far,[170] for, as Shakespeare takes nothing on trust, but interrogates the conventions he employs, so we should beware of being seduced by what the characters claim is taking place or by the emotions the forms used seem naturally to expect.

The Winter's Tale[171] bears this out with bewildering pathos. The last significant action of Greene's *Pandosto*,[172] Shakespeare's source, is committed by Pandosto himself, who 'calling to mind' all the evil he has done 'fell into a melancholy fit, and, to close up the comedy with a tragical strategem, he slew himself'.[173] We could not ask for a clearer statement of generic purpose. However, Greene's syntax is significantly uncertain. We are left in doubt whether the intention of the 'tragical stratagem' is the author's, who would here interpolate this clause as a breezy aside to his audience, or Pandosto's, who would then assume an attitude of frozen self-regard. Such unclarity is richly suggestive, for it invites us to speculate on Pandosto's feelings, but must finally leave us uneasy. If Greene himself is confessing to a 'stratagem', how tawdry his work must seem. It is also an error of taste to have Pandosto kill himself because the comic reconciliation the subtitle, 'The Triumph Of Time', promises is left incomplete. Shakespeare reverses Greene's direction here, and closes up his tragical drama with a comical stratagem.[174]

He also focuses intently on the meaning of the subtitle. In Greene, the shepherd finds the abandoned Fawnia and brings her home. Greene handles the passage of years with great skill. At first the baby is an object whom its foster-parents come to love, 'seeing as it waxed in age so it increased in beauty'.[175] We are told that 'in *a* short time it began to speak and call him Dad and her

Mam'.[176] This touching sequence of domestic vignettes lets us watch the child develop gradually. When 'it was about seven years old'[177] the shepherd sets up on his own account, and when Fawnia is ten 'he set her to keep'.[178] By the time she is sixteen she is a beauty, who makes herself garlands to keep off the sun's heat, 'which attire became her so gallantly as she seemed to be the goddess Flora herself.'[179]

Greene's treatment of Fawnia's childhood is contained in one long paragraph, developed with considerable artistry from its humble beginning to a radiant conclusion. In this movement is the regenerative drive of 'The Triumph of Time'. Shakespeare handles things very differently, by presenting us with Time himself. Time tells us that 'I that please some, try all' (IV.i.1): we are all his subjects.

> Impute it not a crime
> To me, or my swift passage, that I slide
> O'er sixteen years, and leave the growth untried
> Of that wide gap, since it is in my power
> To o'erthrow law, and in one self-born hour
> To plant and o'erwhelm custom.
>
> (ll. 4–9)

Time asks not to be blamed for doing what is his by nature. 'Growth' may suggest regeneration, but it also refers to Perdita's growth and simply to whatever has happened. It invites but does not compel a symbolic understanding. Indeed, Time's description of himself is hardly heartening. He shows himself as a ravening destroyer, who breaks down both the subtle creation of 'law' and the humbler ordering of 'custom'. Shakespeare takes the idea of time with almost pedantic literalness, exploring simply what it does without requiring us to see a meaning in it. He also takes the romance convention of long passages of time with audacious seriousness. In Greene, the passage of years is cunningly elided by the smoothness of the prose, Fawnia's successive ages popping up as milestones to remind us that time is passing, but the scenes in which she is set serving to distract us from the time that flows through them. Shakespeare exposes the skeleton of the plot nakedly, and accepts with the greatest good will that, if Time is to triumph, Time must appear. Shakespeare goes beyond mockery of convention into a severely serious acceptance, one which insists on the truth of the convention's form while hesitating to ascribe a particular meaning to it.[180]

It may be that the idea of personifying time derived in part from Greene's personification of 'Fortune', which, having 'all this while . . . shewed a friendly face, began now to turn her back and to shew a louring countenance, intending as she had given Fawnia a slender check, so she would give her a harder mate; to bring which to pass, she laid her train on this wise'.[181] What happens is that Fawnia meets Dorastus, the model for the complication of the plot by Florizel. 'Fortune' is time interpreted providentially, and here seen as purposeful. Greene uses the imagery of Fortune as a chess-player so that he can pun on 'mate', which is not just the ending of a game but the new beginning of a marriage. Fortune reverses her appearance, just as Time says, 'I turn my glass' (l. 16). What Time means is that he directs his mirror to a new point, and he is seen as a reflecting rather than a controlling agent. 'Imagine me, / Gentle spectators, that I now may be / In fair Bohemia' (ll. 19–21), he asks, indicating that the audience must willingly suspend their disbelief for the play to proceed. Time will 'give my scene such growing / As you had slept between' (ll. 16–17): growth is again simply change.

Time tells us that we shall now see Florizel and Perdita. 'What of her ensues / I list not prophesy; but let Time's news / Be known when 'tis brought forth' (ll. 25–7). He does not even tell us what relationship there may be between the two characters, though it is very unlikely that any audience would not suppose there to be some. Far from promising a 'mate', Time tells us that we shall see what we shall see. 'A shepherd's daughter, / And what to her adheres, which follows after, / Is th'argument of Time' (ll. 27–9). Perdita and what happens to her will be his subject, and will 'follow after' – rather unsurprisingly, in view of what we have already been told.

> Of this allow,
> If ever you have spent time worse ere now;
> If never, yet that Time himself doth say,
> He wishes earnestly you never may.
> (ll. 29–32)

Time hopes that our pleasure in the play will be the least pleasure we ever have, so that if we are enjoying it he wishes us very well indeed and if not he hopes that things will look up for us.[182] These parting lines remind us that Time is an actor, like the other persons of the play, and thus tend to diminish his potential symbolic status. Shakespeare dazzles us by a theatrical coup which carries within it seeds of questioning. Time enters simply to say that time passes.

The next two scenes frustrate us with delay. Camillo and Polixenes appear next, planning to disguise themselves and spy on Florizel and his unknown *inamorata*. We cannot but be certain that the girl is Perdita, particularly because of the details we get of her background (IV.ii.38–45). We sense that her circumstances are fragile and vulnerable, but are withheld from immediate confirmation by the baffling direction 'Enter AUTOLYCUS, *singing*.' Autolycus' bawdy song draws on criminal argot:[183] the lyricism is heavily qualified. Autolycus then tells us who he is, 'a snapper-up of unconsidered trifles' (IV.iii.26). At this point the audience cannot see what Autolycus has to do with the plot, so that his entertaining intrusion is baffling and irksome as well as funny. We watch him fleece the Clown, and learn that a sheep-shearing is to take place (l. 37).

As the play picks up from Time's breach of its narrative flow, it gathers gradually out of shards. We hear of Perdita only marginally, not by name, and see the world she is in as dangerous. It is threatened both by Polixenes' paternal stringency and by Autolycus' amoral laxity. This enforces the understanding of her name as 'the lost one', and gives dramatic tension to what follows, the sheep-shearing itself.

The stage is now crowded with characters. Most are shepherds and shepherdesses in festive attire, but Polixenes and Camillo in disguise are also there, observing Florizel and Perdita, to whom we first attend.

Florizel tells Perdita that, dressed as she is, she seems 'no shepherdess, but Flora/Peering in April's front' (IV.iv.2–3). The festival 'Is as a meeting of the petty gods,/And you the queen on't' (ll. 4–5). Florizel's poetic tone transforms the scene into a symbolic presentation of Perdita's virtue and presents us immediately with one way of seeing it. Perdita is unpersuaded, and feels that only because 'custom' (l. 12) allows it can she tolerate the topsy-turviness of the whole business.

> Your high self,
> The gracious mark o'th'land, you have obscur'd
> With a swain's wearing, and me, poor lowly maid,
> Most goddess-like prank'd up.

(ll. 7–10)

Perdita knows that they are really only playing, and is uneasy at the deception their clothes entail. Florizel's reply is to ignore her and 'bless the time/When my good falcon made her flight across/Thy father's ground' (ll. 14–16). Greene tells us that 'it fortuned that Dorastus, who all that day had been hawking . . . encountered [Fawnia] by the way'.[184] 'It fortuned': Greene nudgingly reminds us that providence is at work, where in Shakespeare they meet purely by chance 'the time/When'. Time here is occasional and contingent. The hawk's free flight happens to bring the two together, and whether we – as Florizel does not explicitly do – see this as less than accidental is left up to us.

Perdita's trepidation comes not just from the falseness of fancy dress but from a realistic fear that the King would not like her in her 'borrowed flaunts' (l. 23). Florizel is confident that no harm would come of it, citing the Olympians' transformations into animals when they loved. His grandiose imaginings prevent his seeing the truth on which Perdita insists, that his determination 'must be' (l. 37) changed by the King. Florizel urges her not 'With these forc'd thoughts' to 'darken . . ./The mirth o'th'feast' (ll. 41–2). He is prepared to renounce his father for her (ll. 42–3). Perdita prays, 'O lady Fortune,/Stand you auspicious!' (ll. 51–2). Here the benevolent goddess is named, but we can see Polixenes and Camillo on stage. Fortune seems a flimsy shield against reality here, and does not stand 'auspicious' at this point. It may be that Fortune operates over a larger range, through the way in which the discovery of Polixenes leads ultimately to Perdita's return to Sicily and the restoration of Hermione, but that is certainly not what Perdita has in mind. Neither can we reasonably think of this at the time, compelled as our feelings are by dramatic urgency. We too want Fortune to side with Perdita, but the weakness of her prayer suggests a frailty in the goddess.

The other celebrants come forward, Florizel urges Perdita to greet them (ll. 52–4) and the Shepherd engagingly reminisces about the past. Shakespeare removes a potential emotional complication by killing the Shepherd's wife (Perdita's feelings must be free to flow towards Hermione), but the Shepherd's recollections (ll. 55–62) give us a vivid picture of the home in which Perdita grew up.

Perdita greets the merry-makers and offers them flowers. To Camillo and Polixenes she gives 'flowers of winter' (l. 79), on which Polixenes jokingly remarks.

> Sir, the year growing ancient,
> Not yet on summer's death nor on the birth
> Of trembling winter, the fairest flowers o'th'season
> Are our carnations and streak'd gillyvors,
> Which some call nature's bastards: of that kind
> Our rustic garden's barren; and I care not
> To get slips of them.
>
> (ll. 79–85)

The rosemary and rue she has given the two men will keep 'all the winter long' (l. 75), and she confesses that she has given them rather early in the year. We are still close to the end of summer, though, which seems very late to be shearing sheep. The lateness of the season emphasises the fragility of the rural order over which Perdita presides, and prevents the pastoral from escaping the world of natural inclemency.[185] Perdita's explanation that she has no appropriate flowers is tantalising, and Polixenes asks the obvious question why she dislikes the customary ones (ll. 85–6).

> Sir, I have heard it said
> There is an art which, in their piedness, shares
> With great creating nature.
>
> (ll. 86–8)

Perdita reveres nature's greatness and creativity and believes that man should not meddle with her. This reverence speaks of the naturalness of her character. She is fit to be a princess though not raised as one.

The nature–nurture debate is familiar. That it is a rehearsal of commonplaces[186] is unimportant, for what matters is the degree of importance given to the debate by the dramatic structure. The dramatic irony by which Polixenes commends in horticulture what he condemns in his family, grafting 'A gentle scion to the wildest stock' (l. 93) is also familiar. Perdita puts a stop to the argument by producing more flowers (l. 103) and it is left unconcluded. Perdita has conceded Polixenes' point (l. 97) but refuses to act on it (ll. 99–100). Her simpler beliefs are clung to in the face of Polixenes' polished rationality. This is appropriate to her status as shepherdess, and reveals how far she is a creature of her background, but makes us feel a health in the rustic world missing from the court. Perdita speaks of 'great creating nature' but Polixenes speaks of it as something to be transformed (l. 96). She commands our sympathy, but Polixenes is right in terms both of plants and, though he does not know it, of humans. We are left with a divided impulse to side with her against our better judgement, which means that 'great creating nature' does not emerge clearly as a symbolic principle to be adhered to but instead offers an attractive way of interpreting the world's processes.

The flowers Perdita now offers are ones 'Of middle summer' (l. 107). The seasonal imagery begins to run backwards, so that she next refers to 'blasts of January' (l. 111) and wishes that she had 'flowers o'th'spring' (l. 113) for Florizel and the girls. The imagination reverses the process of time, but only in imagination. Perdita's invocation of the flowers that 'Proserpina . . . lets fall' (ll. 116–17) is entirely beautiful and entirely without present referent. The flowers she thinks of conjure up images of fragility. They arrive 'before the swallow dares' (l. 119) and 'die unmarried' (l. 123), and though some are 'bold' (l. 125) and some 'imperial' (l. 126) we sense that they are born to die. Perdita's own fears about her relationship with Florizel are latent in this imagery, but the power of the poetry reminds us both that she knows the real natural world in vivid detail and that she can do nothing to stay its course.

The flickering uncertainty about when exactly the sheep-shearing festival is taking place emphasises its incandescent brevity. Perdita is brushed by the transience of things, and the order such festivities embody is seen to be an act of the will. Florizel and Perdita are again observed as they exchange compliments, following which there is a dance. During the dance Polixenes pumps the shepherd for information and the dramatic irony is intensified.

A servant enters to announce the arrival of a 'pedlar' (l. 183). We are told that he has 'the prettiest love-songs for maids, so without bawdry (which is strange); with such delicate burdens of dildoes and fadings, jump her and thump her' (ll. 195–7). These indelicate refrains introduce a new note to the proceedings. If what the pastoral ceremony celebrates is the natural cycle, we are here reminded that that cycle is also latent in the most casual fornication. The pedlar is summoned, but Perdita says he must be warned 'that he use no scurrilous words in's tunes' (ll. 215–16). Her concern that the tone should not be lowered is appealing, but again reminds us how much the occasion depends on willed order.

Autolycus' appearace here is very funny, in that the Clown fails to recognise him. It also changes the emphasis of the scene, for we now watch the rustics engage in banter and japes. Autolycus offers the ballad of 'Two maids wooing a man' (l. 290), which both Dorcas and Mopsa know (l. 293). The Clown takes them off-stage after they and Autolycus have sung it, saying, 'We'll have this song out anon by ourselves' (l. 310). He leaves on his erotic expedition to be followed by Autolycus, who remains on stage a moment to sing a new offer of his wares (ll. 316–24).

After this interlude of rural pleasantry, the Servant reappears to announce a 'gallimaufry of gambols' (l. 329) which is admitted, and we watch a *'dance of twelve Satyrs'*. This burlesque dance is a kind of antimasque to the dance we saw earlier, and the two are appropriately reversed in order because the solemnity with which Perdita treats the sheep-shearing aspires to raise it to the level of a masque but it continually threatens to come apart, which now happens with inexorable rapidity. The focus narrows again to an argument, one between Polixenes and Florizel (ll. 346–418) in which the other characters momentarily take part but which Polixenes dominates. The suspense we feel as Florizel betrays himself is prolonged until Polixenes unmasks. Polixenes leaves threatening punishment for all (ll. 421–42).

Perdita, who has been silent for most of the argument (she refuses to be drawn in at ll. 381–4), now speaks.

> Even here, undone,
> I was not much afeard; for once or twice
> I was about to speak, and tell him plainly,
> The selfsame sun that shines upon his court
> Hides not his visage from our cottage, but
> Looks on alike.
>
>   (ll. 442–7)

This plain-speaking miss recovers her confidence by what might be bluster but conveys a truth. She sees Polixenes as merely pretentious, and her plebeian egalitarianism draws us to share in it. She tells Florizel to see to 'your own state' (l. 449): as for 'this dream of mine −/Being now awake, I'll queen it no inch farther,/But milk my ewes, and weep' (ll. 449–51). She began the scene by rebuking Florizel for decking her out in unbeseeming finery, but now she confesses that she has shared in the 'dream' and makes no attempt to blame him for what has happened. 'I told you what would come of this' (l. 448), she says, but immediately allows that she is at least equally culpable.

At this point, Camillo intervenes (l. 451). We already know that he is homesick for Sicily (IV.ii.4–9), but are not prepared for the opportunism with which he now turns events to his own advantage. That this is his motive is not apparent until ll. 509–14, so that the scene hangs in weary suspense until then. This lack of clear direction suits our feelings after the violent shock of Polixenes' rage and the complete destruction of the atmosphere Perdita has worked so lovingly to preserve. Perdita and Florizel assent to Camillo's plan, and Florizel exchanges clothes with Autolycus. When they leave (l. 669), Autolycus is for a short time alone on stage to tell us that he misunderstands everything. 'This is the time that the unjust man doth thrive' (ll. 673–4), he thinks, and 'The prince himself is about a piece of iniquity' (l. 678).

The Clown and Shepherd reappear to discuss the circumstances of Perdita's arrival in Bohemia. Autolycus listens to their conversation and sees in it a chance for himself. 'Though I am not naturally honest, I am sometimes so by chance' (ll. 712–13). One might see an irony here and feel that nature was indeed working through Autolycus, on whom the resolution of the plot will depend, but we can do so only by refusing to believe what he actually says. Autolycus contributes to the good by fulfilling his nature, which is to seize 'unconsidered trifles', and that he overhears this conversation is entirely a matter of chance.

The Shepherd and Clown are persuaded to let Autolycus act on their behalf. 'We are blest in this man, as I may say, even blest' (l. 829), the Clown says, and the Shepherd replies that 'he was provided to do us good' (ll. 830–1). Where Autolycus sees chance at work, they see providence. We are aware that Autolycus does not intend their good, however, and feel that this invocation of a benevolent force is as fragile as Perdita's was at the start of the scene. We hope that all will be well for the young lovers, but cannot at this point see how. Shakespeare forbids the plot to move too easily forward, so that we see that what from one point of view is providential is from another contingent. When he is alone, Autolycus says that 'If I had a mind to be honest, I see Fortune would not suffer me' (ll. 832–3). Fortune can be a self-serving excuse for villainy, quite as much as an explanation of how things are. Indeed, to accept it is to take the world as it is.

This very long scene moves through an extraordinary range of dramatic effects, from comedy to incipient tragedy. Polixenes' rage is ambiguous, for while it is frightening it is also the comic attribute of a duped father.[187] Our sympathy with Florizel coheres with a dramatic convention by which paternal stiffness is mocked. The masque-like pastoral elements of the scene are set against the raucous bawdry of some of the minor characters. Predictably, the Clown resists Perdita's shaping will and slopes off to allow two women to woo him at once. There is what looks like a deliberate display of dramatic virtuosity here, Shakespeare running through the gamut of what he can do, with spellbinding rapidity. The speed of his art deceives the mind, though, for the scene that began as an approach to unity ends in irresolution.

Nothing in the scene validates any of the terms used in it by the characters. The succession of voices and motives prevents our having a clear sense of providential pattern, however much we desire it. Shakespeare is perfectly aware that romance usually does tell of 'The Triumph of Time', and leaves this scene open to such an interpretation by letting the idea of providence exist in it. If we listen carefully, though, we hear something stranger. The scene presents a series of possible determinations, moments at which the intention of the plot may be revealed, but none of these is carried through. Perdita is unquestionably beautiful and good, which compels us to admire what she praises, but in the debate with Polixenes she is clearly wrong. This division of our response to a single character is reflected formally in the plot's coming to rest on the whimsical, scabrous Autolycus, whose concerns are entirely selfish.

There is a peculiarly beautiful irony at the start of the scene when, in his catalogue of Olympian metamorphoses, Florizel says that among them was 'the fire-rob'd god, / Golden Apollo' (ll. 29–30), who became 'a poor humble swain, / As I seem now' (ll. 30–1). Florizel intends the sheep-shearing to show the transformation of Perdita into a queen, and his metamorphic activity allies him with the god of poetry. This god, though, is one who must flee the country when his father finds out what he has been up to. To claim metaphorical kinship with Apollo is not to take on his powers. The deeper, weirder irony is that the Oracle on whose fulfilment the story rests is Apollo's. Cleomenes prays, 'Great Apollo/Turn all to th'best!' (III.i.14–15) when he has collected the oracular letter, and Dion is sure that when it is read 'something rare/Even then will rush to knowledge' (ll. 20–1). Leontes, of course, refuses to believe the Oracle's verdict and brings about a crisis.

The Oracle is remarkable in two ways. Shakespeare uses Greene's words almost exactly, except that he removes the initial sententious observations that 'SUSPICION IS NO PROOF: JEALOUSY IS AN UNEQUAL JUDGE'.[188] These remarks have a thunderous obviousness which is not really needed, and they tend to turn the scene into an allegory of the kind which Shakespeare always resists. Shakespeare's Oracle opens with hard fact:

> Hermione is chaste; Polixenes blameless; Camillo a true subject; Leontes a jealous tyrant; his innocent babe truly begotten; and the king shall live without an heir, if that which is lost be not found.   (III.ii.132–6)

Its judgements on what has happened could not be plainer, which is striking inasmuch as oracles traditionally offer ambiguous rather than clear judgement. However, the last part is at this moment entirely baffling, because we know Leontes has an heir (Mamilius) and even if he is ill (II.iii.10–17) he is recovering. Leontes refuses to believe what the Oracle has said, but is interrupted by the news of Mamilius' death of grief at his mother's unlucky fate (III.ii.145). 'Apollo's angry, and the heavens themselves/Do strike at my injustice' (ll. 146–7), he says as Hermione faints. When she has been taken away, he prays, 'Apollo, pardon/My great profaneness 'gainst thine Oracle!' (ll. 153–4). He interprets what has happened as a judgement on himself and resolves to set things right.

> I'll reconcile me to Polixenes,
> New woo my queen, recall the good Camillo,
> Whom I proclaim a man of truth, of mercy.
> (ll. 155–7)

Leontes treats what he takes as the Oracle's punishment as a direction to play a new part. He shows little concern for the feelings of those he has wounded, though, choosing rather to 'proclaim' their virtues than to respond to them. Equally, when told of Hermione's death, he orders that she and his son should be interred together:

> Once a day I'll visit
> The chapel where they lie, and tears shed there
> Shall be my recreation. So long as nature
> Will bear up with this exercise, so long
> I daily vow to use it.
>
> (ll. 238–42)

Leontes adopts a frozen posture, 'shame perpetual' (l. 238).

In the course of time, Leontes' court try to persuade him to remarry (v.i). Paulina, though, holds him to his vow, reminding him that

> the gods
> Will have fulfill'd their secret purposes;
> For has not the divine Apollo said,
> Is't not the tenor of his Oracle,
> That King Leontes shall not have an heir,
> Till his lost child be found? which, that it shall,
> Is all as monstrous to our human reason
> As my Antigonus to break his grave.
>
> (ll. 35–42)

Later we hear Hermione tell Perdita the Oracle 'Gave hope thou wast in being' (v.iii.127): hope, no more. Paulina insists that Leontes die without an heir because such is the Oracle's decree. She understands the Oracle's last statement as a moral injunction rather than a prophecy, and Hermione acts throughout on the basic trust

> I must be patient till the heavens look
> With an aspect more favourable.
>
> (ii.i.106–7)

Obedience to the Oracle is the same as obedience to whatever happens, an acceptance of the world. What Paulina counsels Leontes against is the renewed exercise of will.

The Oracle's decree freezes Leontes and Hermione until Perdita is restored. It never says that she will be: 'the king shall live without an heir, if that which is lost be not found'. What it says turns out to be a fact rather than a promise, given how Leontes responds to circumstances. That he does not remarry in the end is thanks to Paulina's knowledge that Hermione is not dead, but she knows that Hermione's hope is beyond reason. Reason appears to be Leontes' forte, in that he is the character who sets out to interpret the behaviour of others, notably Polixenes and Hermione, and that this leads him quickly into unreason suggests that trust and acceptance of others' opacity is to be preferred to judgement.

At the end of the play, Leontes seems to have learnt little, requiring Paulina to marry Camillo (v.iii.135–45) without seeking her opinion. He then asks Paulina to

> Lead us from hence, where we may leisurely
> Each one demand, and answer to his part
> Perform'd in this wide gap of time.
>
> (ll. 152–4)

He still believes that people can give full accounts of their behaviour, and that they are essentially actors. He shows no sense of providence's having intervened: if this is a didactic, symbolic drama, it falls at the first hurdle. His matchmaking is a kind of stage-management, though he does thank the 'heavens' (l. 150) for bringing Perdita and Florizel together.[89] Leontes is unwilling to relinquish control over what happens. Hermione speaks not to him but to Perdita, because there is really nothing to be said.

Paulina tells Leontes that 'That she is living, / Were it but told you, should be hooted at / Like an old tale: but it appears she lives' (ll. 115–17). Leontes must trust to the appearance and not seek an explanation behind it, which would necessarily be risible. He must accept that Hermione appears to be a statue but turns out to be a flesh-and-blood woman whose wrinkles (l. 28) show that even in retirement she cannot escape the vicissitudes of time. Time continues to flow whatever people do, and just as it makes pastoral fragile so it prevents people from achieving entirely symbolic status. Hermione steps out of statuehood into life and embraces Leontes, but the ageing shows that life has continued to work within her, and her silence shows a wish to forget which we fear may be irked in future by his garrulous belief in causal explanation.

The Winter's Tale shows that people may take on for one another symbolic functions, but in the cases where this is shown as an artistic achievement we see art being undone. Perdita's pastoral is disrupted, and Hermione must step down if her sequestration is to have had any meaning. The purely symbolic, the purely aesthetic, is hostile to life, although it embodies the characters' deepest longings. The Oracle sets a condition for Leontes to have an heir, and that condition is satisfied, but we are shown no evidence that that is not a matter of chance. Hermione and Paulina might well have plotted in vain, as Paulina's words to Leontes suggest that she recognises. Hermione relies on hope and patience, but these qualities invalidate her both for the drama Leontes arranges (her trial, where she throws herself on the Oracle's verdict) and for an active part in the play Paulina arranges. She is a character who must be moved by others, and the play shows us two manipulators in conflict.

On the other hand we have Leontes, who has a forensic ambition to see motives exposed and to find the world confirming his view of it. His certainty that Hermione is unfaithful makes that a fact. The dramatic form to which he is naturally drawn is therefore a trial, in which all must be disclosed. When that fails, he is magnamimous to himself by acting as though he can undo everything, vicious to others by not seeing that he can really have hurt them. He wants to be loved for what he is, not to change. Paulina, on the other hand, acts by emblematic display. She takes Leontes to see the dead bodies of his son and his queen, and she produces the show of Hermione's statue.[190]

Leontes' drama aims at final knowledge. Paulina's, on the other hand, is knowingly deceptive. Hermione is neither dead nor a statue. It appears from what Hermione says, that she has 'preserv'd/Myself to see the issue' (v.iii.127–8), that Paulina produces Hermione's scripts, and both of these direct that she be presented as a visual object, a corpse or a statue. These appearances inspire feeling, but have no meaning, no useful attachment to life – they are simply figures for Leontes' guilt – until she returns from the aesthetic world to reality. In the conflict between Leontes' telling and Hermione's showing, it is the latter that wins.

Hermione claims no purpose beyond a wish 'to see the issue', an outcome which may also be a child, and shows no certainty, only 'hope', that the issue will indeed be her daughter. She is not to be taken as having superhuman powers. Leontes claims insight and intention, but the former is shown to be vitiated by the latter. Hermione's stepping-down shows him that the patterns of art must yield to everyday life in its unpredictable, unknowable variety. He now has to live with her again.

The symbolic, then, only has meaning when it can rejoin life and work on us there. Of itself it can do nothing but be seen, and is likely to be deceptive. Without it, though, life is the world of reason without faith which Leontes inhabits, and conducive to a kind of insanity in which all behaviour, all events are interpreted in the light of personal obsession. Time is seen as a presenter rather than an agent, Fortune shown to be the excuse of knaves and the creed of gulls quite as much as a determining beneficence. If we trust to this entirely we do nothing, like Hermione in seclusion, and to do nothing is merely to endure. If we mistrust it, though, we run into folly. The gods of this play are ambiguous and inscrutable, the Oracle a series of announcements which have in the end no enigma but no prophetic power. The Oracle's judgements say how things are but not how they are going to be. The play's extraordinary achievement is to take the symbolic form of romance and ironise it in such a way that we both believe and disbelieve at the same time. Not to find it absurd, we must trust its appearance, but examined closely its appearance carries the spores of disintegration. To unify the whole as redemptive is an effort of the audience's will for which the play does not in the end give an adequate justification.

Hermione appears to Leontes as a statue because he so wills it: his suspense of disbelief is an act of the imagination. It is one to which he is attracted because in remembering her he can remember only a woman who is dead, a past life transformed into a mental object, an icon. Were she truly a statue, the play's ending would be most unsatisfactory. Patience on a monument is haunting, but we can do nothing for her. The purely aesthetic object is dead, and even if it tells us that we must change our life[191] we can have no developing relationship with it. Whether it succeeds in telling us to change is up to us – Angelo is not moved by Isabella's direct appeal to the example of God Himself (*Measure for Measure*, II.ii.73–9). The statue surprises Leontes by being wrinkled, surpassing art by containing the passage of time. That it proves finally not to be a statue at all returns us to the world of marriage and continuity, a future without a form.[192] Hermione's pose embodies the nature of Shakespearean drama, which is to present us with the possibility that we are seeing our highest aspirations in symbolic form but to remind us that they can only snatch at such forms in passing if they are to remain alive.

Conclusion

To be hostile to drama is to be hostile to life:[1] a statue cannot act.
The dramatic invites us to falsify, though, to speak rhetorically
and act according to our conception of our own character. Othello
is exemplary of men who do so, and his end is disaster. At the
moment when the play seems to have ended, and the Venetians
have tied up the loose ends of the plot, Othello says, 'Soft you; a
word or two before you go' (*Othello*, v.ii.337). 'You' rather than
'we' because he has no intention of leaving. Lodovico, who has
been giving the orders, is triumphantly upstaged. 'I have done
the state some service, and they know't' (l. 338), Othello goes on,
playing down his past with becoming modesty but reminding
everyone that he is first and foremost a martial figure. 'I pray you,
in your letters, / When you shall these unlucky deeds relate, / Speak
of me as I am' (ll. 339–41). Othello knows that he will be written
about and wants to manage his own publicity, just as Hamlet,
who has occupied the stage for an unusually long time, dies
imposing on Horatio the duty to 'tell my story' (*Hamlet*, v.ii.363).
Hamlet has no story, for the play shows him delighting in his
own ability to change roles and acting finally only because Laertes
trumps him. He leaps into Ophelia's grave and tells Laertes that
whatever signs of grief he shows

> I'll do't. Dost thou come here to whine?
> To outface me with leaping in her grave?
> Be buried quick with her, and so will I.
> (v.i.299–301)

'Nay,' he says, 'an thou'lt mouth, / I'll rant as well as thou' (ll.
305–6). Plunged into drama, Hamlet loses the imaginative freedom
in which he could count himself a 'king of infinite space' (ii.ii.265),
a freedom against which his own resolution for revenge proves
ineffectual. Hamlet naturally resists the narrowness of dramatic
performance, and is finally only stung into it by rivalry. His
'story' is the story of what happens to him, not of what he does.

Othello does not seek imaginative freedom at all, but clings
obstinately to his role. He has said earlier, should the amorous

part of his life conflict with the military, 'Let housewives make a skillet of my helm' (*Othello*, I.iii.274). Emilia's 'O gull! O dolt!' (v.ii.161) shows that he has indeed made himself ridiculous, but this he refuses to see. He directs Lodovico how to write of him, then tells him,

> And say besides, that in Aleppo once,
> Where a malignant and a turban'd Turk
> Beat a Venetian and traduc'd the state,
> I took by the throat the circumcised dog,
> And smote him thus.
>
> (v.i.351–5)

Othello produces an instance of his past worthiness and turns it against himself. Killing a Venetian he has become an enemy of the state, so he must logically kill himself. The deliberate adherence to a mistaken role is shown to be not merely destructive but ultimately suicidal.

The symbolic pose Othello adopts is compelling and bogus at the same time. Cleopatra's triumph is entirely persuasive, though equally suicidal. Shakespeare does not present a single-minded view of man's wish for magnificence. However, we should remember that the magnificent, the imposing, are characteristic of the Romantic sublime, for Shakespeare does achieve sublimity, but of a very peculiar kind. If the sublime defines our mental horizon, being the point at which understanding becomes conscious of its own organisation and can go no further, Shakespeare finds that horizon to be internal. The sublime is inside other men and women, the 'glassy essence' of which Isabella speaks.

To know this is not in Shakespeare's world enough. Isabella's knowledge gives her no practical help. Her silence at the end of the play is awesome because we are suddenly aware that she has a core of being beyond what we have yet seen, a core which continues to live and is capable of surprising us. Her silence is, I have argued, a moment of realism rather than of symbolism or allegory. This implies that for Shakespeare the realistic and the sublime are the same. He uses the dramatic device of silence to shock us into an appreciation of reality beyond the point at which we understand or can predict it.

When Pandarus invites Troilus and Cressida to see themselves if their love fails as falling into the typical roles they will truly fall into, the paradox is that they earn those roles only because of the muddled, haphazard nature of their behaviour. In a better world they would have acted otherwise, and it is precisely because the world is not better that they come to have the typical status for us they do. The enduring symbol comes about when life is seen retrospectively, and is utterly divorced from it: because Pandarus can suggest that they may not succeed in their love, we feel that Cressida is morally culpable rather than determined, but because we know that she is determined by the future we find her harder to judge. The ambivalence gives an effect of reality which Shakespeare consistently pursues elsewhere.

The characteristic Shakespearean effect is one of doubleness, which may also be duplicity. Time and again, we find characters whom we mock but sympathise with, admire but dislike, hate but feel for, despise but are awed by. This is a deliberate artistic end, of which *The Winter's Tale* is in all ways exemplary. At the formal level, the tension between our emotional adherence to the romance plot and all that it conventionally implies is set against our awareness that we never see providence or time as an agent, only as a presenter or a 'wide gap' people must muddle through. Hermione may appear to be symbolic of virtue helpless in a cruel world, but at the end of the play we must want to know what she has done in the intervening period. It is glib and inadequate to say, as some critics will, that the drama elides the point. We, like Leontes, are free to wonder, and our questioning about the reality contributes to the emotions I discussed above, our sense of the ethereal fragility of the absolute presentations for which we yearn.

The Winter's Tale is double at the formal level, then. This tension is universal in Shakespeare's work. At the level of character, we find Leontes repugnant and deeply sympathetic because his jealousy is one to which any lover is prone. Leontes shares our deep fears and cannot therefore simply be dismissed as a villain.

This doubleness can be described as duplicitous because it is all a result of artistic method. Shakespeare clearly sets out to complicate and divide our responses, and his work is unusually hospitable to interpretation. This is related to the world in which he worked. Shakespeare's audiences are able to respond to their utmost capacity, but he does not simply dismiss the groundlings to laugh at coarse jokes and propose to the intellectuals that they relish Hamlet's philosophy. The groundlings are made uncomfortably aware that Shylock has feelings, the intellectuals that Hamlet is a victim of his own pride. Anyone who enters the theatre with any knowledge of contemporary (by which I mean Elizabethan and Jacobean) drama does so with a knowledge of conventions, however inarticulate. In *The Winter's Tale* we see how Shakespeare can apparently fulfil conventional demands and gratify our wishes while at the same time offering no evidence that what happens is more than accidental. His purpose is to come down on neither side, but to divide us between aesthetic pleasure and doubt, to give us the mingled pleasure and pain which are the hallmarks of the sublime.

The proper response to a Shakespearean play is 'Yes'. None of his plays resolves itself into a paraphrasable meaning, though each proposes a multiplicity of interpretations. This leaves it open to us to choose between two kinds of response. The first is to deal with Shakespeare polemically, to approach him with purposes of our own and find them fulfilled there. This is an attractive method because there is more than enough in the plays to reward the attentions of systematic thinkers.

The other response is to try to deal with the plays as objects without meanings, to analyse their appearances as aesthetic artefacts, and it is in this direction that I have tried to move. It is ultimately an impossibility, because unless we are drawn to the plays for some personal reason we shall never wish to think about them, and that personal motive will always be lesser than the multiplicity of the plays. Shakespeare is a mirror in which the critic may see his own face.

Reading him with an eye to his avoidance of meaning, though, focusing on his happy acceptance of the conditions imposed by a bare stage and a heterogeneous audience, may help us to read other literature differently. The Romantic symbol attempts to impose on us its own truthfulness, where the symbols at the heart of systematic allegory rest on generally received faiths. We misunderstand both if we forget the part imagination must play in giving them aesthetic form. Shakespeare may be the supremely sceptical writer, but literary form is itself scepticism realised.[2]

When Spenser presents us with the vision on Mount Acidale, he presents us with what all his work had tended towards. It is a moment at once brazenly public and hermetically private. Its effect rests not on faith but on its place in the logic of a book and a career, and the verbal ingenuity with which it is made significant.

Milton's verbal universe comes from his head, not heaven. The poet of 'Kubla Khan' must deliberately re-create the pleasure-palace. At the same time, without faith Spenser would not have conceived of his vision, without the help of nature the poet would have no strength. All are rhetoricians, and aim at what rhetoric intends, to carry conviction. We are offered not objects of knowledge but their simulacra, so that we feel our powers exercised without mundane motives.[3]

Poetry mingles conscious and unconscious motives and agencies. Its sources are often obscure to the poet, but its means are capable of being entirely controlled. The imagination takes beauty for truth, and presents us with concepts towards which we are drawn. They are not yet concepts of reason, and maybe they never can be. They should not therefore be judged by reason. When Paul de Man, whom I take as representative of a widespread variety of criticism, reproves Wordsworth for being untruthful in the face of temporality, he misapprehends the nature of art, which is to give us not meaning but the feeling of meaning.

When we return to the world from art, we carry with us that sense of meaningfulness. We see sunsets as Turneresque, old men as Wordsworthian. Art gives us ways of coping with the world we inhabit. That coping is always, necessarily, provisional. Poetry has no axioms and can reach no indisputable conclusions. By inviting us to participate in the visions of others it invites us to feel our common humanity. Shakespeare, our supreme poet, shows us that sublimity, the place where the mind falters, is in and of ourselves. Reading him, we become greater than we know, for this accessible, popular art has the humility to tell us nothing. In its silence we hear the sound of our own thoughts, thoughts now without an object, and are liberated from the concerns and motives that make us what we are. So we learn what we are, and may appreciate the possibilities or responsibilities that open up for us. In our search to find meaning in experience, we are enabled by art to know how meaning would feel: if we accept an artistic vision, we accept that the feeling of meaning in it (which may for the writer be, and usually is, a meaning experienced as true) satisfies our desires. Shakespeare the aesthete was the man who knew more than any other how to turn his meanings into the sensation of meaningfulness which strikes like revelation.

Notes

CHAPTER 1

1. Frederick S. Boas, *Shakspere and His Predecessors* (London: John Murray, 1896) p. 27.
2. All quotations are from G. K. Hunter (ed.), *All's Well That Ends Well*, New Arden edn (London and New York: Methuen, 1967), to which I am indebted for much information. A useful critical history is Joseph G. Price, *The Unfortunate Comedy: A Study of 'All's Well That Ends Well' and Its Critics* (Toronto: University of Toronto Press, 1968).
3. For instances, see Madeleine Doran, *Endeavors of Art: A Study of Form in Elizabeth Drama* (Madison: University of Wisconsin Press, 1954) pp. 212–14.
4. Hunter, Introduction to *All's Well*, pp. xxx–xxxi.
5. E. M. W. Tillyard, in *Shakespeare's Problem Plays* (London: Chatto and Windus, 1950), p. 113, says that 'by the standards of real life there is nothing surprising in Helena's having fallen for Bertram's handsome outside, his high rank, and her unconscious knowledge that she could dominate him and give him moral backbone, granted the chance.' I am not happy that Bertram's rank is involved.
6. Hunter (ed.), *All's Well*, p. 16.
7. Sir Arthur Quiller-Couch, in his Introduction to *All's Well That Ends Well* (Cambridge: Cambridge University Press, 1929) p. xxxi, finds of Helena that 'the general unpleasantness of the plot helping, we detect in her a strain of the modern young woman familiar to us in modern dramas and novels; a heroine of the pushing, calculating sort, that knows its own mind and will get its own way to its own ends without inconvenient scruple – and if affection help advancement, so much the better! Be it observed that all Shakespeare's heroines, save Helena, have royal or noble blood; that she alone belongs to what we call the upper-middle class. . . . She is perhaps too "efficient" to engage our complete sympathy.' As will be seen, I have some but not complete sympathy with this view, and I share also some of Quiller-Couch's defensive feelings about Bertram (see ibid., pp. xxvii–xxviii).
8. A. P. Rossiter, in *Angel with Horns and Other Shakespeare Lectures*, ed. Graham Storey (London: Longman, 1961) p. 87, sees law as important because through it the King can appear as the exemplary judge, a moralistic view with which I disagree, preferring the drier view of Leo Salingar, who in *Shakespeare and the Traditions of Comedy* (Cambridge: Cambridge University Press, 1974) p. 302, notes that 'trickery and luck' alone are inadequate to the dangerous worlds of the problem plays.
9. The same quotations are brought together in Ann Pasternak Slater, *Shakespeare the Director* (Brighton: Harvester, 1982) p. 156.

10. Hunter, in his Introduction to *All's Well*, pp. xviii–xx, discusses the evidence for and dismisses the idea as a serious possibility.
11. John Kerrigan, in *'Love's Labour's Lost* and the Circling Seasons', *Essays in Criticism*, xxviii, no. 4 (Oct 1978), observes that the characters leave the play for reality (pp. 280–1) to be reconciled in due course by the seasonal cycle the songs represent (pp. 270, 273).
12. Sir Walter Ralegh, 'The Nymph's Reply', in Christopher Marlowe, *The Complete Poems and Translations*, ed. Stephen Orgel (Harmondsworth: Penguin, 1971), p. 212.
13. Christopher Marlowe, 'The Passionate Shepherd to his Love', ibid., p. 211.
14. C. L. Barber, in *Shakespeare's Festive Comedy: A Study of Dramatic Form and Its Relation to Social Custom* (Princeton, NJ: Princeton University Press, 1959) p. 118, finds that these songs give 'the conclusion of the comedy what marriage usually provides: an expression of the going-on power of life.'
15. 'Gloucestershire is a state of mind I am very fond of', Falstaff observes, intelligently mentalising the landscape, in Robert Nye, *Falstaff* (London: Hamish Hamilton, 1976) p. 314.
16. W. H. Auden, *The Dyer's Hand and Other Essays* (London: Faber and Faber, 1975) pp. 182–208. See esp. pp. 195–7.
17. Ibid., p. 184.
18. Geoffrey Hill, 'The Guardians', *For the Unfallen: Poems 1952–1958* (London: André Deutsch, 1959) p. 40.
19. Cf. Peter Conrad, *Shandyism: The Character of Romantic Irony* (Oxford: Basil Blackwell, 1978) p. 9.
20. Cf. M. M. Reese, *The Cease of Majesty: A Study of Shakespeare's History Plays* (London: Edward Arnold, 1961) pp. 255–6.
21. This is significantly different from the source in Painter, where 'the Lady . . . purposed to finde meanes, to attaine the two thinges, that thereby she might recover her husbande', and where the pilgrimage is clearly an elaborate ruse. See Hunter (ed.), *All's Well*, pp. 148–9.
22. It is worth remarking at this point that, although her soliloquy of love is reported to the Countess, it is transformed in the telling to 'Her matter was, she loved your son. Fortune, she said, was no goddess, that had put such difference betwixt their two estates; Love no god, that would not extend his might only where qualities were level; [Diana no] queen of virgins, that would suffer her poor knight surpris'd without rescue in the first assault or ransom afterward. This she deliver'd in the most bitter touch of sorrow that ere I heard virgin exclaim in' (i.iii.106–14). The Steward's account omits the 'ambition' (i.i.88) that Helena owns to, and her own tone with the Countess is submissive and respectful, but not as ceremonious as that she employs with the King. The Countess can be seen therefore as having 'the tenderest and most capacious sympathy for youth in love' (Rossiter, *Angel with Horns*, p. 83), but it should not be thought that she knows Helena entirely.
23. *OED* sense 2, 'An expedient or remedy to be tried', is clearly also available.

24. John Donne, 'An Anatomy of the World: The First Anniversary', ll. 205–13, *The Complete English Poems*, ed. A. J. Smith (Harmondsworth: Penguin, 1971) p. 276.
25. See Norman Rabkin, *Shakespeare and the Problem of Meaning* (Chicago and London: Chicago University Press, 1981) esp. pp. 19–27, for a discussion of this concept.
26. Anne Barton, in *Ben Jonson, Dramatist* (Cambridge, London, New York: Cambridge University Press, 1984), describes this kind of naming (p. 167) but shows that Jonson himself only came to such naming gradually and later moved away from it (see esp. pp. 175–7).
27. Cf. Hunter, *All's Well*, New Arden edn, p. xxxiii.
28. John Bayley, in *Shakespeare and Tragedy* (London, Boston and Henley: Routledge and Kegan Paul, 1981) p. 81, finds Parolles 'engagingly complacent' here.
29. 'A tragi-comedy is not so called in respect of mirth and killing, but in respect it wants deaths, which is enough to make it no tragedy, yet brings some near it, which is enough to make it no comedy': John Fletcher, 'To the Reader', in Francis Beaumont and John Fletcher, *Select Plays*, ed. M. C. Bradbrook (London: Dent, 1962) p. 242.
30. The view of W. W. Lawrence, in *Shakespeare's Problem Comedies* (Harmondsworth: Penguin, 1969) pp. 59–61, that they will be happy because convention requires it, does too little justice to the characters' reality to be accepted.
31. See Joseph G. Price, *The Unfortunate Comedy*, pp. 80–1, and for Schlegel, p. 83.
32. William Hazlitt, 'All's Well That Ends Well', *The Round Table/Characters of Shakespeare's Plays*, ed. Catherine Macdonald Maclean (London: Dent, repr. 1969) p. 329.
33. Samuel Taylor Coleridge, *Coleridge on Shakespeare: A Selection of the Essays Notes and Lectures of Samuel Taylor Coleridge on the Poems and Plays of Shakespeare*, ed. Terence Hawkes (Harmondsworth: Penguin, 1969) p. 277.
34. Ibid.
35. Ibid.
36. Pandarus' final address to the audience is, I shall argue below, of a different kind.
37. Originally this emphasis goes back to the second or third century AD. See Gilbert Highet, *The Classical Tradition: Greek and Roman Influences on Western Literature* (Oxford: Clarendon Press, 1949) pp. 51–5.
38. Text from W. W. Skeat (ed.), *Chaucerian and Other Pieces* (Oxford: Clarendon Press, 1897) pp. 327–46.
39. Ibid., p. 327.
40. Ibid.
41. Ibid.
42. Ibid., p. 328.
43. Ibid., p. 328. On p. 521 Skeat says, 'Read *lusty*, to avoid the repetition of *worthy*', going against his copy-text, Chalmers' 1824 reprint of the edition printed by Charteris (Edinburgh, 1593) (Skeat, *Chaucerian and Other Pieces*, p. lv). I have amended his reading, while obeying his

change from '-ie' to '-y' (ibid.) because the repetition seems to me a deliberate poetic effect. 'Lusty' says little about Chaucer's Troilus and makes even less sense in Henryson's context. The Charteris-text reading can be found in G. Gregory Smith (ed.), *The Poems of Robert Henryson*, III (Edinburgh: Scottish Text Society, 1908) 4, the Thynne-text reading on p. 175. It is of particular interest to note that Sir Francis Kinaston's *The Sixt and last booke of Troilus and Creseid written by Mr Robert Henderson and called by him The Testament of Creseide* (1639–40) has 'lusty' on p. 478, but that Kinaston cheerfully tells us in his Latin translation (ibid.) that Chaucer wrote 'ab eruditissimo / De Creseida & Troilo dignissimo', finding the ideas of lustiness and worthiness interchangeable. The manuscript from which my reading is taken is in the Bodleian Library (MS Add. C. 287); a transcription can be found in G. Gregory Smith (ed.), *The Poems of Robert Henryson*, I (Edinburgh: Scottish Text Society, 1914) cv–clx, and a description of the manuscript on pp. xcvii–cii.

44. Skeat, *Chaucerian and Other Pieces*, p. 328.
45. Ibid., p. 329.
46. Ibid.
47. Ibid.
48. Ibid., p. 327.
49. Cf. John Bayley, *The Characters of Love: A Study in the Literature of Personality* (London: Chatto and Windus, 1968) pp. 86, 105–7.
50. Henri Matisse, 'Notes of a Painter' (1908), tr. Jack D. Flam, in Jack D. Flam, *Matisse on Art*, paperback edn (Oxford: Phaidon, 1978) p. 38.
51. I have used the recording of Walton's *Troilus and Cressida* made at the Royal Opera House, Covent Garden, issued by EMI in 1977. Quotations from the libretto by Christopher Hassall are from the booklet contained in that set (SLS 997), referred to hereafter as 'SLS 997 booklet'.
52. Geoffrey Chaucer, *Troilus and Criseyde*, *The Works of Geoffrey Chaucer*, ed. F. N. Robinson, 2nd edn (London: Oxford University Press, 1966) pp. 389–479.
53. Cf. Bayley, *The Characters of Love*, p. 82.
54. Jean Racine, *Bérénice*, ed. Gabriel Spillebout (Paris: Bordas, 1970).
55. Cf. Bayley, *The Characters of Love*, p. 107.
56. Hassall, libretto to Walton's *Troilus and Cressida*, SLS 997 booklet, p. 9.
57. Ibid., p. 10.
58. Ibid., p. 17.
59. Ibid., p. 16.
60. It is fair to acknowledge that Walton knew this was pornographic: see Gillian Widdicombe, Introduction to Walton's *Troilus and Cressida*, ibid., p. 5.
61. Chaucer, *Troilus and Criseyde*, III.1240–414.
62. Cf. Bayley, *The Characters of Love*, pp. 111–12.
63. Hassall, libretto to Walton's *Troilus and Cressida*, SLS 997 booklet, p. 20.
64. Ibid., p. 21.

65. Though they had fallen out, she knew that he was writing it. See John Pearson, *Façades: Edith, Osbert and Sacheverell Sitwell* (London: Fontana, 1980) p. 417. Cf. Widdicombe, Introduction to Walton's *Troilus and Cressida*, SLS 997 booklet, p. 5.
66. Text from Skeat, *Chaucerian and Other Pieces*, p. 343.
67. Cf. Bayley, *The Characters of Love*, pp. 103–4.
68. Text from Skeat, *Chaucerian and Other Pieces*, p. 344.
69. See n. 43 above.
70. Skeat's heavily pointed text offers no comma after 'steill', but there is one in Robert Henryson, *Poems and Fables*, ed. H. Harvey Wood (Edinburgh: Oliver and Boyd, 1933), p. 123, which is based on the Charteris text (see pp. xxv–vi), and in the poetically sensitive selection by Hugh MacDiarmid, *Henryson* (Harmondsworth: Penguin, 1973) p. 39. Neither the Charteris nor the Thynne text, as reprinted in Smith, *The Poems of Robert Henryson*, III 22, 195, has a comma. Charles Elliott in his selection, Henryson, *Poems* (Oxford: Clarendon Press, 1963) p. 105, has no comma and takes the phrase to refer to the swoon alone (p. 155n.), but admits that the 'punctuation is editorial' (p. xxi). The Kinaston manuscript (see n. 43 above) is again of interest, offering as a Latin translation (p. 506)

> Vt Creseida amoris sensit pingus
> Rigidior chalibe ea deueniebat
> Et tremor omnia ossa percurrebat.

This takes the phrase to apply to Cresseid alone, and recognises its polyvalence by making such a decision. At the very least, there is an audible caesura, emphasised by the line's alliterative structure, sufficiently forceful to justify my reading.
71. Text from Skeat, *Chaucerian and Other Pieces*, p. 346.
72. Ibid.
73. Ibid.
74. See Highet, *The Classical Tradition*, pp. 52, 53.
75. Ibid., p. 55.
76. Robert Kimbrough, *Shakespeare's 'Troilus and Cressida' and Its Setting* (Cambridge, Mass.: Harvard University Press, 1964) pp. 25–39.
77. All quotations are from Kenneth Palmer (ed.), *Troilus and Cressida*, New Arden edn (London and New York: Methuen, 1982), to which I am indebted for much information.
78. See ibid., p. 203n.
79. Ibid., p. 242.
80. John Bayley, in *Shakespeare and Tragedy*, p. 100, observes of this play that 'the act of poetry is itself a slave to limit, and in the act of fulfilling itself divides what it says from the freedom of unvoiced apprehension. We label ourselves by utterance', and on p. 116 remarks that Cressida is 'discontinuous with any notion of personality'.
81. Christopher Marlowe, *The Complete Plays*, ed. J. B. Steane (Harmondsworth: Penguin, 1969) pp. 105–78.

82. Cf. John Bayley, *The Uses of Division: Unity and Disharmony in Literature* (London: Chatto and Windus, 1976) p. 205.
83. Palmer (ed.), *Troilus and Cressida*, p. 6. Cf. W. W. Greg, *The Shakespeare First Folio: Its Bibliographical and Textual History* (Oxford: Clarendon Press, 1955) pp. 346–7.
84. R. A. Foakes, *Shakespeare, the Dark Comedies to the Last Plays: From Satire to Celebration* (London: Routledge and Kegan Paul, 1971) p. 58.
85. Cf. Conrad, *Shandyism*, pp. 2–3; and T. S. Eliot, *Selected Essays*, 3rd edn (London: Faber and Faber, 1951) pp. 129–31.
86. Good introductions to the post-structuralism to which I refer are Jonathan Culler, *Structuralist Poetics: Structuralism, Linguistics and the Study of Literature* (London: Routledge and Kegan Paul, 1975) pp. 241–54; and Christopher Norris, *Deconstruction: Theory and Practice* (London and New York: Methuen, 1982).
87. Kimbrough, *Shakespeare's 'Troilus and Cressida'*, pp. 73–4.
88. See Palmer (ed.), *Troilus and Cressida*, pp. 307–10, for a full discussion of this theory.
89. Ibid., p. 56.
90. Samuel Johnson, 'Preface to Shakespeare', *Rasselas, Poems, and Selected Prose*, ed. Bertrand H. Bronson, 3rd Ed. (New York: Holt, Rinehart and Winston, 1971) p. 274.
91. Cf. Kimbrough, *Shakespeare's 'Troilus and Cressida'*, pp. 174–5.
92. Ibid., p. 74.
93. On the way in which preconscious material can be brought to consciousness by speech with another, see Sigmund Freud, *An Outline of Psycho-Analysis*, tr. and ed. James Strachey (London: Hogarth Press/Institute of Psycho-Analysis, 1973) pp. 17–20.
94. Cf. Conrad, *Shandyism*, pp. 2–3.
95. Cf. Barbara Everett, 'The Inaction of *Troilus and Cressida*', *Essays in Criticism*, xxxii, no. 2 (Apr 1982) pp. 120–1.
96. Cf. Bayley, *Shakespeare and Tragedy*, pp. 62–3.
97. All quotations are from Kenneth Muir (ed.), *Macbeth*, New Arden edn, corr. repr. (London and New York: Methuen, 1972), to which I am indebted for much information.
98. Cf. Bayley, *Uses of Division*, p. 222.
99. Cf. Bayley, *Shakespeare and Tragedy*, p. 196.
100. The Old Man of ii.iv.1–20 is, as Bayley (*Shakespeare and Tragedy*, pp. 195–6) notes, too pregnant with meaning to be taken as central to the play's purpose.
101. Muir (ed.), *Macbeth*, p. 125n.
102. On Shakespeare's use of the word, see Anne Barton (Anne Righter), *Shakespeare and the Idea of the Play* (Harmondsworth: Penguin, in association with Chatto and Windus, 1967) e.g. pp. 81–6.
103. Muir, Introduction to *Macbeth*, p. xi.
104. Cf. Conrad, *Shandyism*, pp. 2–12.
105. Bayley, in *Uses of Division*, p. 190, applies this specifically and uniquely to *Troilus and Cressida*.
106. For the view that 'Drama abstracts from reality the fundamental forms of consciousness' and that tragedy 'reflects the basic structure

of personal life', see Susanne K. Langer, *Feeling and Form: A Theory of Art Developed from 'Philosophy in a New Key'* (London: Routledge and Kegan Paul, 1953) pp. 327, 351, and more generally pp. 326–66. The opposing view, that genre is much more subject to historical and cultural transformation, is clearly put in Alastair Fowler, *Kinds of Literature: An Introduction to the Theory of Genres and Modes* (Oxford: Clarendon Press, 1982) esp. pp. 45–52.

CHAPTER 2

1. P. B. Shelley, *Poetical Works*, ed. Thomas Hutchinson, rev. G. M. Matthews (London, Oxford, New York: Oxford University Press, 1970) pp. 411–24.
2. Samuel Taylor Coleridge, *Poems*, sel. and ed. John Beer, rev. edn (London: Dent, 1973) pp. 167–8.
3. Cf. Humphry House, *Coleridge: The Clark Lectures 1951–52* (London: Rupert Hart-Davis, 1953), p. 117.
4. For the history of the idea, see M. H. Abrams, *The Mirror and the Lamp: Romantic Theory and the Critical Tradition* (London, Oxford, New York: Oxford University Press, 1953); and James Engell, *The Creative Imagination: Enlightenment to Romanticism* (Cambridge, Mass., and London: Harvard University Press, 1981).
5. Cf. John Beer, *Coleridge's Poetic Intelligence* (London and Basingstoke: Macmillan, 1977), p. 117.
6. George Watson, in *Coleridge the Poet* (London: Routledge and Kegan Paul, 1966) pp. 122–30, interprets the two halves of the poem as signifying respectively fancy and imagination – for which see Samuel Taylor Coleridge, *Biographia Literaria, or Biographical Sketches of My Literary Life and Opinions*, new edn, ed. George Watson (London: Dent, 1975) p. 167.
7. Cf. Coleridge, 'Letter to Sara Hutchinson, April 4, 1802 – Sunday Evening', *Poems*, pp. 272–80.
8. See Thomas McFarland, *Coleridge and the Pantheist Tradition* (Oxford: Clarendon Press, 1969) esp. pp. 53–62.
9. In a symbol, 'the concept is one which only reason can think, and to which no sensible intuition can be adequate': Immanuel Kant, *Critique of Aesthetic Judgement: The Critique of Judgement*, tr. James Creed Meredith (Oxford: Clarendon Press, 1952) p. 221.
10. On typology, see Erich Auerbach, 'Figura', *Scenes from the Drama of European Literature: Six Essays* (New York: Meridian, 1959) pp. 28–76, and *Mimesis: The Representation of Reality in Western Literature*, tr. Willard R. Trask, paperback edn (Princeton, NJ: Princeton University Press, 1968) pp. 73–6, 156–62, 194–202. See also Northrop Frye, *The Great Code: The Bible and Literature* (London, Melbourne and Henley: Routledge and Kegan Paul, 1982) pp. 78–101.
11. Matthew Arnold, 'Stanzas from the Grande Chartreuse', *Poems*, new edn, intro. Kenneth Allott (London: Dent, 1965) p. 321.

12. Shelley, *Poetical Works*, p. 443.
13. 'Life, like a dome of many-coloured glass, / Stains the white radiance of eternity' (ibid.).
14. See Richard Holmes, *Shelley: The Pursuit* (London: Weidenfeld and Nicolson, 1974) pp. 635–7, for the biographical background to Shelley's allegory.
15. See Paul de Man, 'The Rhetoric of Temporality', *Blindness and Insight: Essays in the Rhetoric of Contemporary Criticism*, 2nd edn (London: Methuen, 1983) p. 207.
16. G. K. Chesterton, *Heretics* (London: John Lane, The Bodley Head, 1905) p. 293.
17. Thus we are told in Maurice Merleau-Ponty, *Signs*, tr. Richard C. McCleary (Evanston, Ill.: Northwestern University Press, 1964), that 'the spoken word (the one I utter or the one I hear) is pregnant with a meaning which can be read in the very texture of the linguistic gesture . . . and yet is never contained in that gesture, every expression always appearing to me as a trace, no idea being given to me except in transparency, and every attempt to close our hand on the thought which dwells in the spoken word leaving only a bit of verbal material in our fingers' (p. 89), and that 'Language is much more like a sort of being than a means, and that is why it can present something to us so well. A friend's speech on the telephone brings us the friend himself' (p. 43). Language conveys a presence beyond analysis. The implicit promotion of speech over writing is one to which Derrida has been consistently hostile, and explores most fully in *De la grammatologie* (Paris: Editions de Minuit, 1967). For his analysis of problems in Husserl's thought, see '"Genèse et structure" et la phénoménologie', *L'Ecriture et la différence* (Paris: Editions du Seuil, 1967) pp. 229–51. See Vincent Descombes, *Modern French Philosophy*, tr. L. Scott-Fox and J. M. Harding (Cambridge, London, New York: Cambridge University Press, 1980) pp. 136–45, for an analysis of the Derridan position *vis-à-vis* phenomenology.
18. See de Man, 'The Rhetoric of Temporality', *Blindness and Insight*, p. 191.
19. Dylan Thomas, 'A Refusal to Mourn the Death, by Fire, of a Child in London', *Collected Poems 1934–1952*, paperback edn (London: Dent, 1971) p. 94.
20. Shelley, *Alastor; or, the Spirit of Solitude, Poetical Works* p. 18. On the essential passivity of mind here, see Jay Macpherson, *The Spirit of Solitude: Conventions and Continuities in Late Romance* (New Haven, Conn., and London: Yale University Press, 1982) pp. 83–4.
21. All quotations from Spenser are from *Poetical Works*, ed. J. C. Smith and E. de Selincourt, paperback edn (London, Oxford, New York: Oxford University Press, 1970). Page references to *The Shepheardes Calender* relate to this edition and appear in the text.
22. See Richard Helgerson, *Self-Crowned Laureates: Spenser, Jonson, Milton and the Literary System* (Berkeley, Los Angeles, London: University of California Press, 1983) pp. 63, 67–8.
23. David Norbrook, in *Poetry and Politics in the English Renaissance*

(London, Boston, Melbourne and Henley: Routledge and Kegan Paul, 1984) pp. 145–7, sees Colin as a 'prophetic, anti-courtly' figure whose 'vision embodies . . . courtesy', but a 'courtesy . . . of a paradoxically uncourtly nature: the appearance of the courtier Calidore interrupts the poet's vision, and at the centre of the dance stands not an image of Queen Elizabeth but . . . the poet's own love'. However, the imagination remains 'essentially political'. He notes that Ralegh saw himself as Calidore, and he sets the vision in the context of Irish problems, Colin's vision being 'in part a vision of the beautiful poetry which will help to persuade all inhabitants of Ireland that their best interests are served by English rule'. This view of latent political implication, respecting the poet's autonomy, is more rewarding than that of Anthea Hume, who in *Edmund Spenser: Protestant Poet* (Cambridge: Cambridge University Press, 1984) p. 143, sees Colin as belittled by representing Spenser in his pastoral role, subject to the patronage of the epic author of *The Faerie Queene*.

24. Kathleen Williams, in *Spenser's Faerie Queene: The World of Glass* (London: Routledge and Kegan Paul, 1966) p. 215, sees this as 'foreshadowed' by the Graces' disappearance.
25. Calidore's arrival will represent the Harrowing of Hell: see A. C. Hamilton, in his edition of *The Faerie Queene* (London and New York: Longman, 1980) p. 621, for a survey of various interpretations.
26. Virginia Woolf, 'The Faery Queen', *The Moment and Other Essays* (London: Hogarth Press, 1947) p. 27.
27. Cf. Williams, *Spenser's Faerie Queene*, p. 222.
28. A. C. Hamilton, *The Structure of Allegory in 'The Faerie Queene'* (Oxford: Clarendon Press, 1961) p. 199.
29. John Erskine Hankins, *Source and Meaning in Spenser's Allegory: A Study of 'The Faerie Queene'* (Oxford: Clarendon Press, 1971) pp. 177–8.
30. Alastair Fowler, *Spenser and the Numbers of Time* (London: Routledge and Kegan Paul, 1964) p. 222.
31. W. B. Yeats, 'The Scholars', *Collected Poems*, 2nd edn (London and Basingstoke: Macmillan, 1950) p. 158.
32. Spenser, *Poetical Works*, pp. 536–45.
33. During his stay in London he had published the first half of *The Faerie Queene* and readied *Complaints* for the press. See Introduction to Spenser, *Poetical Works*, pp. xxviii, xxxi.
34. Williams, in *Spenser's Faerie Queene*, p. 216, observes that 'The likeness of the poet's mountain to Dame Nature's Arlo Hill is the measure of how close the poet's nature is to the true nature of things.' The repeated verbal form helps to join them together.
35. Quoted in Hankins, *Source and Meaning in Spenser's Allegory*, p. 288.
36. Fowler, *Spenser and the Numbers of Time*, pp. 232–3.
37. Ben Jonson, 'To Penshurst', *Poems*, ed. Ian Donaldson (London, Oxford, New York: Oxford University Press, 1975) p. 89.
38. All quotations are from John Milton, *Paradise Lost*, ed. Alastair Fowler (London: Longman, 1971).
39. See ibid., pp. 3–6.

40. Roger B. Rollin, '*Paradise Lost*: "Tragical-Comical-Historical-Pastoral"', *Milton Studies*, v, ed. James D. Simmonds (Pittsburgh: University of Pittsburgh Press, 1973) pp. 4 and 6, where Books I–XII are 'The History Play of the Son of God', I–X 'The Tragedy of Satan', IV–XII 'The Pastoral Tragicomedy of Adam and Eve'.
41. See Dennis H. Burden, *The Logical Epic: A Study of the Argument of 'Paradise Lost'* (London: Routledge and Kegan Paul, 1967) pp. 58–60.
42. Milton, *Paradise Lost*, ed. Fowler, p. 115n.
43. T. J. B. Spencer, '*Paradise Lost*: The Anti-Epic', in C. A. Patrides (ed.), *Approaches to 'Paradise Lost': The York Tercentenary Lectures* (London: Edward Arnold, 1968) p. 82.
44. Milton, *Paradise Lost*, ed. Fowler, pp. 210–11nn.
45. Frank L. Huntley, 'Before and After the Fall: Some Miltonic Patterns of Systasis', in Patrides (ed.), *Approaches to 'Paradise Lost'*, p. 5.
46. Ibid.
47. See John Milton, 'An Apology against a Pamphlet', *Complete Prose Works*, I, ed. Don M. Wolfe (New Haven, Conn., and London: Yale University Press, 1953) p. 890.
48. Donald F. Bouchard, *Milton: A Structural Reading* (London: Edward Arnold, 1974) p. 89.
49. J. B. Broadbent, 'Milton's "Mortal Voice" and His "Omnific Word"', in Patrides (ed.), *Approaches to 'Paradise Lost'*, p. 104.
50. *Paradise Regained* presents a different picture. Barbara Kiefer Lewalski, in *Milton's Brief Epic: The Genre, Meaning, and Art of 'Paradise Regained'* (London: Methuen, 1966), indicates that Milton probably saw no classical kind as corresponding to the biblical brief epic (p. 37), shows that his poem consummates an already Christian genre (pp. 102–29), and speaks of his 'conscious manipulation of this generic tradition' (p. 103). At the same time, Milton does employ some classical typology in the poem, so that Christ is related, for instance, to Hercules (pp. 227–41) and Socrates (pp. 241–9).
51. See Maryann Cale McGuire, *Milton's Puritan Masque* (Athens, Ga: University of Georgia Press, 1983).
52. William Wordsworth, *Poetical Works*, ed. Thomas Hutchinson, rev. Ernest de Selincourt, paperback edn (London, Oxford, New York: Oxford University Press, 1969) p. 590. This passage has only two accidental differences from the newly edited text in Jonathan Wordsworth, *William Wordsworth: The Borders of Vision*, corr. edn (Oxford: Clarendon Press, 1984) p. 388.
53. Ezra Pound, *The Cantos* (London: Faber and Faber, 1975) p. 802.
54. Wordsworth, *Poetical Works*, p. 590.
55. All quotations from Marvell are from *The Complete Poems*, ed. Elizabeth Story Donno (Harmondsworth: Penguin, 1972). For 'The Garden', see pp. 100–2.
56. Federico García Lorca, 'Walking Asleep', *The Gypsy Ballads of Federico García Lorca*, tr. Rolfe Humphries (Bloomington, Ind., and London: Indiana University Press, 1953) pp. 25–6.
57. William Empson, *Some Versions of Pastoral*, 3rd imp. (London: Chatto and Windus, 1968) pp. 131–2.

58. Marvell, *Complete Poems*, p. 94.
59. Empson, *Some Versions of Pastoral*, p. 131.
60. John Keats, *The Complete Poems*, ed. John Barnard (Harmondsworth: Penguin, 1973) pp. 346–8.
61. Wallace Stevens, 'Of Mere Being', *The Palm at the End of the Mind: Selected Poems and a Play*, ed. Holly Stevens (New York: Vintage, 1972) p. 398.
62. Keats, *Complete Poems*, p. 345.
63. Empson, *Some Versions of Pastoral*, p. 124.
64. Michael Long, *Marvell, Nabokov: Childhood and Arcadia* (Oxford: Clarendon Press, 1984) p. 129, finds the floral clock in the Latin but not the English version of the poem.
65. William Wordsworth, *The Prelude: A Parallel Text*, ed. J. C. Maxwell, corr. edn (Harmondsworth: Penguin, 1972). Quotations are from the 1805 text.
66. Cf. Milton, *Paradise Lost*, xii.646.
67. Richard Hurd, *Letters on Chivalry and Romance with the Third Elizabethan Dialogue*, ed. Edith J. Morley (London: Henry Frowde, 1911) pp. 121–3.
68. '. . . the poem is not an allegory of human life: rather, our life is an allegory of the poem which reveals our life as it should be' is the sympathetic view of A. C. Hamilton in *The Structure of Allegory in 'The Faerie Queene'*, p. 221.
69. See Joseph Anthony Wittreich, Jr, 'Perplexing the Explanation: Marvell's "On Mr Milton's Paradise Lost"', in C. A. Patrides (ed.), *Approaches to Marvell: The York Tercentenary Lectures* (London, Henley and Boston: Routledge and Kegan Paul, 1978) pp. 298–302.
70. *Letters of John Keats: A New Selection*, ed. Robert Gittings, corr. edn (London, Oxford, New York: Oxford University Press, 1975) p. 37.
71. Keats, *Complete Poems*, pp. 312–24.
72. Ibid., p. 425
73. Cf. Christopher Ricks, *Keats and Embarrassment* (London, Oxford, New York: Oxford University Press, 1976) p. 133.
74. Keats, *Complete Poems*, p. 299.
75. Ibid., pp. 435–49.
76. Ibid., pp. 82–93.
77. Keats 'hoisted himself up, and looked burly and dominant, as he said, "What an image that is – sea-shouldering whales!"': Cowden Clarke, quoted in Aileen Ward, *John Keats: The Making of a Poet* (London: Secker and Warburg, 1963) p. 30.
78. Dante, *The Selected Works*, ed. Paolo Milano (London: Chatto and Windus, 1972) p. 30.
79. Keats, *Complete Poems*, pp. 219–20.
80. Ibid., p. 345.
81. De Man, 'The Rhetoric of Temporality', *Blindness and Insight*, p. 197.
82. It is likely that it receives a full examination in the study of Hegel which he had nearly finished when he died. See Geoffrey Hartman, 'Paul de Man's Proverbs of Hell', *London Review of Books*, 6, no. 5 (15 Mar – 4 Apr 1984) p. 8.

83. De Man, 'The Rhetoric of Temporality', *Blindness and Insight*, pp. 206–8, 211.
84. Ibid., pp. 213–16.
85. Angus Fletcher, *Allegory: The Theory of a Symbolic Mode* (Ithaca, NY: Cornell University Press, 1965) pp. 124–5.
86. Ibid., pp. 243–4.
87. Ibid., p. 307.
88. Ibid., pp. 305–6.
89. Ibid., pp. 321–2.
90. Ibid., p. 357.
91. Ibid., p. 65.
92. Ibid., pp. 313–15. See also pp. 237–8.
93. Joseph Addison, *The Spectator*, III, ed. Donald F. Bond (Oxford: Clarendon Press, 1965), no. 357 (19 Apr 1712) pp. 336, 338, 338.
94. Milton, *Paradise Lost*, ed. Fowler, p. 126n.
95. Samuel Johnson, 'Milton', *Lives of the English Poets*, I, intro. Arthur Waugh (London, New York, Toronto: Oxford University Press, 1952) p. 113.
96. See above, p. 99 and n. 45.
97. Conrad, *Shandyism*, p. 19.
98. Ibid.
99. Ibid., p. 20.
100. Marvell, *Complete Poems*, pp. 55–8.
101. C. A. Patrides, '"Till prepared for longer flight": The Sublunar Poetry of Andrew Marvell', in Patrides (ed.), *Approaches to Marvell*, p. 34.
102. See Paul Hamilton, *Coleridge's Poetics* (Oxford: Basil Blackwell, 1983), to which (esp. pp. 129–34) my use of Kant is indebted.
103. It thus seeks the impossible, which is why it stops. For poetry's incapacity to produce objects of knowledge, and Kant's views on this, see ibid., pp. 47–54, esp. p. 49.
104. Kant, *Critique of Aesthetic Judgment*, p. 223.
105. Ibid., p. 222.
106. Ibid., p. 223.
107. Cf. Angus Fletcher, *Allegory*, pp. 70–1.
108. Cf. Kant, *Critique of Aesthetic Judgement*, 'The beautiful is the symbol of the morally good' (p. 223) – and we may take it that the categorical imperative has in Kant's thought an objective existence; it 'brings even our higher cognitive faculties into common accord' and 'it finds a reference in itself to something in the Subject itself and outside it . . . the supersensible – a something in which the theoretical faculty gets bound up into unity with the practical in an intimate and obscure manner' (p. 224). The 'supersensible' is, presumably, the unknowable reality behind appearances. For Schelling's obliteration of the separateness of poetry and knowledge, see Paul Hamilton, *Coleridge's Poetics*, p. 54.
109. Shelley, *Poetical Works*, p. 808. See Holmes, *Shelley: The Pursuit*, p. 182.
110. Milton, *Paradise Lost*, ed. Fowler, p. 31.
111. Mary W. Shelley, *Frankenstein or the Modern Prometheus*, ed. M. K.

Joseph (London, New York, Toronto: Oxford University Press, 1969) pp. 15, 16. Jay Macpherson, in *The Spirit of Solitude*, p. 186, observes the significance of the framing narrative.

112. Tillyard, *Shakespeare's Problem Plays*, pp. 123–8.
113. Philip Edwards, *Shakespeare and the Confines of Art* (London: Methuen, 1968) p. 109.
114. Ibid., p. 118.
115. Ibid., p. 119.
116. Ibid., pp. 118–19.
117. Ibid., p. 117.
118. J. W. Lever (ed.), *Measure for Measure*, New Arden edn (London: Methuen, 1967) p. lvii. All quotations from the play are from this edition, to which I am indebted for much information. A useful critical history is Rosalind Miles, *The Problem of 'Measure for Measure': A Historical Investigation* (London: Vision Press, 1976).
119. Edwards, *Shakespeare and the Confines of Art*, p. 118.
120. Wallace Stevens, 'Asides on the Oboe', *The Palm at the End of the Mind*, p. 187.
121. Ibid.
122. Cf. Lever (ed.), *Measure for Measure*, p. 46n.
123. G. Wilson Knight, *The Wheel of Fire: Interpretations of Shakespearean Tragedy with Three New Essays*, rev. edn (London: Methuen, 1960) p. 91.
124. Lever (ed.), *Measure for Measure*, p. 148n.
125. Cf. Clifford Leech, 'The "Meaning" of *Measure for Measure*', *Shakespeare Survey*, 3, ed. Allardyce Nicoll (Cambridge: Cambridge University Press, 1950) p. 70. W. W. Lawrence, in *Shakespeare's Problem Comedies*, pp. 100–1, argues that the Duke symbolically unites State and Church, but overlooks the fact that the audience are always conscious that the Friar's garb is a disguise.
126. Knight, *The Wheel of Fire*, p. 79.
127. Ibid., p. 95.
128. Edwards, *Shakespeare and the Confines of Art*, p. 117.
129. Bayley, *Shakespeare and Tragedy*, pp. 38–9.
130. Ibid., p. 43.
131. Ibid., pp. 43–4.
132. Robert Browning, 'How It Strikes a Contemporary', *Men and Women*, ed. Paul Turner (Oxford: Oxford University Press, 1972) p. 111.
133. Bayley, *Shakespeare and Tragedy*, p. 43.
134. All quotations are from John Ford, *The Broken Heart*, ed. Brian Morris (London: Ernest Benn, 1965).
135. Clifford Leech, *John Ford and the Drama of His Time* (London: Chatto and Windus, 1957) pp. 12, 74.
136. Dorothy M. Farr, *John Ford and the Caroline Theatre* (London: Macmillan, 1979) pp. 80, 98, 98.
137. Una Ellis-Fermor, *The Jacobean Drama: An Interpretation*, paperback edn (London: Methuen, 1965) p. 232.
138. Eliot, *Selected Essays*, p. 199.
139. Ellis-Fermor, *The Jacobean Drama*, p. 242.

140. Keats, 'Ode to a Nightingale', *Complete Poems*, p. 347.
141. Cf. J. B. Bamborough, *Ben Jonson* (London: Hutchinson, 1970) pp. 126–7.
142. All quotations are from Ben Jonson, *Works*, ed. C. H. Herford and Percy Simpson, corr. edn (Oxford: Clarendon Press, 1954) v, 163–271.
143. Cf. on this passage Barton, *Ben Jonson, Dramatist*, p. 131, for a slightly harsher view: the same author does, though, find an increasing sympathy for Morose on Jonson's part as the play progresses (pp. 134–5).
144. Edmund Wilson, 'Morose Ben Jonson', *The Triple Thinkers: Twelve Essays on Literary Subjects* (London: John Lehmann, 1952) pp. 203–20.
145. Jonas A. Barish, *Ben Jonson and the Language of Prose Comedy*, 2nd imp. (Cambridge, Mass.: Harvard University Press, 1967) p. 297.
146. Quotations from Webster are from *Three Plays*, ed. D. C. Gunby (Harmondsworth: Penguin, 1972).
147. Cf. Conrad, *Shandyism*, p. 4; and Lee Bliss, *The World's Perspective: John Webster and the Jacobean Drama* (Brighton: Harvester, 1983) pp. 112, 113.
148. All quotations are from John Marston, *The Malcontent*, ed. Bernard Harris (London: Ernest Benn, 1967).
149. Cf. Conrad, *Shandyism*, pp. 5–6.
150. All quotations are from John Marston, *Antonio and Mellida: The First Part*, ed. G. K. Hunter (London: Edward Arnold, 1965).
151. See Anthony Caputi, *John Marston: Satirist* (Ithaca, NY: Cornell University Press, 1961) p. 105.
152. If, like Lee Bliss in *The World's Perspective*, we see the Duke as a witty intriguer, we must agree that 'in the Duke's play role is identity, personality is subsumed in function' (p. 48). Oscar James Campbell, in *Shakespeare's Satire* (London, New York, Toronto: Oxford University Press, 1943) p. 127, finds him to be a satiric commentator modelled on instances in Marston; Ernest Schanzer, in *The Problem Plays of Shakespeare: A Study of 'Julius Caesar', 'Measure for Measure', 'Antony and Cleopatra'* (London: Routledge and Kegan Paul, 1963), believes him to be merely a dramatic convenience realised as a Renaissance ruler for whom ends justify means (p. 113) and believes that he keeps Claudio's survival secret simply for purposes of 'dramatic excitement' at the end of the play (p. 127). The two latter views do not sufficiently distinguish between the Duke's play and Shakespeare's.
153. Brian Gibbons, in *Jacobean City Comedy: A Study of Satiric Plays by Jonson, Marston and Middleton*, new edn (London and New York: Methuen, 1980), sees *Measure for Measure* as a court comedy (p. 68) with city-comedy elements (pp. 117–18).
154. Herman Melville, 'The Coming Storm', *Collected Poems*, ed. Howard P. Vincent (Chicago: Packard, 1947) p. 94.
155. The text I have used is in Herman Melville, *Billy Budd, Sailor and Other Stories*, sel. and ed. Harold Beaver, rev. edn (Harmondsworth: Penguin, 1970) pp. 59–99.

156. See Elizabeth Hardwick, 'Bartleby in Manhattan', *New York Review of Books*, xxviii, no. 12 (16 July, 1981) 27–31.
157. Melville, 'Bartleby', *Billy Budd, Sailor and Other Stories*, p. 99.
158. Ibid.
159. Ibid.
160. See Nicolas J. Perella, *The Critical Fortune of Battista Guarini's 'Il Pastor Fido'* (Florence: Leo S. Olschki, 1973) pp. 26–9. See also Doran, *Endeavors of Art*, pp. 203–9.
161. See John Bayley, *Pushkin: A Comparative Commentary* (Cambridge: Cambridge University Press, 1971) pp. 185–93; and Tatiana A. Wolff, 'Shakespeare's Influence on Pushkin's Dramatic Work', *Shakespeare Survey*, 5, ed. Allardyce Nicoll (Cambridge: Cambridge University Press, 1952), p. 102.
162. W. H. Auden, 'The Sea and the Mirror: A Commentary on Shakespeare's *The Tempest*', *Collected Poems*, ed. Edward Mendelson (London: Faber and Faber, 1976) pp. 311–41.
163. Ibid., p. 317.
164. Ibid.
165. Ibid., p. 316.
166. Ibid.
167. See Harry Levin, 'Two Magian Comedies: *The Tempest* and *The Alchemist*', *Shakespeare Survey*, 22, ed. Kenneth Muir (Cambridge: Cambridge University Press, 1969) p. 51.
168. Auden, 'The Sea and the Mirror', *Collected Poems*, p. 317.
169. In a sense this is done by Madeleine Doran in *Endeavors of Art*.
170. See Barton (Righter), *Shakespeare and the Idea of the Play*, p. 81.
171. All quotations are from J. H. P. Pafford (ed.), *The Winter's Tale*, New Arden edn (London: Methuen, 1966), to which I am indebted for much information.
172. Robert Greene, *Pandosto. The Triumph of Time*, ibid., pp. 182–225.
173. Ibid., p. 225.
174. E. C. Pettet, in *Shakespeare and the Romance Tradition* (London: Methuen, 1970) p. 162, notes that paradoxically this brings Shakespeare closer to romance than Greene.
175. Greene, *Pandosto*, in Pafford (ed.), *The Winter's Tale*, p. 201.
176. Ibid.
177. Ibid.
178. Ibid.
179. Ibid., p. 202.
180. Cf. Pafford (ed.), *The Winter's Tale*, pp. 168–9; and Foakes, *Shakespeare, the Dark Comedies to the Last Plays*, pp. 130–1. E. A. J. Honigmann, in *The Stability of Shakespeare's Text* (London: Edward Arnold, 1965) pp. 144–5, suggests that this scene belongs to a different stage of composition from that of its neighbours and that Time might have opened the play as well. If correct, this hypothesis would bear out his function as presenter.
181. Pafford (ed.), *The Winter's Tale*, p. 202.
182. This is disentangled by Pafford, ibid., pp. 76–7n.
183. Ibid., pp. 80–1nn.

184. Ibid., p. 204.
185. Cf. Rabkin, *Shakespeare and the Problem of Meaning*, pp. 136–7.
186. Pafford (ed.), *The Winter's Tale*, pp. 169–70.
187. On Shakespeare's use of this device in the equally incongruous circumstances of *King Lear*, see Susan Snyder, *The Comic Matrix of Shakespeare's Tragedies: 'Romeo and Juliet', 'Hamlet', 'Othello', and 'King Lear'* (Princeton, NJ: Princeton University Press, 1979) pp. 143–4.
188. Pafford (ed.), *The Winter's Tale*, p. 196.
189. That is, unless 'heavens directing' expresses a wish that they should do so: the phrase is ambiguous.
190. Cf. Pafford, Introduction to *The Winter's Tale*, p. lxxv; and Foakes, *Shakespeare, the Dark Comedies to the Last Plays*, pp. 143–4.
191. See R. M. Rilke, 'Archaic Torso of Apollo', *Selected Works* ii: *Poetry*, tr. J. B. Leishman (London: Hogarth Press, 1968) p. 143.
192. I do not understand the position of Kenneth Muir, in *Shakespeare's Comic Sequence* (Liverpool: Liverpool University Press, 1979) p. 175, that 'The characters at the end of the play are redeemed from the flux of time', common though that position is.

CONCLUSION

1. Jonas Barish, in *The Antitheatrical Prejudice* (Berkeley, Los Angeles, London: University of California Press, 1981), observes that 'Antitheatricalism opposes itself . . . to an institution, and, even more fundamentally, to a mode of experience and a form of life, to certain characteristics shared by all men' (p. 469), but this it is 'rash to dismiss as mere prejudice. We do wish for men to be what they seem. . . . We do cling to a belief in ourselves as distinct beings, with stable identities, however much latitude we wish to extend to self-experimentation and self-transformation' (ibid.; cf. pp. 476–7). For the fear of drama as a fear of self-multiplication, see, for example, pp. 91–2, 311–13, 418–19.
2. 'C'est un art de profond sceptique que la poésie savante. Elle suppose une liberté extraordinaire à l'égard de l'ensemble de nos idées et de nos sensations': Paul Valéry, 'Au sujet d'Adonis', *Oeuvres*, ed. Jean Hytier, i (Paris: Gallimard, 1957) 482.
3. Kant, *Critique of Aesthetic Judgement*, p. 224: the beautiful 'pleases *apart from all interest'*.

Works Cited

EDITIONS OF WORKS BY SHAKESPEARE

Craig, W. J. (ed.), *The Complete Works of William Shakespeare* (London, New York, Toronto: Oxford University Press, 1963 repr. of 1943 resetting).

Hunter, G. K. (ed.), *All's Well That Ends Well*, New Arden edn (London and New York: Methuen, 1967).

Lever, J. W. (ed.), *Measure for Measure*, New Arden edn (London: Methuen, 1967).

Muir, Kenneth (ed.), *Macbeth*, New Arden edn, corr. repr. (London and New York: Methuen, 1972).

Pafford, J. H. P. (ed.), *The Winter's Tale*, New Arden edn (London: Methuen, 1966).

Palmer, Kenneth (ed.), *Troilus and Cressida*, New Arden edn (London and New York: Methuen, 1982).

Quiller-Couch, Sir Arthur (ed.), *All's Well That Ends Well* (Cambridge: Cambridge University Press, 1929).

EDITIONS OF ROBERT HENRYSON, *THE TESTAMENT OF CRESSEID*

Elliott, Charles (sel. and ed.), *Poems* (Oxford: Clarendon Press, 1963).

Kinaston, Sir Francis (ed. and Latin tr.), *The Sixt and last booke of Troilus and Creseid written by Mr Robert Henderson and called by him The Testament of Creseide* (1639–40, Bodleian MS Add. C 287).

MacDiarmid, Hugh (sel.), *Henryson* (Harmondsworth: Penguin, 1973).

Skeat, W. W. (ed.), *Chaucerian and Other Pieces* (Oxford: Clarendon Press, 1897).

Smith, G. Gregory (ed.), *The Poems of Robert Henryson*, I and III (Edinburgh: Scottish Text Society, 1914 and 1908).

Wood, H. Harvey (ed.), *Poems and Fables* (Edinburgh: Oliver and Boyd, 1933).

OTHERS

Where several titles are the work of one author they are listed alphabetically, with the proviso that editions follow original works.

Abrams, M. H., *The Mirror and the Lamp: Romantic Theory and the Critical Tradition* (London, Oxford, New York: Oxford University Press, 1953).

Addison, Joseph, *The Spectator*, III, ed. Donald F. Bond (Oxford: Clarendon Press, 1967) no. 357 (19 Apr 1712) pp. 329–39.

Arnold, Matthew, *Poems*, new edn, intro. Kenneth Allott (London: Dent, 1965).

Auden, W. H., 'The Prince's Dog', *The Dyer's Hand and Other Essays* (London: Faber and Faber, 1975) pp. 182–208.

——, 'The Sea and the Mirror: A Commentary on Shakespeare's *The Tempest*', *Collected Poems*, ed. Edward Mendelson (London: Faber and Faber, 1976) pp. 311–41.

Auerbach, Erich, 'Figura', *Scenes from the Drama of European Literature: Six Essays* (New York: Meridian, 1959) pp. 11–76.

——, *Mimesis: The Representation of Reality in Western Literature*, tr. Willard R. Trask, paperback edn (Princeton, NJ: Princeton University Press, 1968).

Bamborough, J. B., *Ben Jonson* (London: Hutchinson, 1970).

Barber, C. L., *Shakespeare's Festive Comedy: A Study of Dramatic Form and Its Relation to Social Custom* (Princeton, NJ: Princeton University Press, 1959).

Barish, Jones A., *The Antitheatrical Prejudice* (Berkeley, Los Angeles, London: University of California Press, 1981).

——, *Ben Jonson and the Language of Prose Comedy*, 2nd imp. (Cambridge, Mass.: Harvard University Press, 1967).

Barton, Anne, *Ben Jonson, Dramatist* (Cambridge, London, New York: Cambridge University Press, 1984).

—— (Anne Righter), *Shakespeare and the Idea of the Play* (Harmondsworth: Penguin, in association with Chatto and Windus, 1967).

Bayley, John, *The Characters of Love: A Study in the Literature of Personality* (London: Chatto and Windus, 1968).

——, *Pushkin: A Comparative Commentary* (Cambridge: Cambridge University Press, 1971).

——, *Shakespeare and Tragedy* (London, Boston and Henley: Routledge and Kegan Paul, 1981).

——, *The Uses of Division: Unity and Disharmony in Literature* (London: Chatto and Windus, 1976).

Beer, John, *Coleridge's Poetic Intelligence* (London and Basingstoke: Macmillan, 1977).

Bliss, Lee, *The World's Perspective: John Webster and the Jacobean Drama* (Brighton: Harvester, 1983).

Boas, Frederick S., *Shakspere and His Predecessors* (London: John Murray, 1896).

Bouchard, Donald F., *Milton: A Structural Reading* (London: Edward Arnold, 1974).

Broadbent, J. B., 'Milton's "Mortal Voice" and His "Omnific Word"', in C. A. Patrides (ed.), *Approaches to 'Paradise Lost': The York Tercentenary Lectures* (London: Edward Arnold, 1968) pp. 99–117.

Browning, Robert, *Men and Women*, ed. Paul Turner (Oxford: Oxford University Press, 1972).

Burden, Dennis H., *The Logical Epic: A Study of the Argument of 'Paradise Lost'* (London: Routledge and Kegan Paul, 1967).

Campbell, Oscar James, *Shakespeare's Satire* (London, New York, Toronto: Oxford University Press, 1943).

Caputi, Anthony, *John Marston, Satirist* (Ithaca, NY: Cornell University Press, 1961).

Chaucer, Geoffrey, *Troilus and Criseyde, The Works of Geoffrey Chaucer,* ed. F. N. Robinson, 2nd edn (London: Oxford University Press, 1966) pp. 389–479.

Chesteron, G. K., *Heretics* (London: John Lane, The Bodley Head, 1905).

Coleridge, Samuel Taylor, *Biographia Literaria, or Biographical Sketches of My Literary Life and Opinions,* new edn, ed. George Watson (London: Dent, 1975).

——, *Coleridge on Shakespeare: A Selection of the Essays, Notes and Lectures of Samuel Taylor Coleridge on the Poems and Plays of Shakespeare,* ed. Terence Hawkes (Harmondsworth: Penguin, 1969).

——, *Poems,* sel. and ed. John Beer, rev. edn (London: Dent, 1973).

Conrad, Peter, *Shandyism: The Character of Romantic Irony* (Oxford: Basil Blackwell, 1978).

Culler, Jonathan, *Structuralist Poetics: Structuralism, Linguistics and the Study of Literature* (London: Routledge and Kegan Paul, 1975).

Dante, *The Selected Works,* ed. Paolo Milano (London: Chatto and Windus, 1972).

Derrida, Jacques, *De la grammatologie* (Paris: Editions de Minuit, 1967).

——, ' "Genèse et structure" et la phénoménologie', *L'Ecriture et la différence* (Paris: Editions du Seuil, 1967) pp. 229–51.

Descombes, Vincent, *Modern French Philosophy,* tr. L. Scott-Fox and J. M. Harding (Cambridge, London, New York: Cambridge University Press, 1980).

Donne, John, *The Complete English Poems,* ed. A. J. Smith (Harmondsworth: Penguin, 1971).

Doran, Madeleine, *Endeavors of Art: A Study of Form in Elizabethan Drama* (Madison: University of Wisconsin Press, 1954).

Edwards, Philip, *Shakespeare and the Confines of Art* (London: Methuen, 1968).

Eliot, T. S., *Selected Essays,* 3rd edn (London: Faber and Faber, 1951).

Ellis-Fermor, Una, *The Jacobean Drama: An Interpretation,* paperback edn (London: Methuen, 1965).

Empson, William, *Some Versions of Pastoral,* 3rd imp. (London: Chatto and Windus, 1968).

Engell, James, *The Creative Imagination: Enlightenment to Romanticism* (Cambridge, Mass., and London: Harvard University Press, 1981).

Everett, Barbara, 'The Inaction of *Troilus and Cressida',* *Essays in Criticism,* XXXII, no. 2 (Apr 1982) 119–39.

Farr, Dorothy M., *John Ford and the Caroline Theatre* (London: Macmillan, 1979).

Fletcher, Angus, *Allegory: The Theory of a Symbolic Mode* (Ithaca, NY: Cornell University Press, 1964).

Fletcher, John, 'To the Reader', in Francis Beaumont and John Fletcher, *Select Plays,* ed. M. C. Bradbrook (London: Dent, 1962), p. 242.

Foakes, R. A., *Shakespeare, the Dark Comedies to the Last Plays: From Satire to Celebration* (London: Routledge and Kegan Paul, 1971).

Ford, John, *The Broken Heart*, ed. Brian Morris (London: Ernest Benn, 1965).

Fowler, Alastair, *Kinds of Literature: An Introduction to the Theory of Genres and Modes* (Oxford: Clarendon Press, 1982).

——, *Spenser and the Numbers of Time* (London: Routledge and Kegan Paul, 1964).

Freud, Sigmund, *An Outline of Psycho-Analysis*, tr. and ed. James Strachey (London: Hogarth Press/Institute of Psycho-Analysis, 1973).

Frye, Northrop, *The Great Code: The Bible and Literature* (London, Melbourne and Henley: Routledge and Kegan Paul, 1982).

Gibbons, Brian, *Jacobean City Comedy: A Study of Satiric Plays by Jonson, Marston and Middleton*, new edn (London and New York: Methuen, 1980).

Greene, Robert, *Pandosto, The Triumph of Time*, in William Shakespeare, *The Winter's Tale*, New Arden edn, ed. J. H. P. Pafford (London: Methuen, 1966) pp. 182–225.

Greg, W. W., *The Shakespeare First Folio: Its Bibliographical and Textual History* (Oxford: Clarendon Press, 1955).

Hamilton, A. C., *The Structure of Allegory in 'The Faerie Queene'* (Oxford: Clarendon Press, 1961).

Hamilton, Paul, *Coleridge's Poetics* (Oxford: Basil Blackwell, 1983).

Hankins, John Erskine, *Source and Meaning in Spenser's Allegory: A Study of 'The Faerie Queene'* (Oxford: Clarendon Press, 1971).

Hardwick, Elizabeth, 'Bartleby in Manhattan', *New York Review of Books*, XXVIII, no. 12 (16 July 1981) 27–31.

Hartman, Geoffrey, 'Paul de Man's Proverbs of Hell', *London Review of Books*, 6, no. 5 (15 Mar – 4 Apr 1984) 8–10.

Hazlitt, William, 'All's Well That Ends Well', *The Round Table/Characters of Shakespear's Plays*, ed. Catherine Macdonald Maclean (London: Dent, repr. 1969) pp. 329–32.

Helgerson, Richard, *Self-Crowned Laureates: Spenser, Jonson, Milton, and the Literary System* (Berkeley, Los Angeles, London: University of California Press, 1983).

Highet, Gilbert, *The Classical Tradition: Greek and Roman Influences on Western Literature* (Oxford: Clarendon Press, 1949).

Hill, Geoffrey, *For the Unfallen: Poems 1952–1958* (London: André Deutsch, 1959).

Holmes, Richard, *Shelley: The Pursuit* (London: Weidenfeld and Nicolson, 1974).

Honigmann, E. A. J., *The Stability of Shakespeare's Text* (London: Edward Arnold, 1965).

House, Humphry, *Coleridge: The Clark Lectures 1951–52* (London: Rupert Hart-Davis, 1953).

Hume, Anthea, *Edmund Spenser: Protestant Poet* (Cambridge: Cambridge University Press, 1984).

Huntley, Frank L., 'Before and After the Fall: Some Miltonic Patterns of Systasis', in C. A. Patrides (ed.), *Approaches to 'Paradise Lost': The York Tercentenary Lectures* (London: Edward Arnold, 1968) pp. 1–14.

Hurd, Richard, *Letters on Chivalry and Romance with the Third Elizabethan Dialogue*, ed. Edith J. Morley (London: Henry Frowde, 1911).

Johnson, Samuel, 'Milton', *Lives of the English Poets*, I, intro. Arthur Waugh (London, New York, Toronto: Oxford University Press, 1952) pp. 63–134.

——, 'Preface to Shakespeare', *Rasselas, Poems, and Selected Prose*, ed. Bertrand H. Bronson, 3rd edn (New York: Holt, Rinehart and Winston, 1971) pp. 261–307.

Jonson, Ben, *Epicoene, or The Silent Woman, Works*, ed. C. H. Herford and Percy Simpson, corr. edn (Oxford: Clarendon Press, 1954) V, 163–271.

——, *Poems*, ed. Ian Donaldson (London, Oxford, New York: Oxford University Press, 1975).

Kant, Immanuel, *Critique of Aesthetic Judgement, The Critique of Judgement*, tr. James Creed Meredith (Oxford: Clarendon Press, 1952).

Keats, John, *The Complete Poems*, ed. John Barnard (Harmondsworth: Penguin, 1973).

——, *Letters of John Keats: A New Selection*, ed. Robert Gittings, corr. edn (London, Oxford, New York: Oxford University Press, 1975).

Kerrigan, John, '*Love's Labour's Lost* and the Circling Seasons', *Essays in Criticism*, XXVIII, no. 4 (Oct 1978) 269–87.

Kimbrough, Robert, *Shakespeare's 'Troilus and Cressida' and Its Setting* (Cambridge, Mass.: Harvard University Press, 1964).

Knight, G. Wilson, *The Wheel of Fire: Interpretations to Shakespearean Tragedy with Three New Essays*, rev. edn (London: Methuen, 1960).

Langer, Susanne K., *Feeling and Form: A Theory of Art Developed from 'Philosophy in a New Key'* (London: Routledge and Kegan Paul, 1953).

Lawrence, W. W., *Shakespeare's Problem Comedies* (Harmondsworth: Penguin, 1969).

Leech, Clifford, *John Ford and the Drama of His Time* (London: Chatto and Windus, 1957).

——, 'The "Meaning" of *Measure for Measure*', *Shakespeare Survey*, 3, ed. Allardyce Nicoll (Cambridge: Cambridge University Press, 1950), pp. 66–73.

Levin, Harry, 'Two Magian Comedies: *The Tempest* and *The Alchemist*', *Shakespeare Survey*, 22, ed. Kenneth Muir (Cambridge: Cambridge University Press, 1969) pp. 47–58.

Lewalski, Barbara Kiefer, *Milton's Brief Epic: The Genre, Meaning, and Art of 'Paradise Regained'* (London: Methuen, 1966).

Long, Michael, *Marvell, Nabokov: Childhood and Arcadia* (Oxford: Clarendon Press, 1984).

Lorca, Federico García, *The Gypsy Ballads of Federico García Lorca*, tr. Rolfe Humphries (Bloomington, Ind., and London: Indiana University Press, 1953).

McFarland, Thomas, *Coleridge and the Pantheist Tradition* (Oxford: Clarendon Press, 1969).

McGuire, Maryann Cale, *Milton's Puritan Masque* (Athens, Ga: University of George Press, 1983).

Macpherson, Jay, *The Spirit of Solitude: Conventions and Continuities in Late*

Romance (New Haven, Conn., and London: Yale University Press, 1982).

Man, Paul de, 'The Rhetoric of Temporality', *Blindness and Insight: Essays in the Rhetoric of Contemporary Criticism*, 2nd edn (London: Methuen, 1983) pp. 187–228.

Marlowe, Christopher, *The Complete Plays*, ed. J. B. Steane (Harmondsworth: Penguin, 1969).

——, *The Complete Poems and Translations*, ed. Stephen Orgel (Harmondsworth: Penguin, 1971).

Marston, John, *Antonio and Mellida: The First Part*, ed. G. K. Hunter (London: Edward Arnold, 1965).

——, *The Malcontent*, ed. Bernard Harris (London: Ernest Benn, 1967).

Marvell, Andrew, *The Complete Poems*, ed. Elizabeth Story Donno (Harmondsworth: Penguin, 1972).

Matisse, Henri, 'Notes of a Painter' (1908), tr. Jack D. Flam, in Jack D. Flam, *Matisse on Art*, paperback edn (Oxford: Phaidon, 1978) pp. 35–40.

Melville, Herman, 'Bartleby', *Billy Budd, Sailor and Other Stories*, sel. and ed. Harold Beaver, rev. edn (Harmondsworth: Penguin, 1970) pp. 59–99.

——, *Collected Poems*, ed. Howard P. Vincent (Chicago: Packard, 1947).

Merleau-Ponty, Maurice, *Signs*, tr. Richard C. McCleary (Evanston, Ill., Northwestern University Press, 1964).

Miles, Rosalind, *The Problem of 'Measure for Measure': A Historical Investigation* (London: Vision Press, 1976).

Milton, John, 'An Apology against a Pamphlet', *Complete Prose Works*, I, ed. Don M. Wolfe (New Haven, Conn., and London: Yale University Press, 1953) pp. 868–953.

——, *Paradise Lost*, ed. Alastair Fowler (London: Longman, 1971).

Muir, Kenneth, *Shakespeare's Comic Sequence* (Liverpool: Liverpool University Press, 1979).

Norbrook, David, *Poetry and Politics in the English Renaissance* (London, Boston, Melbourne and Henley: Routledge and Kegan Paul, 1984).

Norris, Christopher, *Deconstruction: Theory and Practice* (London and New York: Methuen, 1982).

Nye, Robert, *Falstaff* (London: Hamish Hamilton, 1976).

Painter, William, 'Giletta of Narbona', in William Shakespeare, *All's Well That Ends Well*, New Arden edn, ed. G. K. Hunter (London and New York: Methuen, 1967) pp. 145–52.

Patrides, C. A., '"Till prepared for longer flight": The Sublunar Poetry of Andrew Marvell', in Patrides (ed.), *Approaches to Marvell: The York Tercentenary Lectures* (London, Henley and Boston: Routledge and Kegan Paul, 1978) pp. 31–55.

——, *Approaches to 'Paradise Lost': The York Tercentenary Lectures* (London: Edward Arnold, 1968).

Pearson, John, *Façades: Edith, Osbert and Sacheverell Sitwell* (London: Fontana, 1980).

Perella, Nicolas J., *The Critical Fortune of Battista Guarini's 'Il Pastor Fido'* (Florence: Leo S. Olschki, 1973).

Pettet, E. C., *Shakespeare and the Romance Tradition* (London: Methuen, 1970).

Pound, Ezra, *The Cantos* (London: Faber and Faber, 1975).

Price, Joseph G., *The Unfortunate Comedy: A Study of 'All's Well That Ends Well' and Its Critics* (Toronto: University of Toronto Press, 1968).

Rabkin, Norman, *Shakespeare and the Problem of Meaning* (Chicago and London: Chicago University Press, 1981).

Racine, Jean, *Bérénice*, ed. Gabriel Spillebout (Paris: Bordas, 1970).

Reese, M. M., *The Cease of Majesty: A Study of Shakespeare's History Plays* (London: Edward Arnold, 1961).

Ricks, Christopher, *Keats and Embarrassment* (London, Oxford, New York: Oxford University Press, 1976).

Righter, Anne: *see* Barton, Anne.

Rilke, R. M., *Selected Works*, ii: *Poetry*, tr. J. B. Leishman (London: Hogarth Press, 1960).

Rollin, Roger B., '*Paradise Lost*: "Tragical-Comical-Historical-Pastoral"', *Milton Studies*, v, ed. James D. Simmonds (Pittsburgh: University of Pittsburgh Press, 1973) pp. 3–37.

Rossiter, A. P., *Angel with Horns and Other Shakespeare Lectures*, ed. Graham Storey (London: Longman, 1961).

Salingar, Leo, *Shakespeare and the Traditions of Comedy* (Cambridge: Cambridge University Press, 1974).

Schanzer, Ernest, *The Problem Plays of Shakespeare: A Study of 'Julius Caesar', 'Measure for Measure', 'Antony and Cleopatra'* (London: Routledge and Kegan Paul, 1963).

Shelley, Mary W., *Frankenstein or the Modern Prometheus*, ed. M. K. Joseph (London, New York, Toronto: Oxford Univesity Press, 1969).

Shelley, P. B., *Poetical Works*, ed. Thomas Hutchinson, rev. G. M. Matthews (London, Oxford, New York: Oxford University Press, 1970).

Slater, Ann Pasternak, *Shakespeare the Director* (Brighton: Harvester, 1982).

Snyder, Susan, *The Comic Matrix of Shakespeare's Tragedies: 'Romeo and Juliet', 'Hamlet', 'Othello', and 'King Lear'* (Princeton, NJ: Princeton University Press, 1979).

Spencer, T. J. B., '*Paradise Lost*: The Anti-Epic', in C. A. Patrides (ed.), *Approaches to 'Paradise Lost': The York Tercentenary Lectures* (London: Edward Arnold, 1968) pp. 81–98.

Spenser, Edmund, *The Faerie Queene*, ed. A. C. Hamilton, corr. edn (London and New York: Longman, 1980).

——, *Poetical Works*, ed. J. C. Smith and E. de Selincourt, paperback edn (London, Oxford, New York: Oxford University Press, 1970).

Stevens, Wallace, *The Palm at the End of the Mind: Selected Poems and a Play*, ed. Holly Stevens (New York: Vintage, 1972).

Thomas, Dylan, *Collected Poems 1934–1952*, paperback edn (London: Dent, 1971).

Tillyard, E. M. W., *Shakespeare's Problem Plays* (London: Chatto and Windus, 1950).

Valéry, Paul, 'Au sujet d'Adonis', *Oeuvres*, ed. Jean Hytier (Paris: Gallimard, 1957) i, 474–95.

Walton, Sir William, and Hassall, Christopher, *Troilus and Cressida*, EMI 3-record set SLS 997, with enclosed booket (1977).

Ward, Aileen, *John Keats: The Making of a Poet* (London: Secker and Warburg, 1963).

Watson, George, *Coleridge the Poet* (London: Routledge and Kegan Paul, 1966).

Webster, John, *Three Plays*, ed. D. C. Gunby (Harmondsworth: Penguin, 1972).

Widdicombe, Gillian, Introduction to Walton's *Troilus and Cressida*, EMI 3-record set SLS 997, booklet (1977).

Williams, Kathleen, *Spenser's Faerie Queene: The World of Glass* (London: Routledge and Kegan Paul, 1966) pp. 280–305.

Wilson, Edmund, 'Morose Ben Jonson', *The Triple Thinkers: Twelve Essays on Literary Subjects* (London: John Lehmann, 1952) pp. 203–20.

Wittreich, Joseph Anthony Jr, 'Perplexing the Explanation: Marvell's "On Mr Milton's Paradise Lost"', in C. A. Patrides (ed.), *Approaches to Marvell: The York Tercentenary Lectures* (London, Henley and Boston: Routledge and Kegan Paul, 1978) pp. 280–305.

Wolff, Tatiana A., 'Shakespeare's Influence on Pushkin's Dramatic Work', *Shakespeare Survey*, 5, ed. Allardyce Nicoll (Cambridge: Cambridge University Press, 1952) pp. 93–105.

Woolf, Virginia, 'The Faery Queen', *The Moment and Other Essays* (London: Hogarth Press, 1947) pp. 25–9.

Wordsworth, Jonathan, *William Wordsworth: The Borders of Vision*, corr. edn (Oxford: Clarendon Press, 1984).

Wordsworth, William, *Poetical Works*, ed. Thomas Hutchinson, rev. Ernest de Selincourt, paperback edn (London, Oxford, New York: Oxford University Press, 1969).

——, *The Prelude: A Parallel Text*, ed. J. C. Maxwell, corr. edn (Harmondsworth: Penguin, 1972).

Yeats, W. B., *Collected Poems*, 2nd edn (London and Basingstoke: Macmillan, 1950).

Index